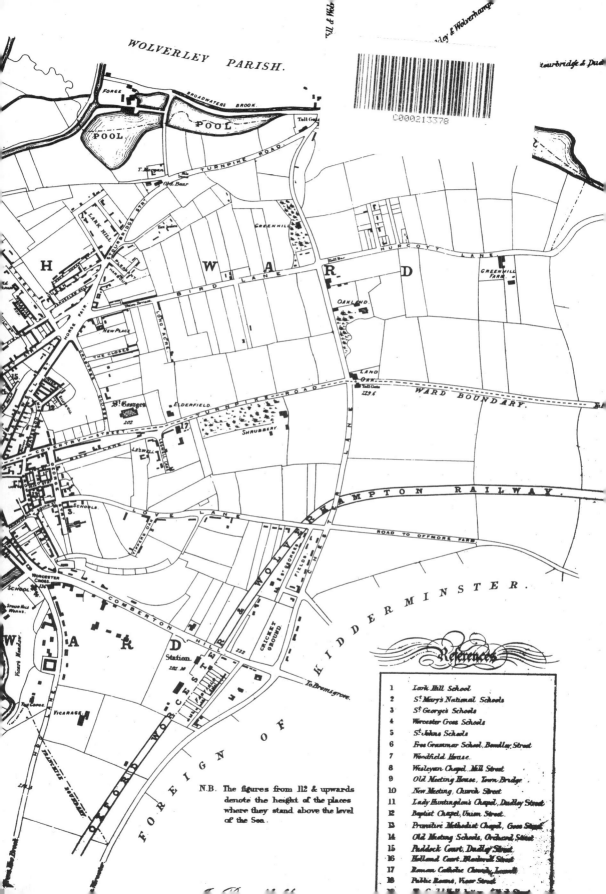

WOLVERLEY PARISH.

POOL

POOL

FORGE    BROADWATERS    BROOK.

Toll Gate

T. Morgan

Old Bear

TURNPIKE    ROAD

H                    W                A                R                D

GREENHILL

HURCOTT    LANE

GREENHILL FARM

LARK HILL

BIRD    LANE

OAKLAND

NEW PLACE

LONG ACRE

THE CLOSES

LAND    OAK

122.6    Toll Gate

WARD    BOUNDARY.

St Georges
202

ELDERFIELD

17

SHRUBBERY

TURNPIKE    ROAD

COVENTRY    STREET

BIRD    LANE

LEASWELL

SCHOOLS

3.

LOVE    LANE

ROAD TO OFFMORE FARM

AMPTON    RAILWAY.

WORCESTER CROSS

W        A        R        D

COMBERTON    HILL

Station.

202.10

CRICKET GROUND

222

To Bromsgrove.

FOREIGN    OF    KIDDERMINSTER.

VICARAGE.

WORCESTER

OXFORD

N.B. The figures from 112 & upwards
denote the height of the places
where they stand above the level
of the Sea.

*A History of*
# KIDDERMINSTER

Comberton Hall, Comberton Road. Though much modernised, this house presumably incorporated the original buildng thought to date from *c*.1600. Its demolition in the 1970s was so routine that I have been unable to find any record of it. Yet this act deprived us of a rare surviving link in the built environment to one of the major submanors to grow out of Domesday Kidderminster.

*A History of*

# KIDDERMINSTER

*Nigel Gilbert*

Phillimore

2004

Published by
PHILLIMORE & CO. LTD
Shopwyke Manor Barn, Chichester, West Sussex, England


© Nigel Gilbert, 2004


ISBN 1 86077 309 5



Printed and bound in Great Britain by
MPG BOOKS LTD
Bodmin, Cornwall

# Contents

# Acknowledgements

I am particularly grateful to Don Gilbert for the many conversations we have enjoyed through recent years. His influence has been substantial in certain sections of the book, although any errors are of course my own. I owe a debt also to those whose writings have pioneered a trail through aspects of Kidderminster's history. I must mention Roy Lewis, who studied the cloth industry nearly fifty years ago, and whose work still needs to be developed; Len Smith, whose study of the hand-loom carpet weavers massively enhanced our understanding of the industrial history of the town, including the great strike of 1828; the late Arthur Marsh, whose book on the carpet weavers' union contained so many references for me to work on; Melvyn Thompson, whose recent book on the history of the town's carpet industry saved me a lot of work; and the Wolverley and Cookley Historical Society, whose journals have inspired much of my thinking on prehistoric times.

I would especially like to thank the staff of Kidderminster Library, whose excellent collection has provided much of the material for this book. In particular I am grateful to Lesley Hart, who retired shortly before the completion of this book, and Jeremy Hamblett for their help and encouragement. Similarly I must thank Deborah Overton at the Historic Environment Record at Worcester University for her considerable assistance. I thank also those at Bewdley Museum who helped me with access to the picture and photograph collection, especially Liz Cowley, Liz Jenkins, and Angela and Charles Purcell. I have received further valuable help from staff at Worcester Record Office, the History Centre in Worcester itself, Worcester Cathedral Library, Birmingham Reference Library and Stafford Record Office.

Illustrations 6, 15, 17-19, 21, 22, 24, 25, 35, 36-8, 45, 47, 48, 50, 51, 55, 56, 60, 63, 64, 70, 72, 74-7, 79, 82, 84, 85, 91, 96 and the frontispiece are reproduced by permission of Kidderminster Public Library; front cover, 1, 8, 11-13, 30, 43, 44, 49, 54, 69, 80, 86, 88, 89 and 93 are reproduced by permission of Bewdley Museum; 10, 33, 34, 39, 53 and 95 are reproduced by permission of Len Smith; 2-5, 9, 31, 32, 42, 61 and 62 are reproduced by permission of Worcester Record Office; 28 and 71 are reproduced by permission of Belinda Stretton; 7, 46, 68, 78, 81, 90, 92, 97-100 and 102 are reproduced by permission of the

*Kidderminster Shuttle*; 40 and 41 are reproduced by permission of Patrick Lea; 57 and 83 are reproduced by permission of the Historic Environment Record at University College, Worcester; 94 and 103 are reproduced by permission of Stephen Bragginton; 58, 59, 66 and 73 are reproduced by permission of Liz Payne-Ahmadi; 52 is reproduced by permission of Charles Talbot; 65 is reproduced by permission of Stephen Smith; 16 is reproduced by permission of Bob Green; 23 is reproduced by permission of the Charles Hastings Education Centre at Worcester Royal Hospital; 67 is reproduced by permission of Sotheby's; 101 is reproduced by permission of Melvyn Thompson. Illustration 20 is reproduced from Benjamin Hanbury's *Extracts from the Diary of Joseph Williams*; 26 is reproduced from T.R. Nash's *Collections for the History of Worcestershire*; 29 and 87 are reproduced from E.D. Priestley Evans' *History of New Meeting House*. Illustrations 14, 27 and 104 belong to the author.

Many individuals have helped me. They include John Berrow, Steve Bragginton, Ken Briggs, Alan Brooks, John Combe, John Cotterell, Richard Davies, Andrew Dickens, David Everett, Carole Gammond, Mick Kelly, Liz Payne-Ahmadi, Scott Pettitt, Richard Pugh-Cook, Cedric Quayle, Jamie Shaw, Brian Smith, Charles Talbot, Dr Richard Taylor, Ian Walker, John Wardle, Richard Warner, Ron White and Colin Young.

Finally, I understand now why writers often offer profuse thanks to their family. In recent weeks I have become increasingly difficult to live with. I am most appreciative of the support of my wife, Ingra, and my two sons, David and Jim, who have been denied their customary access to the computer, and my dog, Woody, who has endured shorter walks than usual.

# Introduction

The story of Kidderminster is an extraordinarily colourful one. Rarely has the town been quiet for very long. Its history is one of struggle, as befits an industrial town. This may be a surprise to some, because many still remember the post-war decades into the 1970s when the carpet industry was flourishing and harmony reigned. Certainly, when I began to research the history of the town, I was taken aback to find a record of classic 19th-century industrial conflict, including a five-month strike in 1828 which had many parallels with the 1983 miners' strike. The long view, cast back over the centuries, must be that Kidderminster people have a proud record of nonconformity and awkwardness. In recent years they have done something to restore that reputation.

Some towns, such as neighbouring Bewdley, can confidently be described as 'historic', because they stand there in all their glory for any visitor to see. Unfortunately, the large part of historic Kidderminster has been destroyed. Probably no town has failed so much to do justice to its history. It could have been a town of great character, capable of attracting many visitors. Instead, much of the landscape is devoid of interest and Kidderminster has become a byword for architectural vandalism. Yet at Domesday the principal manor of the locality was that of Kidderminster, with the surrounding area, including what would later be Bewdley, subordinate to it. Any sense of this historical pedigree has been lost and the town does not even have a museum.

Kidderminster's history contains a high degree of mystery. Probably the most intriguing is the question of the monastery. It is almost certain that there was one here, but we cannot say exactly where it was situated or what it was like. Unless there is a surprising archaeological discovery, it is unlikely that we will ever properly lay the question to rest. We know little of Kidderminster in the late Middle Ages. We know it had a cloth industry, but it is by no means clear how successful it was. As we enter a better-documented age, it becomes easier to unravel mysteries, such as the difficulty of locating streets supposedly built by Lord Foley around 1753. Yet even the modern period leaves us with unanswered questions, like the fate of some of the town's looted landmarks, such as the Horsefair clock and the Blakebrook drinking fountain. Or what happened to the record of the named vote by councillors which led directly to the demolition of the old library buildings in Market Street?

Apart from the inherent difficulty of certain issues or periods, a major problem confronted me in writing a new history of the town. There has never been a chronological history of Kidderminster. All the previous major histories of the town have been organised on the basis of topics, including those by Burton and by Tomkinson and Hall. Both these books have been extremely helpful to me, but they are of only limited use in showing how one thing led to another. My book represents a first effort to study the sequence of events, and it will need to be built upon.

Inevitably the story of the carpet industry runs through the second half of the book. The achievement of this small town has been astonishing. For the best part of two centuries Kidderminster has been well known across the world, because of the skill and hard work of its citizens. Yet this success has come at a price. It is ironic that, whilst supplying a luxury product, there have been many long periods of struggle and hardship for Kidderminster people.

I

# *Before Kidderminster*

W hat did the area we now know as Kidderminster look like in the Stone Age? Were the Romans here, and did they find a primitive landscape covered in wild woodland? When was the settlement founded from which emerged the town of Kidderminster? Where were the early hamlets and villages which were to make up the medieval manor and later the parish of Kidderminster? A complete answer to all these questions will require a major archaeological breakthrough, but we can summarise the evidence so far.

In recent years historians have recognised that human intervention in the landscape occurred earlier than had previously been thought. It is no longer believed, for example, that the invading Anglo-Saxons had to fight their way through dense primeval forests. Mesolithic (middle stone-age) man may have been clearing woodland and creating heathland in the period 8000-4000 BC. The process quickened with the arrival from Europe of people with the knowledge of agriculture before 4000 BC. This marked the beginning of the Neolithic or new stone age. Clearance continued through the Bronze Age into the Iron Age. One distinguished expert is prepared to hazard the guess that by 500 BC half of England had ceased to be wildwood.[1]

The limited archaeological information confirms this general picture. Just north of Wribbenhall, at Lightmarsh Farm, analysis of samples taken revealed charred hazelnut shells giving a radiocarbon date of the earlier eighth millennium BC. Mesolithic man is known to have eaten well of the nuts of the hazel tree, which was abundant after the Ice Age. These Mesolithic men may have been based around the Severn. Looking at the Stour Valley in 1949, the much respected local historian, A.J. Perrett, found an axe from the Neolithic period (4000-2500 BC) at Oldington Wood south of the railway line between the Stourport Road and the Stour. This certainly opens up for us the vision of Neolithic man farming the Stour Valley from the Severn up to Kidderminster and beyond. Yet there is so little archaeological evidence. The best we have takes us forward into the Bronze Age (2500 to 750 BC) with the finding of axes in 1927 near the junction of Chester Road and Hillgrove Crescent and in 1978 at Tomkinsons old carpet factory in Church Street.[2] At least these suggest a very early settlement on the site which would one day develop into the historic town of Kidderminster.

We must go beyond our parish into the neighbouring parish of Wolverley for further evidence of significant activity by Stone-Age man in our area. A number of finds have been recorded by the energetic Wolverley and Cookley Historical Society. These included evidence that Mesolithic hunter-gatherers had visited areas on either side of Kinver Edge. Flints were found at both Blakeshall and Little Kingsford. Whilst farming at the latter site, Geoffrey Gilley made other exciting discoveries. The large number of flints recovered there suggested the former presence of a Neolithic farm. Additional proof of a permanent settlement was provided when a number of 'boiling stones' were also found. Further archaeological exploration may reveal other sites closer to the Severn in the Stour Valley.

Flints do not occur naturally in our local landscape. These finds reveal something about the travel and trade of Stone-Age man, who used the rivers and watercourses. Another discovery dramatically emphasised the progress of early man along such river systems as the Severn and the Stour and into tributaries like the Horse Brook, which flows near Little Kingsford. Above that farm, on Castle Hill, in 1989 Verna Johansen found a 'polished stone axe head with a perfect cutting edge'. A subsequent examination at Birmingham University revealed that it was manufactured about 3000 BC in a Neolithic 'factory' at Mount's Bay, near Penzance in Cornwall. Neolithic people are known to have been skilled in woodland management, and they may have started a process of grubbing out woodland, which was to gather pace in the Bronze Age and the Iron Age. Recent excavation by the Stour has enabled geologists to study the soil layers, and it is thought that there was massive soil erosion in the Bronze and Iron Ages due to forest clearance.[3]

## BORDER COUNTRY

Until a comprehensive archaeological survey of Kidderminster and its environs is undertaken, much of its prehistory must remain uncertain. It is possible that the area was relatively wild because it was border country, situated at the edge of regions inhabited by the principal British tribes at the time of the Roman invasion. The Cornovii were based around what is now Shropshire, but moved into adjoining parts such as Staffordshire. The Dobunni had Cirencester as their capital, but they extended northwards into the southern part of the Severn valley. The presence of three hill forts in the countryside north west of Kidderminster is a reminder that for many centuries there may have been a fierce struggle for control of the area. One lies on the west of Habberley Valley in Wassell Wood. Another is to be found in Arley Wood, a remote area approached from Witnells End beyond Shatterford Lakes. The path becomes increasingly overgrown as it leads to the promontory, still containing the ditches of the fort. Trees and bushes cover the site, which has not been properly surveyed. The boundary of Boddenham Farm lies not far away, but it is a mysterious place and it is easy for the visitor to become disoriented. The third fort is at Solcum, above the Drakelow underground factory and adjoining Blakeshall. This is another promontory, and today a field slopes gently on to one side, which still shows the old ramparts. Access is very difficult to the other three sides, which are steep and overgrown, but anybody who stands above these cliffs, looking across towards Arley Wood, gets a clear impression of border country. This fort also remains to be excavated.

Even allowing for the occurrence of fighting and territorial disputes, there is little doubt that by the time of the Roman invasion the Stour Valley would have been fully given over to agriculture. Wildwood had vanished forever from the river flood plains and England was almost as agricultural as it is now. An ancient field system is thought to have been identified just above the flood plain where the Puxton estate is now, but it can be dated anywhere between 2500 and 500 BC.[4] Britain was already a hedged land when the Romans came. In addition to the development of the low-lying fertile soils, some use was being made of higher and less fertile land. It is thought that the heathland west of Kidderminster, part of which survives on the Devil's Spittleful and Rifle Range nature reserves, was created for grazing at least by 500 BC.

## ROMAN REMAINS

Evidence of human activity during the Roman period is scattered across the region. The finds suggest that land had been well developed by then, though perhaps not over the higher ground. There is a concentration of evidence in the area north of Wribbenhall. The analysis of material collected at Lightmarsh Farm and neighbouring Hoarstone Farm in 1994 revealed the site of a farmstead and ditched enclosure in the latter part of the Roman occupation. The finds were dated predominantly to the third and fourth centuries. In 1984 Roman coins dating from the same period were found by a metal-detector in nearby Crundalls Lane. Confirmation that the area may well have been a centre of human activity is provided by the finding of a Roman fibula or brooch at Grey Green Farm. We may be fairly sure that farming has been underway at Habberley for many centuries. A number of Roman coins and brooches have been discovered in the fields between possibly the two oldest farm sites at Low Habberley, the Lane and Low Habberley Farm itself.[5]

1. Hoarstone Farmhouse: one of many farms where occupation dates from Roman times or before.

On the other side of the Severn, in what is now Wyre Forest, it was once claimed that the remains of a Roman villa had been discovered. At Hawkbatch several coins were dug up and there was once a bridge there.[6] It is reasonable to suppose that on the Kidderminster side of the river the low-lying land would by then have been claimed for agriculture. Almost certainly there would have been farms at Eymore, Netherton and Blackstone, for example, but there has been little archaeological endeavour to prove it. However, a Roman camp was discovered in 1958 at Brant Farm, just south of Blackstone. This was thought to date from the late part of the first century, in the early years of the Roman occupation, when the Severn was the furthest extent of their advance. Fragments of Iron-Age pottery were found, indicating that the land had been settled for some time.[7]

The scarcity of the evidence may simply reflect the fact that the Kidderminster area has received insufficient archaeological attention. The exception is where the Wolverley and Cookley Historical Society has been active. They have recorded Romano-British pottery found at several places around Caunsall. Roman coins have been recovered near Gloucester Coppice, which is on the west bank of the Stour north of Wolverley. This is further confirmation that the Stour valley had long been settled. Pottery of the period has been found also at Blakeshall and Little Kingsford, again confirming these places as long-established settlements. At Lower Birch Farm, high up on the north-east side of the Bridgnorth Road approaching Shatterford Lakes, the discovery of pottery is a rare indication that higher ground had been cleared for agriculture and that many of the farms we know today may already have been established by Roman times. However, although a road called the Portway ran from Wribbenhall to Wroxeter in Roman times, no such finds have been found at the Trimpley farms which lay on its route.

The historic core of Kidderminster contains buried archaeological deposits, which are judged to have high potential. So far the town has yielded only a small number of finds to suggest a settlement was established there by the time of the Roman occupation. In 1879 a fourth-century coin and quern stones were found at the late lamented *Three Tuns* in Vicar Street. More recently, in 1980, Roman coins were found at St Mary's church. Other possible evidence has been lost. In 1872, when Barton's premises were built in Vicar Street, 'a set of ancient oak piles black with age' was found between the street and the Stour. 'There were no marks of the saw upon them, but had been roughly dressed with the axe.'[8]

## THE ANGLO-SAXONS

After the Romans withdrew from Britain in the early fifth century, the population declined as the country became prey to invading forces. It is possible that it did not start to recover for over 500 years. Although the invading Anglo-Saxons had reached the area across the West Midlands from Cannock Chase to Warwickshire by the seventh century, it is thought they did not take the Stour valley area into the kingdom of Mercia until the eighth century. To some extent they may have lived alongside the native British before finally taking over, and the occupant of a pagan burial found near Hoarstone Farm in 1992 may have been Anglo-Saxon or British. This period was once known as the 'Dark Ages', partly because little was known about it and partly because classical Roman culture and civilisation gave way to barbarism. Whilst this is now seen as a gross simplification, it has to be said that there remain many unanswered questions about life in the Stour valley during the centuries which followed the departure of the Romans. Certainly, the area was border country between the lands of various peoples or folk groups and may well have been relatively under-populated. In such frontier regions woodland might have been allowed to regenerate. North Worcestershire might have been a region where wastes or commons were shared between folk groups. In a recent book, Sarah Zaluckyj has concluded that 'the area was heavily wooded and under-developed during the earlier Anglo-Saxon period.'[9] We cannot be sure exactly who was living there, but these lands of north Worcestershire became known as the boundary of a people called the *Hwicce*, whose kings were first mentioned by Bede writing in 731. They may have been Anglo-Saxon.[10]

## THE KIDDERMINSTER MONASTERY

Suddenly, in 736, we have a momentary glimpse of the land on which Kidderminster would one day stand. In that year, by a charter, King Aethelbald of Mercia granted land to his earldorman Cyneberht for the foundation of a *coenubium* (monastery). The gift may possibly be seen as the spoils of war after the Anglo-Saxons had finally advanced into the Stour valley, and it was as follows:

> a small portion of land, that is 10 *cassati*, in the province to which the name *Husmerae* has been assigned from ancient times, beside the river called Stour with all necessary things belonging to it, with fields and woods with fisheries and meadows; the above mentioned estate is in circuit on both sides of the above-named river (*ex utraque parte supranominati fluminis*) having on its northern side the wood they call Kinver (*Cynibre*) and on the west indeed another whose name is *Moerheb* of which woods the greatest part belongs to the aforesaid estate. The estate whose name is *Brochyl* is moreover in the said wood called *Moreb* (and is included).[11]

There has been some argument about the location, but scholars are now generally agreed that this is Kidderminster. The precise location may never be clear, because the boundaries are not fully described, and certainly we do not know the precise site of the monastery. One problem is the uncertain size of the estate indicated by the Latin 'cassati'. This is taken to refer to the Saxon 'hide', a unit of assessment reckoned to be the amount of arable land which one plough team could till in a year. Alternatively, it might be viewed as the amount of land required to support one household. It then becomes a measure of soil productivity rather than the actual size of the land, so that a hide could mean 40 acres in Wiltshire and 120 acres in Cambridgeshire.[12] The problem of estimating the extent of Cyneberht's estate is magnified by having to add in other types of land, such as woods, pasture, heathland and fisheries. Conventionally the hide is taken as 120 acres of arable land, so ten of them gave Cyneberht about two square miles for his monastery. This was not a huge area, even when the additional four hides of *Brochyl* are taken into account. Several parts of the Stour valley could potentially have contained the estate. However, the description of an estate lying on both sides of the river with Kinver wood on its north side seems to fit only the Kidderminster area. It is unlikely to have stretched down to the Severn because the charter does not mention such an obvious landmark.

The identity of the wood, *Moerheb*, has generated a good deal of discussion. In an excellent article, Peter King has suggested that it should be identified as the area later known as Kidderminster Heath, stretching south from below Wassell Wood across to Oldington and the Stour. I believe his arguments are sound, but they can equally well identify *Moerheb* with Wassell Wood itself and the top of Trimpley, and in many ways that would be a far more preferable

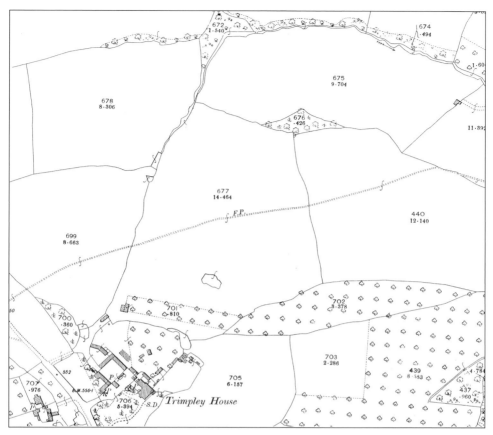

2. Trimpley 1903. The medieval hamlet is likely to have been situated close to Trimpley House. Carole Gammond has identified the ridge and furrow of ancient agriculture in fields numbered 677 and 440. At the top of the map the Honey Brook gathers strength and tumbles down towards Easthams Farm. Any attempt to locate the lost Saxon estate of *Brochyl* should start here.

conclusion. First, his suggestion might pull the estate slightly too far south to be bounded on the north by Kinver Wood. Second, he does not suggest where the estate called *Brochyl* (or Brook Hill) might be in a lower lying area, whereas the Honey Brook flows down the hillside beneath what is now Trimpley Farm and on past the remote and mysterious Easthams Farm. Perhaps *Brochyl* in the wood of *Moerheb* is the land on which one or both of these farms were later built.

The full importance of Trimpley and Habberley to the early history of Kidderminster has yet to be properly documented. Attention has tended to concentrate on land east of the town around the waters and pools of Wannerton or Broadwaters Brook which might have given rise to the name *Husmerae* in the charter. Yet the charter specifically emphasises that the land is on both sides of

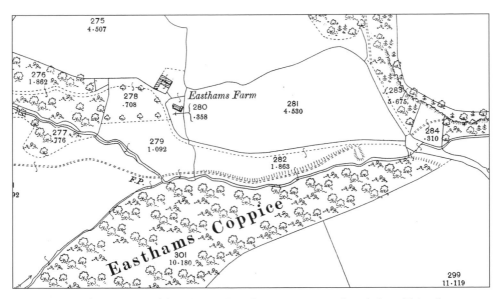

3. Easthams 1902. The Honey Brook continues its flow below Trimpley past the mysterious timber-framed farmhouse. The map clearly shows the embankment and dam, which are evidence of a former mill pond.

the Stour, so we must presume that there was something of significance across the river. The theory that Trimpley was *Moerheb* may be strengthened by considering its possible link with the medieval forest of *Morfe*. The latter name survives in the names of three farms north east of Enville. In the 13th century Morfe was a forest stretching across south Shropshire into Staffordshire, but it did not extend south to take in an area west of Kidderminster. However, there seems no reason to discount the possibility that at one time it did so. After all, Trimpley is the final south-westerly point of high ground which begins with the Enville Sheepwalks.

After all the analysis, a further powerful reason for placing the monastery at Kidderminster is simply the very name 'Kidderminster'. As Margaret Gelling has said, 'when the name of Kidderminster came into use there must have been either a monastery or an important church there'.[13] The Anglo-Saxons used the word *mynster* in both senses, but the charter uses the Latin word *coenubium*, which is generally translated as 'monastery'. We should not, however, imagine pious monks moving among stone cloisters, whose foundations now lie buried somewhere under the modern town. Almost certainly the monastery would have been made of timber with wattle and daub infilling, leaving no trace today. It was probably the kind of family monastery denounced by Bede in 734, when he complained that 'numberless people have been found who call themselves abbots'. Stenton has argued that it was a kind of Saxon equivalent of a tax dodge:

> The typical monastery of this period was an independent house – the creation of a founder who did not feel himself compelled to initiate any particular form of religious organisation … In England the lands which supported a religious community were exempt from most kinds of secular service, and there was an obvious temptation for the head of a family to evade his duties to the state by converting his household into a pseudo-monastery.[14]

Apart from the name 'Kidderminster', there is other evidence that the monastery was built. Cyneberht certainly began to call himself 'Abbot', because he is named as such when witnessing a charter in 757. His son, Ceolfrith, also called himself Abbot when signing a charter giving two estates to Worcester Abbey in the reign of King Offa, who died in 796. One of the estates was for 14 hides *aet Sture*. In 816 the Bishop of Worcester granted to Coenwulf, King of Mercia, 14 hides at *Sture*. Scholars are satisfied that this is the estate from the charter of 736, including the extra four hides of *Brochyl*.[15] In these charters there is no specific mention of a monastery, but given their proliferation it might simply have not been worth mentioning. Its ultimate fate is unknown. In his pioneering history of the town the Rev. Burton points out the likelihood of its having been destroyed by invading Danes, who advanced up the Severn in the last decade of the ninth century and are known to have attacked Ribbesford and Wolverley.

We now enter a period of complete uncertainty, with no documentary material to aid us until the Domesday survey of 1086, by which time the main settlement was known as Kidderminster. It is perfectly possible that the name had already come into being by the time of the charter of 816, but was not important enough to supplant the name *Sture* of the general locality. In fact we may make a general observation about the lack of landmarks mentioned in the charters. This suggests that the area consisted of scattered farms and no significant concentrations of population. After the Danish attacks, partly for reasons of security, it is likely that people came together to form a nucleated settlement. Given the usefulness of religion to leaders, it is very likely that a church was built to replace the monastery destroyed by the Danes, and so the new village took its name. There is an obvious derivation of the name of Kidderminster. Christianity was not fully established in the Saxon kingdom of Mercia until the founding of the episcopal see at Lichfield in 669. The first bishop was St Chad or Ceada, and for two years he undertook missionary work throughout Mercia before dying of plague in 672. He was renowned for his commitment to Christianity and his simple living, so much so that a cult grew around his name. It would have been quite natural for Cyneberht to call his monastery 'Ceada's minster' or for the founder of any new church to do the same. This explanation satisfied some 19th-century scholars such as the Rev. Dr McCave and the Rev. Burton, and I believe it to be the most convincing one still, even though recent scholarship does not see the matter so simply.[16] At least there seems to be general agreement that the name is of Saxon origin, not Celtic. There was a theory that the name was based on combining the British words *kid*, a hill, and *dwr*, water, with the Saxon *minster*. The suggestion did endure, despite being described by Dr McCave in 1876 as 'monstrous', but it is not now treated seriously, partly because the middle *r* did not appear in the town's name until 1270.[17]

## THE HUSMERAE

The various charters show that the Stour valley was the province of a people known as the *Husmerae*. Their territory was known as *Usmere* or *Ismere*, a name which survives now only in Ismere House situated on the north-west side of the A451 road to Stourbridge near to Churchill. We cannot be sure that this denotes a society based on a particular tribe. The name in fact symbolised racial fusion, *us* being Celtic for stream and *mere* Saxon for pool.[18] Their land lay at the north-west border of the kingdom of the *Hwicce*, which stretched south across what is now Gloucestershire. The *Hwicce* kingdom, which became part of Mercia, was an amalgamation of peoples. The struggle by which this had been achieved had probably left the area in a wild and under-developed state.

Woodland encroached from the north and the west. If we are right to locate *Brochyl* on the eastern slopes of Trimpley, then the woods may have stretched right back from there down to the Severn, encompassing what is now Eymore Wood. Nevertheless, the ancient road continued to pass through it from Wribbenhall on towards Shropshire, for it is mentioned as the Great Made Road, or *Miclan Strete*, in a charter concerning Wolverley of 866. It is quite possible that the settlement at Trimpley, which was to be recorded in the Domesday survey, existed throughout the Saxon period. It is true that the *-ley* suffix indicates a clearing in woodland, but we cannot assume that it was created by the Saxons moving in to clear the trees. The clearing may just as easily have been created by surrounding fields becoming woodland as the population declined after the Romans left. The predominance of trees is further suggested by other place names such as Habberley, Wolverley and Cookley. The latter two names are evidence that Kinver Forest stretched down to the Kidderminster area at the time of the 736 charter.

To the south and east of Kidderminster, or *Ismere*, were almost certainly extensive wastes, commons or heathland. This presumably is the explanation of why the grant to Cyneberht makes no mention of boundaries on those sides. Della Hooke has said that 'by Anglo-Saxon times, at least, it is unlikely that there were any unclaimed zones'. However, she goes on to say that

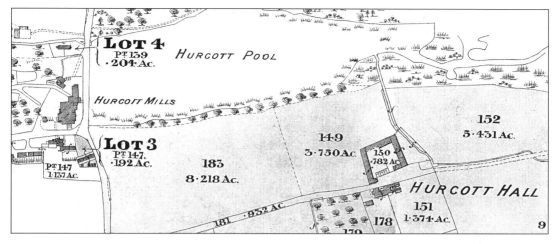

4. Hurcott 1919. This estate agent's plan shows the modern development of the medieval submanor. The mill produced paper for many centuries. The Hall is the probable site of the first manor house of the Blount family. The map shows one of Lord Foley's watercourses diverting water from the Belne Brook past the Hall and into Hurcott pool.

'intercommoning' might have taken place in frontier zones and 'this may have been the normal practice before kingdom boundaries were finally fixed'.[19] Heathland swept round from south of Wassell Wood across to what is now Oldington and the river Stour. To the east, Kinver Forest probably petered out into heaths and wastes around Iverley and Hurcott. Today walkers may get some understanding of the nature of such a landscape by visiting a surviving part of this heathland at Devil's Spittleful, next to Bewdley Safari Park. The most noticeable feature is that there are a large number of trees. Heathland, or wood pasture, was always a balance between trees and good grazing. In the post-Roman period, if the number of animals put out to graze was reducing, then the trees would have gained the upper hand. We may imagine the wood *Moerheb* spilling down from the hills to extend across what was to be called Habberley and Habberley Valley.

Even if it is certain that the landscape of the Kidderminster area became much wilder after the Roman withdrawal due to a drastic fall in population, it cannot be assumed that there was a complete withdrawal from any particular farmstead or hamlet. We have seen that the only archaeological evidence of such a withdrawal, in the case of Hoarstone Farm, is open to doubt. Just as with those place-names ending in *-ley*, it is more than possible that those settlements with names ending in *-ton* existed before the arrival of the Saxons, who renamed them. In the later Saxon period, as Kidderminster grew in importance, an expanding population probably consolidated outlying hamlets such as Sutton, Oldington and Mitton. These 'outliers' of the Domesday survey

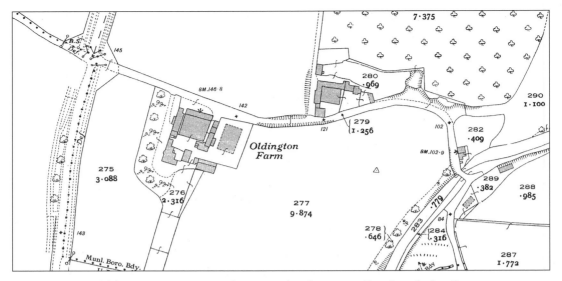

5. Oldington 1938. Lying between the Stourport Road and the Stour, Oldington was one of the most important medieval villages, with a hall probably where the farm was built.

might already have been of considerable antiquity when Cyneberht became an abbot, even though they may have been no more than isolated farmsteads.

## A BLANK IN OUR HISTORY

In his history of our town Burton wrote, 'For more than 200 years from AD 854 there is almost a complete blank in our history, and these two centuries are more sad than any that England passed through since she became a nation.'[20] He is referring not just to the Danish ravages of the late ninth century, but to the subsequent fighting between the Saxon kingdoms which led to the demise of Mercia, and to the renewed Danish incursions of the early 11th century whereby Cnut eventually became King of England in 1016. Since the writing of Burton over 100 years ago, we are no better off in terms of documentary evidence of the history of Kidderminster and its environs. Further progress will depend upon enthusiasts examining the landscape and taking whatever chances present themselves to engage in archaeological excavation.

The domination of Mercia by Wessex led to the implementation of the shire system in the Midlands from the early tenth century. Each county was divided into hundreds and the Kidderminster area was in that of Cresslau. This may indicate that the way of life and the method of organising agriculture was changing. This may have been the point at which the large open field, divided into individual strips of perhaps half an acre, was introduced. Its origins remain a mystery, for it was not a method which the Anglo-Saxons had used in their native countries.[21] Its essential nature was co-operative, because no individual held a block of strips. Instead, his holdings were spread far and wide. The farmers had to work together in terms of agreeing on such matters as which crops should be sown and allowing a field to lie fallow every third year so that the soil should recover. Perhaps we should see the system as based on the principle of unity in adversity, during times of very low population and regular upheavals due to fighting.

The open fields were introduced after the Saxon charters, and then only partially, in what Rackham calls 'peripheral England'.[22] It is a moot point whether this wild part of north Worcestershire would count as peripheral, but it may have done. It is suggested that the growth of Kidderminster occurred no earlier than the tenth century, after the worst depredations of the Danes and the destruction of the monastery. On this view Kidderminster was the outcome of a partial withdrawal from the isolated farmsteads and small hamlets in favour of the larger and closer-knit 'nucleated' settlements which characterised the open-field areas. Three large open fields lay to the east of the town and one to the west. Undoubtedly there were others in the surrounding countryside. Nevertheless, upheavals were in store, and certainly the agricultural system had to be renewed after the Norman Conquest.

## II

# The Middle Ages

In Domesday Book of 1086 Kidderminster, or *Chideminstre*, emerged as the main manor of the area, stretching across the Severn to incorporate Ribbesford and almost certainly what is now Bewdley. Yet the entry contained the dramatic words: 'The whole of this manor was waste.' The most likely reason for the destruction of arable land was the 'harrying of the north' by William the Conqueror in the 1060s. Wolverley too had suffered. In 1066 it had been worth £4, but at the time of the survey its value was only 30s. Some recovery in Kidderminster had been made, but the note that '20 more ploughs possible' indicates that there was still a way to go.

The full Domesday entry can be translated as follows:

> King William holds KIDDERMINSTER in lordship, with 16 outliers: WANNERTON, TRIMPLEY, HURCOTT, FRANCHE, another FRANCHE, *BRISTITUNE*, HABBERLEY, *FASTOCHESFELDE*, WRIBBENHALL, RIBBESFORD, another RIBBESFORD, SUTTON, OLDINGTON, MITTON, *TEULESBERGE*, *SUDUUALE*. In these lands, including the manor, 20 hides. The whole of this manor was waste. In lordship 1 plough;
>
> 20 villagers and 30 smallholders with 18 ploughs; a further 20 more ploughs possible. 2 male and 4 female slaves.
>
> 2 mills at 16s; 2 salt-houses at 30s; a fishery at 100d; woodland at 4 leagues.
>
> In this manor the reeve holds the land of one riding-man; he has 1 plough and a mill at 5 *ora*.
>
> To this manor belongs 1 house in Droitwich and another in Worcester which pay 10d.
>
> The whole manor paid £14 in revenue before 1066; now it pays £10 4s by weight.
>
> The King has placed the woodland of this manor in the Forest. Of this manor's land William holds 1 hide and the land of one riding-man. He has 1 villager and 8 smallholders who have 4½ ploughs. Value 11s.
>
> Also of this land Aiulf holds 1 virgate. 1 plough and 2 slaves there. Value 2s.[1]

Kidderminster clearly was at the heart of a manor of size and significance. This must increase our confidence that the estate in the charter of 736 was indeed Kidderminster and formed the basis out of which the more extensive manor was able to grow. We may still believe there was a church, because it is known that many churches were omitted from Domesday Book.[2] The names of most of the outlying berewicks can be identified with modern districts. The inclusion of Ribbesford, lying on the west side of the Severn, is conclusive proof that the Domesday manor of Kidderminster was larger than the estate granted in the charter. Cyneberht's land had perhaps not extended as far as Wannerton in the east or to Oldington and Mitton in the south west. I feel certain it had not extended to Wribbenhall, or *Gurbehale* as it is written in Domesday Book. It is possible that the manor of Kidderminster crossed over the river not just to Ribbesford, but to include Bewdley. This was the view of Burton, who noted the continuity between a 13th-century document and one from the 14th century, except that *Wrbehale* had become *Beaulieu*.[3] Some outliers may have been very small, and in certain cases may have been single farmsteads. Franche and 'another Franche', for example, may simply mean two farmsteads in the same vicinity. Four names cannot be identified with any confidence, although A.J. Perrett's belief that *Suduuale* is Caldwall has won acceptance.

That the manor of Kidderminster was relatively remote is confirmed by analysis which shows that the population of the Cresslau hundred was the lowest but one in Worcestershire. Burton arrived at a total population of 264 by assuming that each person mentioned in the survey had a household of four.[4] We can be sure there was much woodland, but its extent is uncertain. Domesday revealed that 40 per cent of the county's land was woodland, as against just under 15 per cent in England as a whole. There were four leagues in Kidderminster. There are real doubts about interpreting this measurement, but one suggestion would reckon this at about seven square miles of woodland.[5] This is a conservative estimate, but it would imply that trees covered not just most of the high ground around Trimpley, extending westwards to the Severn and northwards to Eymore and what was to become Park Attwood, but also the expanse of land to the west and south west of Kidderminster, which would later function as heathland. There would have been still more woodland besides.

## THE FOREST

King William held the manor directly. To further emphasise his supremacy he had 'placed the woodland of the manor in the Forest'. This phraseology makes clear that the forest was more than woodland. Kidderminster's forest may well have incorporated farmsteads and clearings. Certainly it would have included heathland and common grazing land. The term 'forest' refers to the law applied to these areas, which were designed to maintain and encourage wild animals, principally deer, and the greenery on which they depended. The forest law allowed the king to keep his deer on other people's lands. Property rights were maintained and the forest was not purely reserved to the king for hunting. Nevertheless, the forest law was an imposition on local people and by 1150 its main effect was to provide the king with revenue. The royal passion for forests continued through the 12th century, but then began to wane.[6] In 1210 the lord of the manor of Kidderminster, Henry Biset, paid £100 so that his woods, including that of *Borlese* (Burlish) might be de-afforested.[7]

## THE LORD OF THE MANOR

The Biset family acquired Kidderminster when King Henry II relinquished the royal hold on the manor by granting it to his Steward, Manser Biset, between 1155 and 1162. After a period of anarchy the Norman ruling class sought to impose greater order across the country. Biset acquired a poor agricultural community of peasants co-operating to manage the strips of the open fields on a three-year crop rotation basis. The open-field system had been re-established after being laid waste, and the fields were named in medieval documents from the 14th century. There were three on the east side of the village: these were Leswell or Lowswall Field between Comberton Hill and Birmingham Road, Middle Field between Birmingham Road and Stourbridge Road, and Church Field which covered part of the area between Stourbridge Road and the river Stour. To the west of Kidderminster, above the rock face between Mill Street and the road to Bewdley, was another open field called Cursefield or Cussfield.[8] It is uncertain whether the Bisets resided in Kidderminster, but their determination to make the most of their new manor undoubtedly led to the growth of Kidderminster from an agricultural village into the embryonic town.

The use of religion, with its capacity to inspire awe and fear, was an obvious method for the Normans to employ in order to begin the process of maximising Kidderminster's potential. Manser Biset, who died in 1186, provided a church in 1175, and any surviving Saxon church was probably destroyed. Robert of Hurcott was the first rector, and the tenants of the manor would have been compelled to pay a tithe to support him. However, Biset had also already founded a convent for leprous women on his wife's property at Maiden Bradley in Wiltshire, and it was his intention that the church and thus the greater tithes should go to them upon Robert's death. This was to be a matter of some dispute and the rectory was not downgraded to a vicarage until the early 14th century.[9]

There is a legend concerning the origin of the name of the open field, Cursefield. Many centuries ago it was decided to build a church on this high ground, because the existing church in the Stour valley was regularly flooded. Unfortunately, every night the building work was undone by the mysterious transportation of the stones to the site now occupied by St Mary's. One version suggests that demons were responsible, another suggests angels. Eventually, the inhabitants gave in to the inevitable and built the church where the stones were taken. They concluded that the original ground chosen was bewitched and called it the Cursed Field, or Cussfield. Of course, a good story is spoiled by the existence of a deed of 1342, which gives the name as Crousfield. As late as 1725 deeds were still referring to Cursefield or Crossfield as alternatives.[10]

Although the Bisets were probably mostly absentee landlords, it is believed that a manor house would have been built near to the church. Some evidence for the existence of a hall is that King Henry III is known to have visited the town in 1226 and 1233 and would have required suitable accommodation. During 19th-century building in Hall Street workmen found extensive vaults of solid masonry. Unfortunately, the insensitive redevelopment of the area has not permitted any extensive excavation and has probably permanently destroyed the possibility of any future investigation. Kidderminster's own Ian Walker has fought a one-man battle to take what opportunity there was to explore workings before the concrete went down. In 1959, after some street widening at Hall Street, he wrote that excavation had revealed 'twelfth century pottery from a hearth'.[11]

## A TOWN

The close interest of the Biset family in Kidderminster resulted in certain economic changes which saw the settlement grow into a town. Manser Biset was followed by his son, Henry, but the period came to an end in 1241 with the

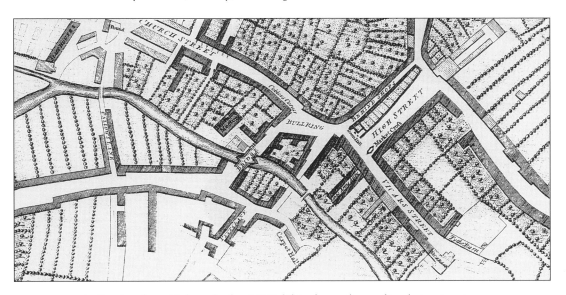

6. Section from Doharty's plan 1753. This shows the medieval street system largely intact, but with a permanent row of buildings dividing the market area to form High Street and Behind Shops.

death of a John Biset, who had no sons. Of course, their interest was not of a paternalistic kind, but one directed at maximising the profit from Kidderminster. The late 12th century was a time of improved agriculture, and they no doubt acted to ensure efficiency was improved. It was also a time when the ruling class was interested in regulating the cloth industry. In 1197 Richard I issued the assize of cloth, which fixed statutory dimensions and assigned four or six men in each borough to enforce the rules. Many of the changes instigated by the Bisets ensured the development of Kidderminster as a place of trade.

Among the rights given to Biset by the king's grant was that of 'toll', enabling him to place a charge on all items sold in the town. The lord clearly thereby had an incentive to encourage the growth of trading in Kidderminster. The system of 'burgage tenure' was duly introduced by one of the Bisets, probably by the start of the 13th century. The occupants were known as 'burgesses', who held freehold tenements and paid a standard rent to the lord of the manor. Their holdings were of a standard width and characterised by a long rectangular shape, which continued to be evident in the town until the wholesale redevelopment of the late 20th century. The privileges enjoyed by burgesses was a way of attracting skilled craftsmen and traders to a town.

Travel at this time was difficult and dangerous. Opportunities for trade in products between distant places were rare and not part of everyday life. In

7. Demolition 1968. This was the last opportunity to explore the medieval cellars and vaults of the Swan Street/High Street area before they disappeared beneath the concrete. The listed *Fox Inn* to the left is about to go, whilst Baxter's House has been reduced to rubble in the foreground.

this respect markets and fairs were vitally important. It is probable that the market was set up at the same time as the burgesses were established. It was certainly in operation by 1240, and in 1266 Thomas de Punchamton, while on his way home from the Kidderminster market, killed Gilbert Athelard who had attacked him. A fair was instituted from 1228.[12] A market cross was erected and was first recorded in 1482. It was shown still standing in Doharty's street plan of 1753, but was pulled down in 1760 when the Guildhall was rebuilt. This was a significant loss, because the medieval market cross was once a common sight and represented 'the emblem of the peace of commercial intercourse'. Markets and fairs constituted the oases of commercialism in a 'wilderness of militancy'.[13]

The developing town of Kidderminster was centred around the market with streets radiating off it. The pattern of those streets is still recognisable today. Thus the early medieval town consisted of the market in the High Street, with Coventry Street, Worcester Street, Vicar Street and the Bull Ring or Church Street leaving the four corners. The burgage plots were situated along these streets. Almost certainly the town at this time would have included Mill Street, as it is generally assumed that one of the two mills listed at Domesday was on the site of the later 'Town Mill', where a building carrying that legend survives today near the Crossley Park junction. Archaeological work has so far failed to prove this assumption.[14]

A key question is whether the growing town supported an early cloth industry of any significance. It has been argued that Kidderminster was a town specialising in the manufacture of cloth from the 13th century, and certainly fullers and dyers are recorded at that time. However, the absence of references to weavers themselves suggests that, like all the local towns, Kidderminster had a cloth industry but it was not outstanding. The fuller, the dyer and the master weaver may have been figures of local importance, but the ordinary weaver was not of high status. The Lay Subsidy Rolls of 1275 and 1327, which list local people to be taxed, contain no names from which 'weaver' can be derived. It is possible that these lists included only burgesses and other propertied people. Weavers may have been of a lower class called 'tencers', possibly immigrants from the surrounding countryside. Their inferior status required the payment to the lord upon their death of a 'heriot', from which burgesses were exempt. The details of this heriot are revealed in a document from 1333: 'The Customs of the Lords of Kidderminster'. It was 'a two horse wain with ironbound wheels, half the pigs, half the bacon, the horses but not the mares, half the bee hives, and half the cloth not assized'. The reference to cloth 'not assized' is a strong clue that weavers were indeed among this subordinate class.[15]

*Overleaf:*   8. Bottom of Swan Street 1926. Such tall buildings once gave Kidderminster a true urban character, but most of them have been lost.

## THE BREAK UP OF THE MANOR

The feudal system of the Middle Ages saw the Normans impose themselves upon a peasant economy which they allowed to continue as before. Gradually the system began to disintegrate. Duties owed to the lord, such as military service or ploughing, were transformed over time into money payments. Lands changed hands so that the original manor dominated by one lord and his steward was no longer recognisable. In Kidderminster the fragmentation of the manor was particularly clear. When John Biset died in 1241, his manor of Kidderminster was split between his three daughters, thereby creating three manors. The share belonging to Ela became known as Kidderminster Biset. Her second husband was John de Wotton, but their son John took the name Biset. The share taken by another daughter, Isabel, became known as Kidderminster Burnell, after Robert Burnell, the Bishop of Bath, who had acquired the manor by the end of the century. The third share was given to the eldest daughter, Margery, who married Robert Rivers, and their son John inherited the share. He passed it to the priory of Maiden Bradley, which was to maintain its holdings in Kidderminster until the Reformation.

The leper colony founded by Manser Biset had become an Augustinian priory in 1184. From then on it received occasional gifts of land interests in Kidderminster, which it already held before acquiring the third share of the manor. The complex network of rights and possessions enjoyed by the priory included the hamlets of Oldington and Comberton, transferred to them by Ralph de Auxeville by 1227. Today there is nothing left of the community that was Oldington, but in the latter part of the 13th century it seems to have been one of the most populous hamlets in the manor of Kidderminster. According to a document seen by Burton there were 13 tenants, and the Lay Subsidy Roll of 1275 listed 15 householders.[16] The lost village probably occupied the site of Oldington Farm, which has now been obliterated by a trading estate on both sides of Oldington Lane off the Stourport Road opposite Brinton's sports ground. Here too, apparently, was a 'hall', the principal residence of the Maiden Bradley manor, for which a lock was purchased in 1281.[17] Good use was made of the river. There was a weir, which would have provided fish stocks. Further downstream there was a mill at Mitton, which was also part of the manor held by the monks of Maiden Bradley.

Monasteries are known to have managed their manors tightly, and it is possible that the stewardship of the priory bore a heavier touch than in the other two thirds of the manor. Nevertheless, they struggled to take possession of Manser Biset's gift of the church. It took Papal Bulls of 1334 to pave the way for the recovery of their property. It had been claimed that the 'simplicity and ignorance' of the monks had reduced them to 'great poverty'. The Bishop of Worcester acted at once and converted the Rectory into a Vicarage. He ordered a valuation of the living, which clearly showed the property involved in the settlement between the priory and the vicars. At first the vicars were to have a house near 'the south side of the church', but eventually they obtained a more favourable agreement, by which they took the house and manor at Hurcott, where there was a mill and where the rents of 58s. 3d. suggested that the tenants were numerous.[18] The assertion of their rights helped the monks to evade poverty. In 1380 the priory of Maiden Bradley was to be rebuilt, assisted by the steady profit extracted from Kidderminster.

## KIDDERMINSTER BISET AND BURNELL

We have a very different coroner's inquest nowadays, but once its function was to determine the rights of the Crown concerning the property and estates of a deceased person. The Inquisitiones Post Mortem of 1307 revealed quite a lot about John Biset's holdings in Kidderminster when he died.[19] The Biset manor contained the heart of the town, because 63 'free burgesses' were paying rents of just over 115s. The names of some of his agricultural tenants link them to places such as Hoarstone, Habberley, North Wood, Puxton, Aggborough and Caldwall. This does not mean that these areas formed the agricultural part of the Biset manor, but is more likely to imply that certain tenants were accumulating a number of holdings in all three manors. Hugh de Caldewelle, for example, is thought to have been a man of substance, and Caldwall itself was part of the Maiden Bradley manor by the 14th century. It is likely that the arable strips of the Biset manor were in the open fields adjacent to the town and were gradually being acquired by the wealthier and more enterprising tenants. There is no mention of a hall or manor house in the demesne estate, held directly by the lord of the manor, yet it has generally been assumed for no obvious reason that the hall close to the church belonged to this manor. The demesne estate did include ten acres of meadow, 160 acres of arable land and a half interest in no fewer than three water mills.

Inquests in 1293, 1294 and 1315 after deaths in the Burnell family hint at both development and neglect in their share of the manor. They were certainly absentee landlords. In 1293 a fulling mill is recorded, which is early evidence of an emerging cloth industry. The location is unclear, as are the 210 acres of arable land and 8½ acres of meadow. There is an indication that the process of enclosure was under way with the reference to a 'certain park, the pasture whereof, beside feeding the deer, is worth half a mark yearly'. The difficulties of absentee landlords were exposed by the 1294 inquest which commented that Burnell was 'unable to sustain' his land at Eymore. Indeed, by 1315 the family had relinquished it. On the eastern edge of Kidderminster the Burnells held Dunclent of Stephen de Bosco (or Attwood), who is believed to have held land at Trimpley also and was clearly a power in the area. In general it is very difficult to tell where the Burnell lands were. The impression is of a manor consisting of land lying some way from the town. Also, given that the 1293 and 1294 inquests refer to a half share in only one water mill, the likelihood is that the Burnell portion was less closely entwined with the Biset share than was that of Maiden Bradley. By a process of elimination it must be likely that this manor consisted of land to the west of the town, from Habberley and Franche across to the Severn.

It has not been possible to locate Trimpley in these inquests, but I would have been inclined to suggest that it formed the heart of the Burnell manor, although it has generally been thought to have belonged to the Attwood family, who definitely held the distinct manor of Park Attwood. Like Oldington, there is much to suggest that Trimpley was of great significance in the medieval period prior to the Black Death of 1349. The list of tenants examined by Burton showed eight tenants at Trimpley in the late 13th century, paying a total rental of 27s. 6¾d. The Lay Subsidy Roll of 1275 gave extraordinary importance to the vill of Trimpley by listing 59 taxpayers as against only 58 for Kidderminster itself. A vill was a medieval administrative unit, rather than a village itself, and that of Trimpley must be taken to have included places such as Franche and Habberley, which were not separately listed. The permission obtained from the king in 1210 for de-afforestation by Henry Biset probably boosted the value of Trimpley and it is likely that much woodland was cleared from the high ground in the following period. On the hillside north east of Trimpley Farm, above where the Honey Brook flows down past Easthams Farm, traces of ridge and furrow have been observed.[20] If this was indeed the location of an open field, and possibly even the Saxon estate of *Brochyl*, then the lost village of Trimpley may well have been near where Trimpley Farm lies today. Around the medieval village the woodland was gradually stripped away, perhaps leaving wood-pasture for grazing. This may have been happening even when the forest law applied. Since most royal forests were subject to common rights held by surrounding settlements, there was a tendency for the woodland to degrade to wood pasture, and eventually common. The end result of this process was Trimpley Common, which by the early 20th century was relatively open, but which today in the absence of grazing is covered by trees.

That only two of the manors shared the town of Kidderminster is shown by the 1333 document, 'The Customs of the Lords of Kidderminster', which stated that the profits of strays within the borough belonged to only the 'two lords', while those of the foreign belonged to the 'three lords'. This is the earliest documented mention of the division of the parish between the borough and the 'foreign', that is the surrounding countryside. It was in the borough where privileged access to profit from industry and trade could be given. As we shall see, conflict would occur when efforts were made to engage in industry in the countryside in the early 16th century. We do not know the extent to which cloth weaving took place in rural areas, nor do we know when it started, but it is possible that even at this early time weaving was taking place in places such as Oldington and Trimpley, thus explaining why they were more populous than other hamlets such as Franche, Habberley and Puxton.

## PRIVATE ESTATES AND DEER PARKS

The Burnell inquests hint at enclosure and the growth of estates. That process was to come to fruition during the 14th century. Eymore was given by Edward Burnell to the Prior and Convent of Worcester in 1312. Soon afterwards the prior obtained a licence to impark his new land.[21] Up to this time the perplexing transfer of manors, lands and other rights had probably had the effect of simply changing or adding to those members of the Norman élite who were taking profit from the labouring classes. The creation of a park was of a potentially more serious nature. It was generally surrounded by a deer-proof boundary consisting of a palisade of oak stakes. It is likely that the grazing rights and the ability of the peasants to collect wood were affected. Also, it is possible

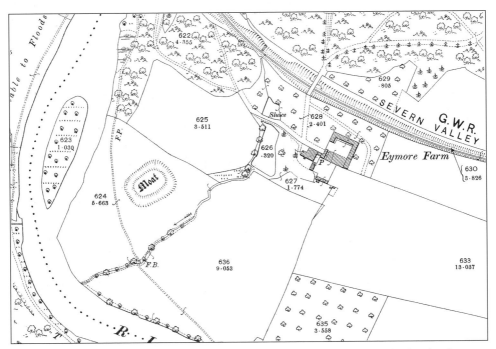

9. Eymore Farm 1904. The moat can be seen today, close to the bank of Trimpley Reservoir. It is probably the site of a farmhouse from the medieval period.

that there were evictions. In 1294 Eymore, which consisted of 26 acres of land and several acres of pasture, had free tenants, who paid 18s. 4d. rent each year. We do not know the effect of the enclosure on them, but the occupation of Eymore for many centuries by the ecclesiastical élite of Worcester was to be another illustration of the adept business practices of religious bodies. The land concerned here is the low-lying area by the Severn, where Eymore Farm was until the reservoir was constructed in the 1960s. An outline of a moat can still be seen in a field near the river, and this might have been the site of the early manor house. A deer park is documented in a charter of 1278 covering the same ground.[22] Its selection as a deer park illustrates the medieval belief that the fallow deer was a woodland animal, even though their biting of young shoots was one of the causes of shrinking woodland.

There would appear to have been another park at Trimpley held by the church at Worcester. The property concerned in the dispute between the priory of Maiden Bradley and the rectors of Kidderminster included the tithes of the 'woods' or the 'parks' of Trimpley and Eymore. This is further evidence that the high land at Trimpley was heavily wooded during the medieval period.[23]

It is likely that another deer park was established soon afterwards at Caldwall. The single octagonal tower in Castle Road is the most visible relic of this estate and is Kidderminster's oldest building, apart from the church. Efforts have been made to clarify the origins, and to set an earlier date for not just the castle but the creation of the sub-manor of Caldwall. However, there is still uncertainty. Various opinions date the tower to 1347, c.1350 or c.1380. However, archaeological evidence suggests the previous existence of an arcaded hall, perhaps dating from before the Conquest, which was demolished in the early 14th century and replaced by a new two-storey house.[24] The owner of Caldwall by 1327 was Hugh de Cokesey, a member of one of Worcestershire's richest families. In 1335 he was granted free warren at Caldwall and acquired the right given by the Crown to keep animals and birds, and to kill them. This points strongly to the creation of a deer park at this time. Its eastern boundary was, of course, Park Lane. The Park was still named on the 1780 Sheriff map, which showed its other boundaries to be Bewdley Road, Sutton Road and Stourport Road.[25]

A deer park was both a privilege and a status symbol. It is tempting to see the addition of a tower to Caldwall Hall as another status symbol. It is not obvious that it served any useful military purpose, with the castle being overlooked by higher ground on its west side. Yet a certain amount of protection was afforded by the boggy nature of the surrounding land and by the Stour itself. Also, it is likely that Caldwall was built on a raised outcrop of more solid ground. It has even been suggested that the tower is the single one remaining of a 'medieval and moated castle'. This theory argues that the Stour or mill leat divided north of Caldwall, with one channel running past its west side, partly following a straight line now formed by the canal, before turning sharply back to the main channel, thus creating a complete moat around the castle. Stone footings are believed to have been seen extending partially into the Stour, before being buried when the course of the river was recently altered for the Weavers' Wharf development. These could have been the base for another tower.[26]

There is no doubt that this early history of the Caldwall estate is central to an understanding of Kidderminster at the time. The fragmentation of the manor, with its absentee landlords, had created a power vacuum. This created the opportunity for the Cokesey family to become the leading family in the town until the late 15th century. Although they were close to those in power, they were perhaps not quite powerful enough to have been subject to the great gains and losses made by others in a time of conflict and anarchy across the country. They were an important local family, whose main base was at first in nearby Upton Warren just west of Bromsgrove. They held the manor of Great Cooksey from the middle of the 13th century. It is thought that Walter de Cokesey received the custody of the earldom of Warwick in 1325, during the minority of Thomas de Beauchamp. The memorials in St Mary's church leave little doubt they became firmly based at Caldwall. By 1313 Kidderminster's church was established as the main church in the deanery. In that year it was used by the Bishop of Worcester for his Whitsuntide Ordination, when 29 sub-deacons, 68 deacons and 46 priests were all ordained. In 1315 the great altar was consecrated by the Bishop, and it is thought that this fixes the date of the chancel, which is the oldest part of the church and includes a beautiful east window.

## PARK ATTWOOD

In 1362 a licence was granted for another park to John Attwood of Wolverley, the king's yeoman, a person of high status. The Attwood (or de Bosco) family had been growing in power and wealth for some time. They were burgesses in the town of Kidderminster, and we have seen that they may have held the manor of Trimpley, where according to Habington they had lived since ancient times. In 1315 they held land at Dunclent. In the early 14th century they were linked by marriage to the earls of Warwick when Robert Attwood's daughter, Isabel, married John Beauchamp of Holt. The de Cokeseys were closely connected also to the Beauchamp family, so we begin to understand the close ties among the West Midlands ruling élite.

The licence was for a park of 600 acres in Kidderminster and Wolverley. A glance at Park Attwood on today's OS map immediately suggests that the park would have extended east of the house and be contained within the area bounded by the Bridgnorth Road and Hollies Lane. This would have been about 600 acres. Furthermore, it is land which straddles the boundary between Kidderminster and Wolverley. In fact the passage of time appears to have seen it move from the latter to the former. The boundaries described in the Saxon charter of 866, when Wolverley was granted to Wulfferd, seem to have contained this land within them. The sharp slopes below the Bridgnorth Road were once ideally suited to be given over for the enclosure of trees and deer. The park was not necessarily devoted to deer, and land supporting arable, sheep or cattle could have been enclosed as well. The lower ground along Hollies Lane may have been used for such purposes. The estate may not have extended fully into the junction of Bridgnorth Road and Hollies Lane. There was a common there until the Enclosure Act of 1774.

By this time the Attwood family had probably built a private chapel, having obtained the licence in 1350. The chapel survived until suppressed during the Reformation and sold in 1549. Since then its location has become obscure, although there is a tradition that it was near to Trimpley church. With a park and a chapel it might seem that under the Attwoods civilisation had arrived, but we cannot be so sure. In 1305 an Attwood tenant was a member of a robber gang on the Trimpley high road. Furthermore, their relative, John Beauchamp of Holt, was robbing merchant boats on the Severn at much the same time. It has been claimed of the ruling families of this period 'that disorder seems almost to be a by-occupation of the class'.[27]

## KIDDERMINSTER'S IMPORTANCE

In summary, it is likely that Kidderminster grew as a town under the Bisets, but stagnated after the tripartite division in the middle of the 13th century. Its importance lay in being an ecclesiastical centre and perhaps having some strategic significance in military terms. In 1295 it sent two MPs to Parliament, but there were to be no more until the Reform Act of 1832. Its trading and economic value were dubious. According to Bund, Kidderminster in 1307 was 'not then a place of much importance'.[28] Evidently he considered that John Biset's assets, as revealed by the inquest, were not impressive. These included rents from his 63 'free burgesses', whose duties were fixed and minimal. Other tenures were still the villeinage kind, whereby any manner of work might be required. Others still were 'customary tenants' and were obliged to assist the lord to maintain his own property by ploughing, hedging, fencing, carrying crops and mowing on certain days of the year. The burgesses were not truly independent. There was no borough court, just the lord's manorial court. In other words, Kidderminster was a 'seigneurial' borough.[29] An illusion of independence may have been created by having largely absentee lords of the manor for three centuries or so after the division of Kidderminster into three parts. The precise balance of power was set down to some extent in deeds of 1333, which survive in 17th-century copies. One appeared to show the right of burgesses 'to elect Bailiffs on the first Monday after Michaelmas'. It also claimed that bailiffs might hand over the lord's tolls 'without an account'. Other documents of 1333 were 'The Customs of the Lords of Kidderminster' and 'The Composition of the Manor and Borough'.

Contained within the last-named document were two regulations, one of which was aimed at those producing cloth in the borough and the other at those bringing cloth in to sell. The first stated: 'No manner of man within the Manor and Borough of Kidderminster shall make any woollen cloth, broad or narrow, without the Bailiff's seal; in pain of 20 shillings for every default'. The latter stated: 'No man or woman shall bring to the fair or market any kerseys for to set to sale without a seal'. These rules controlled the quality of the cloth, but also extracted income from trade. Another source of income was a regulation in the Customs document which stated 'the tencers shall make a fine with the Lords in the Borough yearly for their workshops and for carrying on their craft there'. The 14th-century records are scanty, but these documents do at least enable us to be sure there was a cloth industry in Kidderminster and that it was the principal industry of the town. We cannot be sure that the trade was prospering, but clearly the bailiff and the lord of the manor were intent upon making some money from whatever trade there was.

## POPULATION CATASTROPHE

At some point Kidderminster had prospered. Analysis of the available records suggests that by 1300 the number of people living in the manor of Kidderminster was about 800, with about a third living in the town itself.[30] Therefore, there had been something like a tripling of the population since Domesday, due partly to a combination of the recovery of the waste and other agricultural improvements. Also, up to the early 14th century there must have been an influx into the town of weavers and others looking to engage in their craft. This is suggested by the regulation in the Composition of the Manor document requiring tencers to get the bailiff's permission to work in the town. Much of the increase in population probably occurred by the early 13th century. Dark times were ahead. The Black Death of 1349 is generally supposed to have killed half the inhabitants. Even before that Kidderminster's population was decimated. Constant war against the Welsh, Scots and French impoverished the country. In addition there were terrible famines between 1312 and 1322. Between the Lay Subsidy Rolls of 1275 and 1327 the number of tax payers in the manor of Kidderminster was cut by over half.[31]

The subsequent 150 years or more were just as disturbed, and it is unlikely that Kidderminster developed positively before the growth of a nation state under the Tudors. The shortage of agricultural labour after the calamity of 1349 created a position whereby the labourers were more self-confident. The feudal system came under further strain, and the conflict between lords and serfs eventually led to the Peasants Revolt of 1391. This was the background to the trend for landowners to enclose land for sheep farming. In Kidderminster the parks and other enclosures of the 14th century may not have displaced much arable land, but by the 15th century sheep were taking over from people. This did not lead to a drift of people into the town and a replenishing of its population, for the times were not conducive to organised industry. The Hundred Years' War with France, followed by the Wars of the Roses, bred lawless behaviour.

The French war led Edward III, who reigned for fifty years from 1327-77, to prohibit 'idle games' such as football and cockfighting in order to encourage the practice of archery at the butts. In Kidderminster the north-east corner of the Caldwall estate became the Park Butts, a name which survives today. In a divided manor run by absentee lords Caldwall had grown to be the principal residence of the town. The parish church reflects the dominance of the Cokesey family. Sir Hugh Cokesey and his wife Denise are buried in the churchyard. Their son, Sir Walter (d.1407), is commemorated by a brass in the north-east corner of the nave, together with his wife Matilda and her second husband, Sir John Phelip. A Latin inscription states that King Henry V loved Sir John as a friend and that he fought at Harfleur in France where he died in 1415. The church tower dates from the first half of the 15th century and it must be likely that it was made possible by the Cokesey family, who had survived some troubled times.

Their more illustrious friends, the Beauchamps, had not been so successful. Sir John Beauchamp of Holt made his name as a fighting man under Edward III. His wealth eventually extended to the acquisition of two thirds of the manor of Kidderminster. The reversion of the Biset manor was purchased c.1380 and the Burnell manor was purchased in 1382-3.[32] In 1387 his loyalty was rewarded by Richard II with a peerage and barony. He became Lord of Beauchamp and Baron of Kidderminster, but the latter title seems to have been based purely on his ownership of the manors, and there is no reason to believe he took a direct interest in the town. His success did not last long and he was executed in 1388 after a purge of Richard's favourites. The manors were purchased by Thomas Beauchamp, Earl of Warwick and were eventually settled on his younger brother, Sir William Beauchamp, Lord Abergavenny. After his widow Joan died in 1435 the manors descended to her granddaughter Elizabeth, wife of Sir Edward Nevill, and they were to remain with that family for nearly 300 years. These people were among the richest and most powerful in the country and Kidderminster was of little interest to them.

It was possibly Sir Walter de Cokesey who fortified Caldwall, perhaps in the 1380s, at the same time Sir John Beauchamp was rebuilding Holt Castle.[33] When Sir Walter died his Caldwall manor was valued at 100s., a modest amount, but still probably the most valuable estate in Kidderminster. Whatever the real extent of his fortifications, their erection was clearly a wise move given the disorder of the times. Even the vicar of Kidderminster, William Mountford, was in trouble in 1449 for trespass with others in Leicestershire.[34] Another indication of the growing anarchy was the need for an enquiry into the antics of Sir Hugh Cokesey, grandson of Sir Walter. Lady Abergavenny, Joan de Beauchamp, complained that the Caldwall Lord, along with John Lowe a yeoman of Kidderminster and 'other malefactors arrayed in manner of war', had invaded her houses and park at Snyterfield in Warwick. They had hunted there without permission and 'assaulted and beat her men, servants and tenants.'[35]

This kind of marauding across the country by knights was commonplace in the 15th century, but it might have been thought that Cokesey would have shown some restraint on the land of a family with whom his own family was closely tied. Sir Hugh's sister was Lady Joyce Beauchamp, wife of Walter Beauchamp of Powick. Hugh died in 1445 and his tomb is on the north wall of the chancel in the parish church. The tomb of Lady Joyce is built into the wall of the south aisle of the nave. The Cokesey era was coming to an end. Hugh had no children and the estate descended to Joyce's son, Thomas, by her third husband. He took the name Cokesey, but died without issue in 1498.

With the exception of the Cokeseys' diligent refurbishment of the parish church, the period was probably one of stagnation for the town of Kidderminster. Around it enclosure would have been gathering pace. The reference to the 'yoman', John Lowe, companion of Sir Hugh on his Warwick expedition, is an indication of a rising class of independent farmer and of the break up of the open-field system. In 1450 another Kidderminster yeoman, John Reynold, went on a similar adventure with Humphrey Stafford, who was later to be executed for treason. Stafford and his band were accused of entering Oxfordshire where they 'lay in wait to slay certain the king's lieges, wounded them and carried away their goods to no small value and committed other trespasses and riots.'[36] It is worth reflecting that conditions of anarchy, where yeomen and even the vicar of Kidderminster were getting tangled up in the private acts of pillage and robbery, were not conducive to the growth of industry in the towns.

Nevertheless, records of cloth produced annually suggest that around 1418 Kidderminster was holding its own and ranked with Droitwich as a significant centre in the county, although Worcester was by far the most important.[37] A perusal of the Calendars of Patent Rolls for the 15th century reveals some

10. St Mary and All Saints' Church. This engraving from 1814 shows the 15th-century tower. To its right can be seen the chantry built in 1530, in which Thomas Blount later founded the Grammar School.

evidence that Kidderminster was trading widely, with pardons given to townspeople concerning debts to inhabitants of Ludlow, Salisbury and London. However, the same records contain no references to weavers at Kidderminster at all, suggesting that weaving was still not an occupation of any standing. The occupations of those receiving pardons for criminal offences included a draper, three chapmen, a goldsmith, an ironmonger, a 'walker' (fuller) and a gentleman. Perhaps weavers were very well behaved, but it is more likely their status was such that they were not worthy of pardons. They were probably humble countryside dwellers. In a lawless society the cloth industry migrated to the countryside, where it could not be controlled by borough authorities. This change was linked to the enclosure of arable land for sheep pasture. Perhaps Lowe and Reynold were early examples of farmers who took this course, which ensured a plentiful supply of wool for the cloth industry. The displaced farm labourers provided a pool of cheap labour for prospective clothiers. Such was the decline of the towns that Henry VIII felt compelled to legislate on this matter in Worcestershire, and specifically in Kidderminster.

# III

# *The Making of a Cloth Town*

The deterioration in Kidderminster's cloth trade was addressed by the Worcestershire Cloth Act of 1533. Protective action was taken by Henry VIII's government to assist the town, along with those of Worcester, Evesham, Droitwich and Bromsgrove. The Act described these places as having been 'in times past well and substantially inhabited' by people making woollen cloths. The poor people worked daily 'spinning, carding, breaking, and sorting of wools'. Weavers, fullers, sheremen and dyers had 'sufficient living by the same, until now within few years passed that divers persons inhabiting in the hamlets, thorps and villages adjoining to the said towns, for their private wealths … have not only ingrossed and taken into their hands divers and sundry farms, and become farmers, grasiers, and husbandmen, but also do exercise the mysteries of cloth-making, weaving, fulling and sheering within their said houses to the great decay and ruin of the said Towns'. The Act went on to limit the making of cloth for sale in the county of Worcestershire to those towns.[1]

The selection of all the principal towns in the county for protection again implies that Kidderminster had not been outstanding as a cloth manufacturing town prior to 1533. The growing importance of the cloth industry in Kidderminster must not be exaggerated. Probably the majority of the inhabitants in the early 16th century were in no way connected with the industry.[2] The legislation seems to have been effective. Certainly by 1575 the Worcester clothiers were of the opinion that the Act was the basis of their prosperity. Kidderminster's growth was based on a cloth trade of a different character from that of Worcester and very definitely subordinate to it. Many of the town's looms were narrow, i.e. ¾-yard wide, as opposed to the broadcloth looms which were twice the width. Whereas Worcester produced fine quality broadcloth, Kidderminster was probably producing a great deal of low-quality cloth, linen as well as woollen, for local consumption.[3] Its cloth makers were men of no great standing, weaving cloth on a very small scale with very limited capital. The Worcester clothiers were selling their export-quality broadcloth through the London market, but those at Kidderminster dealt only with the Worcester clothiers. The days of 'Kidderminster stuff' were still to come. Kidderminster was in no position to challenge Worcester's dominance. Nevertheless, the population of the town was growing. In the middle of the century about 1,100 people lived in the parish, with less than half in the town itself. This figure rose to about 1,600 by the end of the century and it may be that much of the increase was in the town. If that was the case, then the population of the town could have been close to 1,000 by the year 1600.[4] The rise of the cloth industry is indicated further in the fact that Kidderminster clothiers were dealing directly with London by the early 17th century.

## SHEEP ENCLOSURES

The Act of 1533 was just one among many statutes from the ministry of Thomas Cromwell under Henry VIII. He envisaged a nation state, which finally overcame the squabbling of a feudal society. His vision included the strengthening of the cloth trade, in part by attracting Dutch weavers to England. Presumably he saw the entry into the 'mysteries of the cloth trade' by sheep farmers as a retrograde step. The record of John Leland's journeying through Kidderminster around 1540, soon after this legislation, gives a clue as to where these great sheep enclosures might have been.[5]

Leland arrived from Bridgnorth. He crossed a bridge with two or three arches over the Stour. The chief part of the town was on the left bank of the Stour, standing on a hilly piece of ground. Leland appreciated the pretty cross in the market place, having six pillars and arches of stone with a seventh pillar in the middle bearing up the fornix. That Cromwell's Act was already doing its work may have been indicated by his comment that 'The Towne standeth most by cloathinge'. Leland noted that his route from Bridgnorth to Kidderminster was 'mostly by enclosed ground'. This cannot be conclusive, but it suggests that Trimpley, Habberley and Franche had by then lost any open fields they once had and were enclosed. It is generally believed that much of north Worcestershire was enclosed by 1540, although Burton has suggested that this was not the case west of Kidderminster in Wribbenhall and Oldington, where Lord Foley's land in 1704 still consisted of open fields. Furthermore, we start to see wills of yeoman farmers from the early 17th century in these areas around the Bridgnorth Road.

## THE BLOUNT FAMILY

Kidderminster's new prosperity was perhaps signified also by having a resident lord of the manor at last. This was a consequence of the Reformation, which finally robbed the monks of Maiden Bradley of interests in Kidderminster they had held for over three centuries. Their property was taken by the Duke of Northumberland, but after his execution for high treason this third part of the manor of Kidderminster was granted in 1560 to Thomas Blount. He founded the Free Grammar School in 1566, a further indication of a town growing in confidence. Blount died in 1580, and there is a monument to him in St Mary's church. In an altar tomb on the north side of the choir his figure lies in armour, his head under a helmet and a lion at his feet. His son, Sir Edward Blount, is also commemorated in the church. His monument is close to the tower entrance on the left. Sir Edward too is shown in armour, leaning on his elbow.

It was Sir Edward Blount who put the three pieces of the manor of Kidderminster together again, albeit temporarily. Already owning the third formerly belonging to Maiden Bradley, Blount married Mary Nevill, sister of Lord Abergavenny and owner of the other two thirds. Blount leased the rest of the manor from his brother-in-law and thereby became lord of the manor of the whole of Kidderminster until his death in 1630. The original Blount manor house is thought to have been at Hurcott, but Sir Edward lived in the handsome brick manor house close to St Mary's church, which was admired by Nash in the mid-18th century. He may even have built it, although it is possible a substantial house had been there for three or four hundred years already. Blount almost certainly created the industrial mill site at Stack Pool in Broadwaters, having obtained permission to make a 'poole hole' there in 1598.[6]

## FURTHER GROWTH

Until the latter part of the 16th century most people would have lived in houses little better than hovels. Improvements were made at this time in certain streets. When the Swan Street/High Street area was being demolished in 1968, fragments of sandstone foundations and cellars were found during 'emergency excavations' by the irrepressible Ian Walker. There was also a spiral staircase. These were probably the remains of Tudor homes of some of the wealthier townspeople.[7] The sole remaining house of this period surviving today is 12 Church Street, a timber-framed house from c.1600. Mill Street also is likely to have been a prosperous street, and it is probable that some brick houses which stood just below Park Butts until demolition in 1979 were rebuildings of timber-framed houses. Perhaps the clothier, Henry Radford, lived there. His will of 1622 describes a large house in Mill Street.

At the same time as this urban growth, there was evidently wealth in the countryside and some names began to appear which were to be familiar to local people for many generations. In 1601 Gilbert Soley, gentleman, was married in

11. Mill Street below Park Butts 1979. Pictured shortly before demolition, these were the late 18th-century homes of manufacturers such as the Brintons, Brooms, Coopers and Leas, who are known to have lived in the street. It is likely that these houses were rebuildings of a timber-framed range.

Kidderminster. It is likely that he was living at Oldington, because his grandson, Jeremy, died there in 1684. Perhaps the 13th-century 'hall' still survived. The Soley family were to move to Sandbourne House near Wribbenhall, where they still lived in the early 19th century. In 1609 Richard Crane of Habberley died. It is thought that the Cranes occupied the original manor house on the site of Low Habberley Farm from about 1563. For nearly three centuries the family would dominate the farms of the area and ultimately become lords of the manor of Habberley. On the extreme east side of the manor of Kidderminster land was purchased in 1585 by William Sebright, town clerk of London and a major benefactor of Wolverley. This included a 'messuage or dwelling house, garden, orchard, watermill, two blade mills, a meadow lying beneath the said watermill, a pasture of four acres, a mill pound or pool, a watercourse, three other pools'. This large estate incorporated parts of Wannerton, Dunclent, Hagley and Churchill. Another prominent house was Comberton Hall, thought to have been built around 1600, possibly on the site of an earlier 'hall'.[8]

## KIDDERMINSTER STUFF

The coining of the term 'Kidderminster stuff', which was well used by the time of Richard Baxter, is evidence of the significance of the town's cloth trade. Earlier references include one in an inventory of 1619 for Naworth Castle to

12. Rear of *The Fox Inn*, Swan Street. This 1920s picture shows that behind some Georgian frontages of the town's lost buildings were timber-framed structures from the earlier Tudor period.

'seven carpets of Kitterminster stuff'.[9] Another reference from 1634 is contained in the inventory of Lettice, Countess of Leicester, who possessed 'four carpets of Kidderminster stuff'. A 'carpet' of that time was used for wall hanging or furniture covering and was not trodden underfoot. The true Kidderminster stuff was a heavy cloth of this type made from a mixture of linen and worsted, known as 'linsey-woolsey'. Sometimes a looser meaning was given to the term, which was applied to any cloth made in Kidderminster, including cheap cloth of poor quality used for outer clothing. Perhaps partly because of this, 'Kidderminster stuff' acquired a derogatory meaning. Even the expensive heavy variety came to represent something disreputable. It was used exten-sively in the theatre and so the expression came to mean something 'artificial and not true'. For example, in the 18th century the poet Shenstone described poems he disliked as 'Kidderminster stuff'.[10]

Nevertheless, the production of wall hangings and furniture fabrics in the town was an industry to take seriously. Kidderminster broad looms were probably producing Kidderminster stuff in the 16th century, the heyday of Shakespeare and the theatre. Only one 'carpet' weaver was recorded at Worcester in 1591, despite the undoubted demand for furnishing fabrics in the city, and this may well have been due to the specialised competition of Kidderminster in that branch of the trade.[11] Kidderminster was therefore in a better position than Worcester to ride out the crisis in the cloth industry which occurred in the early 17th century caused by the decline in English broadcloth. This was linked to the enclosure of good arable land in order to provide sheep pasture. The consequence was not just undernourished people, but better nourished sheep. The well-fed sheep produced a longer coarser wool, known as worsted, which

13. Vicar Street including the *Three Tuns* c.1890.

was used for the Kidderminster stuff. Traditional English broadcloth, on the other hand, required the finer wool produced by undernourished sheep.[12] The agricultural labourers displaced by enclosure were attracted to the prospect of employment in Kidderminster's cloth industry. In 1616 increased levels of poverty in the town provoked the Borough to petition that the Foreign should contribute to the poor of the whole parish.

## THE SOCIETY OF WEAVERS

The platform for the strength of the Kidderminster cloth industry in the early 17th century was clearly provided by the Act of 1533. Another factor may well have been the development of the Society of Weavers, which enjoyed a monopoly of their craft in the town and acted to ensure quality of their product. The weaver at last attained the status that his skill and labour warranted. There is no record of the inception of the society. It is almost certain that it was formed in the 16th century, either soon after the Act took effect, or perhaps later when new religious ideas found their way into the town. In the wake of the Reformation Puritanism held sway within the Church of England. It was dedicated to the purification of the church from all the ritual and ceremony of Roman Catholicism. Many members of the church considered themselves to be followers of John Calvin, whose work in Geneva was bearing fruit in the latter part of the 1550s. His ideas particularly appealed to the independent-minded yeoman and small craftsmen and traders who were struggling to better themselves. Many of the Kidderminster cloth weavers would have been Calvinists. It may have been that religion provided the impetus for the formation of the Society of Weavers and that religion gave them the authority which sustained them for many years.[13]

14. Rear of Church Street. Behind no. 12, Kidderminster's only surviving timber-framed house, other industrial buildings once stretched back towards the Stour. This house and neighbouring houses were home to clothiers such as Joseph Williams and the Housemans.

## THE CHARTER

Whatever independence of mind existed among the middling classes of Kidderminster, the reality was that the town did not have true independence and remained under the control of the lord of the manor. This was to come to a head shortly after the death of Sir Edward Blount in 1630. Controversy centred around the right to the toll on sales in the market and in particular on the corn toll. In 1612 Sir Edward had given this toll to his servant John Nash. After his death in around 1622 the bailiffs gathered the toll by some agreement with Sir Edward, who had apparently been known to remark that the toll of corn was 'anciently given to the Bailiff' towards his expenses. After Sir Edward had died, the two thirds of the manor which he had leased reverted back to Henry Neville, Lord Abergavenny. In 1631 Neville came to the town, where he met the bailiff and burgesses, who presented him with a cup of wine. The lord then offered them a lease of the toll of corn, but they refused claiming that it 'did properly belong to them and was parcel of their inheritance'. Abergavenny responded to their defiance by granting the lease of all tolls to his servant Abraham Newport. After Newport came to Kidderminster and was obstructed by the bailiff and the burgesses in his efforts to collect the tolls, Lord Abergavenny took action in October 1632 by suing for arrears in the Court of the Exchequer. The result was an inevitable victory for the lord of the manor.

Running through the case was the hard fact that the Borough of Kidderminster had no charter of incorporation, and it was the stimulus for the town finally to seek one. Petitions were made to King Charles I, and the bailiff and burgesses described their town as one of 'great trading and making of cloths and stuffs'.[14] Among the 15 requests for increased powers was one for an MP. Another request was for the 'grant and confirmation of the tolls of their fairs and markets for grain and cattle'. Taken together with their open challenge to Lord Abergavenny in that year, it looks as if Kidderminster's leading citizens were men with a political purpose. Their preparedness to stand up for what they saw as their economic rights was in line with the motive forces which would trigger the civil war in the following decade. Their strength of conviction suggests they were emboldened by religious views.

A charter of incorporation for the town was granted on 4 August 1636. However, the detail showed that most of the new requests had been refused and the independence Kidderminster was to enjoy lagged behind many other towns, including Bewdley. The rights of the lord of the manor had been upheld. The advice of William Noy, the King's Attorney General, included the view that the toll which was desired belonged to the lord. The government of the town in essence remained as it was. There was a High Bailiff, assisted by a Low Bailiff, 12 Capital Burgesses and 25 Assistant Burgesses. The Capital

Burgesses were empowered to issue byelaws. A new provision was the creation of the offices of High Steward and Under Steward. The former was a largely honorary appointment and went to Sir Ralph Clare of Caldwall. In 1640 the Capital Burgesses assembled in the Guildhall to draw up byelaws. Many of the rules they produced concerned public houses. Innkeepers were forbidden to allow anybody except travellers to sit 'tippling' on Sundays or festivals. Powers were given to churchwardens and constables, four of whom were provided for by the charter, to go out of church immediately after the start of the second lesson at Sunday services to search all inns, taverns and alehouses. If they found 'householders and men of worth', they were to present them to the Bishop of Worcester to be dealt with. The Puritan tone is obvious in these byelaws.[15]

## RICHARD BAXTER

In 1641 the Puritan sympathies of the burgesses of Kidderminster were confirmed by their appointment of Richard Baxter as lecturer attached to the parish church. The background was that Charles I had been forced at last to reconvene Parliament from November 1640. One of their first measures was to set up a 'Committee for Scandalous Ministers'. The vicar of Kidderminster, George Dance, aware of his own reputation for frequenting alehouses rather than giving inspirational sermons, feared for his future. He agreed to set aside £60 of his £200 per annum for the support of a lecturer.[16] The adoption of lecturers was by no means unusual at this time. The rising industrial classes were looking for men who could assist the process of diffusing religious and political ideas appropriate for a new age. Among those who invited Baxter to Kidderminster were men of considerable local influence. Indeed, one of them, Daniel Dobbyns, was a London merchant and haberdasher who in 1635 had purchased the Kidderminster Manor House or Hall from Edmund Waller, the poet and Parliamentarian. Waller had briefly purchased part of the former estate of Sir Edward Blount.[17]

Baxter is probably the outstanding person ever to be associated with Kidderminster. He was born in the Shropshire village of Eaton Constantine in 1615 and his time in the town is confined to the period between 1641 and 1661. Even this time was curtailed by his enforced departure for five years from 1642 because of the Civil War. Yet Kidderminster, in his own words, 'had the chiefest of my labours'. After a difficult start he built up a huge congregation so that many additional galleries had to be installed in St Mary's church. His many books and other writings have continued ever since to exercise influence. No book on the Civil War and its aftermath is complete without reference to Baxter. He spent the last thirty years of his life being hounded and persecuted, and eventually in 1685 after appearing before Judge Jeffreys he was imprisoned

15. Blackwell Street 1953. A court behind the north-west end of the street, showing another timber-framed survivor until the building of the ring road, drawn by Miss M. Robinson, whose many pictures from this period are held by Kidderminster library.

for nearly two years. His integrity and refusal to suppress his innermost beliefs exposed him to such treatment.

Baxter's first year in the town was not altogether successful and ended badly. He harboured doubts about certain aspects of the Prayer Book and, in particular, agonised over the merits of infant baptism. He told his parishioners that infants before regeneration were 'loathsome in the eyes of God'. When for good measure he added that 'hell was paved with infants' skulls' the good women of Kidderminster almost stoned him to death. Matters came to a head in 1642 when Parliament ordered the defacing of all images of any person of the Trinity in churches and churchyards. Baxter read the order, and there was trouble when the churchwarden attempted to remove a crucifix from the churchyard cross. In Baxter's own words, 'the rabble of drunken swearing journeymen, who were all for conformity, rose in a tumult with clubs, seeking to kill me and the churchwardens'.[18] Baxter was advised to leave the town and he stayed in Gloucester for a month. He survived his return, but found that the beggarly drunken mob was still in a disturbed state. When King Charles raised his standard at Nottingham on 22 August 1642, the Civil War had begun and Baxter left Kidderminster. He would not return until 1647.

## JOURNEYMEN WEAVERS

The developing class system in the town is indicated by Baxter's identification of 'journeymen' with the mob. Just as merchants and others had once farmed out cloth weaving into the countryside, so by the time of Baxter's arrival in Kidderminster weaving was controlled by master weavers who employed journeymen

16. Richard Baxter. A portrait believed to be by Robert Walker. It was photographed at Rous Lench Court in 1920 by Dr F.J. Powicke and Peter Adam.

to do the weaving for them. The master weavers became 'clothiers'. They purchased yarn and then supervised its transformation through the various processes into the finished cloth. Baxter's own account suggests that the journeymen were not very well paid and it is possible that there was some unemployment among them. It is likely that a considerable increase in the population of Kidderminster had created pressures, which perhaps for the first time saw the appearance of an underclass, or 'mob'. The population of the parish was about 3,100 in the 1640s.[19] This meant that it had doubled in under fifty years. It is likely that by this time the majority lived in the town as continuing enclosure caused a steady exodus from the countryside. It is unlikely they all found good work.

The pressure of poverty must have been intense. Even the clothiers themselves were not very well off. Kidderminster stuffs enjoyed some fame, but although the industry was well established, it was not a source of great wealth. Baxter put it this way:

> My people were not rich; there were among them very few beggars because their common trade of stuff weaving would find work for them all, men, women and children, that were able. There were none of the tradesmen very rich, seeing their trade was poor, that would but find them food and raiment; the magistrates of the town were few of them worth £40 per annum and most not half as much; three or four of the richest thriving masters of the trade got but about £500 or £600 in twenty years and it may be lost £100 of it by an ill debtor. The generality of the master workmen lived but little better than their journeymen but only that they laboured not so hard.

Baxter's natural supporters were not necessarily those who were wealthy, but those who might aspire to be so. Of the 36 who signed his letter of invitation to Kidderminster 12 were clothiers, two were dyers and only one was simply a 'weaver'. Seven were from the gentry and four were yeomen. Six were occupied in other trades, a mercer, a blacksmith, a glover, a tailor, a chandler and an innholder. If not rich, they were independent men, for whom religion was something to be lived and breathed and not handed down from on high. Baxter's thinking and preaching helped them to believe their lives had purpose. The Calvinist tradition lent dignity to the values and aspirations of this embryonic middle class.

## AN EMPTY FARM

There is little doubt that Baxter and his adherents were in a minority at the beginning of the Civil War. They consisted of the most enterprising of the townspeople, but as the fighting began their position was vulnerable, being opposed by the labouring classes and by the country gentlemen of the surrounding districts. Many of them left Kidderminster in 1642, either with Baxter or following him to Coventry, where he stayed. Indeed, Baxter referred to 'some hundreds that went with me, and after me, to the wars'. Although a good number of them actually fought for Parliament, it seems likely that to some extent they were forced out of Kidderminster. According to Baxter, 'some stayed till they had been imprisoned, some till they had been plundered, perhaps twice or three times over'. The loss of the core element of the tradespeople must have done serious damage to the prosperity of the town. To this loss can be added the deaths of the journeymen who fought for the Royalist side. It is hardly surprising that by 1644 Kidderminster was reduced to an 'empty farm'.[21] This interesting description is a reminder to us that, despite its growth, Kidderminster was still a small community constructed tightly around its central streets. It remained an agricultural town with its open fields to the east and one, Cussfield, to the west, all presumably untended as a result of two years of division and destruction.

Kidderminster became a Royalist garrison. Parliament's troops had briefly occupied the town in 1642, but had hastily withdrawn after some scouts from the King's army appeared on the top of Kinver Edge. A casualty of this event is recorded in an entry of 14 October in the parish register. A Parliamentary soldier, Thomas King, was buried after breaking his neck in a fall from 'the rock towards Curstfield into the hollow way that leads to Bewdley'. The men who stepped to the fore in the absence of Parliament's army and supporters included Sir Ralph Clare of Caldwall Hall and his younger brother Francis. Another was Thomas Crane, who was accused in 1645 of sending horses and arms to the King's forces at Hartlebury Castle. Most prominent among the country gentlemen was Edward Broad of Dunclent. In 1644 he was anxious to aid the King's forces besieging Stourton Castle and threatened 'divers of the country people that they should be hanged at their own doors if they would not go with him against the said castle'.[22]

In late 1645 Kidderminster was affected by fighting. On 8 November there was a skirmish, probably at Wassell Wood, in which twenty Royalists were killed and Sir Thomas Aston taken prisoner. Fighting continued in the area, even in Kidderminster itself, and soldiers were buried there on 11 and 14 December.[23] Gradually the first phase of the Civil War was drawing to a close with the defeat of the King. The supporters of Parliament were returning to Kidderminster to the extent that in 1647 a letter was sent to Baxter signed by 264 people, including 45 'souldiers', begging him to return to the town. A new agreement was reached and he took up residence again as a lecturer.

## ORDER RETURNS

Much property was destroyed or changed hands in the course of the Civil War. In 1649 the Eymore estate formed part of the Parliamentary Survey of the Lands of the Dean and Chapter of Worcester. The tenant and woodward for the wood or park of Eymore since 1639 was John Corbyn, a supporter of Richard Baxter. He purchased the estate for £3,000, although the Dean and Chapter recovered their land at the Restoration. There were 21 coppices 'consisting of saplings, black poles, and underwoods' to be fallen together as underwood. In addition there were 1,558 timber oaks in the wood. Corbyn was paid specific rates for certain tasks. For example, he received 8d. for every 100 faggots or every ton of timber he took to the two loading places by the side of the Severn, Green Load and Priors Load. From here the wood and timber were transported by barge to the College of Worcester. In fact the restoration of Worcester Cathedral later in the century was accomplished using wood mainly from Eymore.[24] Corbyn had to 'maintain all the Royalties for Deer Hunting, Hawking and other games there within the premises to the use of the Dean and Chapter'. He was obliged to keep the wood properly hedged and ditched to preserve it from 'waste and spoil'. He had to procure the punishment of thieves and hedgebreakers. Of course, a wood provided some opportunity for warmth and shelter to the poor, and Corbyn had covenanted to assist the Dean and Chapter to pull down cottages 'lately built' on the outer side of the wood and to prevent further cottages being built.

After the troubles a paper mill was certainly operating at Hurcott in 1653.[25] It is not completely clear how easy it was for trade to resume in the town. Bye-laws passed in 1650 stated that the reputation of the Society of Weavers had been much damaged by the 'irregularity' of some in the Borough who had been trading privately in stuffs 'deceitfully made both for measure and workmanship'. A scandal was 'fastened upon ye said Trade', which was decaying to the detriment of the poor 'who formerly by their labour therein

17.  Baxter's House, High Street.

were supported and maintained'. It was thought that weavers and other traders were exploiting the use of apprentices rather than employing journeymen who were paid more. The byelaws sought to restrict the use of apprentices so that for every one of them there would be two journeymen.[26] The regulations applied also to the other three fraternities in Kidderminster, the Societies of Taylors, of Smithes and of Shoemakers.

The success of these byelaws as a means of reconciling the violent clashes between the journeymen and their Puritan employers may be judged by the relative calm in the town which was established after Baxter's return in 1647.

From the outset this must have been in part due to the generous spirit in which Baxter conducted the arrangements for his second spell in the town. He insisted on continuing simply as a lecturer and the old vicar, George Dance, was allowed to stay on at the vicarage supported by an allowance. Baxter himself lived in the High Street in a house situated on its west side two up from the Courthouse or Guildhall. This row represented the growth of permanent buildings where once had been the line of market stalls in the middle of the market place. The street at the back of these buildings was known as 'Behind the Shops' and later became Swan Street. Baxter's house was purchased in 1862 by his admirer, William Hancocks of Blakeshall House, who restored it and put up a board with the legend 'Baxter 1641'. It would have made a fine museum but was destroyed in the demolition work of the 1960s.[27]

Baxter judged that he had 600 regular communicants out of a possible 1,800 or so. Many more came to hear him preach, using the galleries which were added to St Mary's church. Whereas when he first came 'there was about one family in a street that worshipped God and called on his name', later there was no disorder on the streets on the Lord's day and 'you might hear an hundred families singing psalms and repeating sermons, as you passed through the streets'. Baxter was able to appeal to the broad population because he was not a strict Calvinist with the rigid view that only a small minority, the predestined 'elect', could achieve salvation. He adopted a typically moderate position between Calvinism and Arminianism, holding that some were the elect but that others could secure their own salvation.[28] Whilst appealing to the poor, and reassuring them that their poverty was not a sign that they were damned, Baxter was not a threat to the trading classes, because he was always clear about the sanctity of private property. He believed that 'the taking of another man's goods is sinful, though it be to save the taker's life … Therefore, ordinarily it is a duty rather to die than to take another man's goods against his will.'[29]

## BAXTER'S REJECTION

The Restoration of the Monarchy in 1660 did not meet with wholehearted support in Kidderminster. In that year a Mrs Robinson, her two daughters and a man from the town were accused of witchcraft and using magic to prevent the return of Charles II. They were subjected to trial by water and flung into the Severn at Worcester. These unfortunate people perhaps had their own reasons for opposing the king, but no doubt some of Baxter's congregation could see that their preacher might lose his position. It was ironic that, although Baxter always viewed Oliver Cromwell as an usurper, he enjoyed liberty to preach during the Commonwealth. Upon the Restoration such freedom was taken from him under a king to whom he had sworn subjection and obedience.[30] He was forced to leave Kidderminster, and he never returned to the place where

'I once thought my days would have ended'. Even Baxter's moderation was too much for the bishops, who having had their power removed under Cromwell were bent upon regaining their control without compromise. Baxter was among those who argued for a modified form of episcopacy, whereby the rule of the bishops would be reduced by a board of presbyters in each diocese. As a member of the Royal Commission to review the Book of Common Prayer of 1661, or the Savoy Conference as it became known, he argued for modifications in the Prayer Book and for the disuse of certain 'superstitious practices'. All of this was rejected and by the Act of Uniformity 1662 all ministers were compelled to accept the Prayer Book as it stood.

Baxter had been in constant conflict with Sir Ralph Clare of Caldwall Hall. One such battle concerned Holy Communion, which Baxter would administer to his people sitting, standing or kneeling. Clare demanded that he and his party should receive the sacrament kneeling on a day by themselves, but Baxter refused. Clare 'was the principal cause of my removal'. In the end Baxter was undone by the local clergy. The King and his Lord Chancellor, Clarendon, wished to accommodate him and there was talk of offering him the bishopric of Hereford. However, Baxter could see what was coming, that the old unmodified rule of the bishops would be reinstated, and he could not accept it. He wanted to remain in Kidderminster and a petition from 1,600 of the inhabitants supported him. This was to no avail, despite the sympathy of the King and of Lord Clarendon. The incompetent vicar, George Dance, did not reciprocate the tolerance Baxter had always shown him. Dance refused to allow Baxter to remain in Kidderminster on any terms whatsoever. He denied Baxter liberty to preach any more. The newly appointed Bishop of Worcester, Morley, was of no assistance to Baxter, having been his principal opponent at the Savoy Conference. He refused even to grant Baxter an interview. There was to be no farewell service. With no possibility of ever preaching again in the town, Baxter took leave of his congregation and went to London, where he lived for a time with Thomas Foley.[31]

His legacy was to be a lasting one. He left many able followers who, like Baxter himself, were forced by the Act of Uniformity and other repressive legislation to accept the label of nonconformists. At first they thought that one day they would be received back into the Church of England, but this never came to pass. Instead, eventually they formed the congregations whose role in the industrial development of Kidderminster was to be crucial and whose churches are still today a familiar part of the town landscape. At the time of his departure Kidderminster was not a wealthy town and the cloth industry was not flourishing. Yet Baxter had strengthened the roots of the Puritan thinking which lent confidence and dignity to the embryonic industrial class. This was his contribution to the forces which one day would see the carpet industry rise to give Kidderminster its fame.

# The Nonconformists

The religion of the nonconformists would be closely linked with the industrial development of the town for about 150 years after Baxter's departure. Yet the path was not smooth, and there is little evidence of great wealth until the latter part of this period. There were further adjustments in the organisation of the cloth industry, and the class system in Kidderminster underwent change. The weavers had managed to increase their status and had begun to occupy the focal point of their trade. Now their standing was to decline again. The emerging 'clothiers' would oversee all stages of the production of cloth, and often they would have no looms of their own. Just as with spinning and dyeing, the task of weaving could be given to others by the clothiers. The loss of control by the weavers is reflected in the fact that by the early 18th century the Society of Weavers was heard of no more.[1]

That the clothiers were not outstandingly rich, despite their dominance of Kidderminster's industry, indicates that life in Kidderminster was a struggle for the most part, probably for a period extending into the 1750s. It is likely that the town did not change much in the 90 years or so following the Restoration. Doherty's map of 1753 tells us that the population was then 4,000, which represents a modest increase, if any, over Baxter's estimate of three to four thousand in his time. Kidderminster remained a small town built around the medieval streets. One change had been, as already mentioned, that a permanent row of buildings had been erected down the middle of the market place, forming High Street and Behind The Shops. Radiating away from this central area were the key streets of Coventry Street, Black Star Street (later to become Blackwell Street), Worcester Street, Vicar Street, Church Street and the Bull Ring, from which the road led across the bridge to Mill Street. There was little building along Coventry Street, which led quickly to the open fields. Any development had mainly been provided along Worcester Street, where building had not reached Worcester Cross, and especially along Mill Street. Vicar Street, or Vicar's Lane, ended at the 16th-century vicarage, where George Dance lived during Baxter's time and afterwards. This is now the site of

18. Habberley Valley. For many centuries much of the land west of Kidderminster was heathland, where grazing reduced the growth of trees.

the town hall, but then the town opened up there into the Stour meadows. The 1753 plan showed that Kidderminster was not then congested. The properties fronted the streets, but behind them the gardens were not yet being hemmed in by workshops.

One change of significance was the gradual shifting of the centre of gravity of the town to the area of Church Street, Bull Ring and Mill Street. It was here that the most important clothiers lived in their timber-framed houses and carried on their trade. The decline of Blackwell Street goes back to these times. This was the historic quarter inhabited by the dyers, or the 'blacksters', as they were once known. The former street name, Black Star Street, was derived from their occupation. They made use of the water from the meandering Daddle Brook, which once flowed across the street, although it is now culverted and hidden from view. These black dyers would dye either the yarn after spinning or the completed woven cloth. Their name also suggests they dealt largely with the production of cheap cloths requiring plain colours only. Eventually the expanding industry and the need for quality made premises by the Stour more desirable. Dyers were few in number in the 17th century and gradually clothiers took over this process. By the beginning of the 18th century most clothiers had expanded and ran their own workshops. One remaining specialist dyer, William Pebody, who died in 1711, had expensive equipment including 'a jack with which water was drawn from the River Stour'.[2]

## THE FOLEYS AND THE MANOR

At this time Kidderminster continued to lack great houses. The town itself was dominated by two residences, the manor house by the church and Caldwall Hall. After Daniel Dobbyns died in 1663, the identity of the manor house occupants is something of a mystery. The Foley family were becoming the dominating influence in Kidderminster. Thomas Foley had purchased Witley Court in 1655. He wished to set up his three sons with estates and his eldest son, also Thomas, was to hold those at Great Witley and Kidderminster. It is possible that he lived in the manor house until 1677, when he moved to

19. Caldwall c.1930. The medieval tower with the Queen Anne house built by the Clare family.

Witley Court upon the death of his father. After that it was probably leased by prominent citizens, including perhaps the clothier Jonathan Lea (d.1728), who according to a family tree lived at the 'Old Hall'. The second major residence, at Caldwall, was transformed by the building of a new three-storey brick mansion adjoining the tower, probably around 1700 by Francis Clare, nephew and heir of Sir Ralph.[3] Outside the town there was no emergence of country houses occupied by influential 'gentlemen'. Instead, there were indications of the growing strength of the yeoman class. In particular the Crane family were growing in prominence, especially in the Habberley area, but their wills show that they occupied farms in places such as Franche and Puxton, where Godfrey Crane, yeoman, died in 1672. One example of a new house which was perhaps something more than a working farm may have been Franche Hall, a fine three-storey mansion first documented in 1681.[4] The precise origin and early occupants of this outstanding house are unknown. However, one possibility is that even this house was linked to a yeoman farmer, the second cousin of Sir Edward Blount, Francis Blount. In 1646 Blount, a yeoman of Franche, is recorded as transferring land in Meerepoole Lane (Marlpool Lane) to a relative.[5]

Despite the restoration of the monarchy and the bishops, the relentless rise of the industrial classes could not be stopped. The gentlemen who were to have most impact on both the town and countryside in this period were those of the Foley family. Their fortune had been made in nail manufacturing in the Black Country by Richard Foley, who had helped launch the career of Richard Baxter, whom he employed for a year from 1638 at a school he founded in Dudley. This fortune was used to establish estates for Richard Foley's three sons, and by steady purchasing Thomas Foley was to piece together much of the fragmented manor of Kidderminster once more. Foley's first purchase was in 1655 when he bought the manors of Heathy and Dunclent from Edward Broad, who may have been paying for his vigorous support of the Royalist cause in the Civil War. In the following year Foley purchased Oldington. Hurcott and Wannerton were added in 1662 and 1683 respectively.[6] The Foleys then had to wait until 1733 for their major purchase, the manorial rights belonging to the Lords Abergavenny. There were a few sub-manors which the Foleys were never to control, such as Caldwall, Comberton, Mitton, Low Habberley and Trimpley, although they did acquire Park Attwood. In addition there may have been some smaller freehold estates, which had once been sold and severed from the principal manors, and would never become available to the Foleys. Franche Hall was an example of such an estate.

## THE CORPORATION

The wealth made from industry by the Foleys was exceptional. Many more years would elapse before Kidderminster's industry would produce men whose wealth would be conspicuous in the town: let alone the country. In effect, many of them were compelled to concentrate on their business by the disabling laws of Charles II, who acted to reduce the power of corporations thought to contain many radicals, Puritans and others who had supported Parliament in the war. The Corporation Act 1661 required members of corporations to swear allegiance to the King and repudiate the taking of arms against him. They had to reject the Solemn League and Covenant of 1643, which defended the protestant religion. Finally, they were required to take Anglican communion at least once a year. This was too much for the burgesses of Kidderminster and, according to Baxter, most of them were turned out, confirming the supposition that the majority were Puritans.

This was a very uneasy period for Kidderminster and it is by no means clear who would have spoken for the town. Baxter had left, leaving his congregation in the care of Thomas Baldwin, who himself was ejected from his ministry at Chaddesley Corbett. The Five Mile Act of 1665 prevented such men from coming within five miles of places in which they had once preached. More seriously, the Conventicle Act 1664 banned meetings of five or more persons 'under the colour or pretence of any exercise of religion'. Nevertheless, the nonconformists did hold meetings in a room at the bottom of Mill Street on the Stour side, before their first meeting house was built in 1693-4. The site for the new chapel was near the bridge and the Bull Ring, and was purchased by Samuel Bowyer, William Smith, Samuel Read and Thomas Doolittle.[7] The latter two names, at least, are associated with the cloth industry. On the political side Kidderminster still had no representation in Parliament, unlike the smaller but wealthier town of Bewdley, whose population in 1661 has been estimated at 2,880. Thomas Foley was MP there in 1660, but did not serve in the Cavalier Parliament of 1661. He was re-elected to the seat in 1673, but was soon unseated on the grounds of bribery, having entertained the electors to dinner at the *George*.[8]

Yet somebody provided effective representation because in 1671 the town obtained an Act of Parliament for regulating the manufacture of Kidderminster stuffs. This was a revisiting of some of the issues covered by the 1650 byelaws, but this time the Society of Weavers was given extensive powers to enforce the regulations. Despite the disabilities placed on some of their leading members on the grounds of religion, the society remained a respected body for the time being. Once again there was concern about what the Act described as the 'debasing of the said manufacture'. Powers to enter property and seize defective yarn or cloth were given to the president, wardens and assistants of the society. All yarn and cloth was to carry the seal of the society and be sold openly and in a public place. Much of Kidderminster's cloth went to London's Blackwell Hall market and the town's clothiers were highly dependent upon agents called factors to ensure their access to this market. It is possible that some London merchants encouraged weavers to bypass both the regulations and the factors and deal directly with them, ultimately to the detriment of the quality of the cloth. This 'private' trade had been a problem addressed by the 1650 byelaws.

Another problem tackled by the Act was that of poor journeymen 'who have served in the said trade, and are not able to set up for themselves'. The provision of the Act this time specified that every master weaver who employed two apprentices was required to employ two journeymen also.[9] This was a reduction in the quota from the byelaws, which confirms there was no shortage of work. By 1677 there were 417 looms in the town. Of these, master weavers had 157, journeymen 187 and apprentices 115 looms.[10]

Among the most successful clothiers of this period were Thomas Houseman, who died in 1677, and his son John who predeceased his father by a year. The goods in their inventories were valued at £365 and £385 respectively, which were high figures by Kidderminster's standards. They showed that the family was involved in every stage of cloth production. They possessed a dyehouse where they dyed wool prior to the weaving process.[11] The Housemans are known to have lived in Church Street during the 18th century and may have occupied the sole surviving timber-framed house, number 12, behind which on Doharty's 1753 map is a possible dyehouse. Despite the success of the Housemans the cloth industry was in serious decline during the late 17th century, according to Nash. The fame of the town's industry was indicated at Richard Baxter's trial in 1685, when Judge Jeffreys referred to his 'linsey-woolsey doctrine', but his contempt may have alluded to the poor state of the industry. Other cloths were developed to replace linsey-woolsey.

## THE YEOMEN CRANES

A history of sheep enclosures and the supply of wool to Kidderminster must involve the Crane family. By this time the dominance of the local farms by men with that surname was quite extraordinary. We have already mentioned Godfrey Crane of Puxton, yeoman (probate 1672). Others included Samuel Crane of Franche, yeoman (1677), John Crane of Habberley, yeoman (1684), Joseph Crane of Arley Kings, yeoman (1692), William Crane of Dunclent, farmer (1700), John Crane Snr. of Habberley, yeoman (1726), John Crane the elder of Oldington, yeoman (1741), Edward Crane of Wolverley, yeoman (1747) and Joseph Crane of Horseley, yeoman (1754). In later years wills would show the Cranes holding other farms such as Greenhill and the Brant. Furthermore, it is clear that, in Habberley at least, several farms were occupied by the family. At this stage the Cranes were not yet 'gentlemen' and certainly not lords of the manor. Yet although yeomen were ranked clearly below gentlemen, there was some blurring at the edges. The progress of the Cranes, and perhaps the support given by Thomas Crane to the Royalist cause in the Civil War, might lead us to believe there was always influence in the family. They even appear to have received financial assistance when the Habberley manor house, which was situated on the site of Low Habberley farm, was burnt down in 1717. It belonged to the above John Crane. The house, which had seven bays, was destroyed in 12 hours.[12] The total loss was estimated at just over £869. This included a 'great quantity of wool' owned by Henry Crane, John's son and the woolstapler of Church Street, Kidderminster. Henry probably departed from the predominant beliefs of his family by becoming a leading member of the town's nonconformist community. We shall speak of him and his wealth at his death later, but it is clear that by 1717 there was already an unusual amount of wealth in the family. This is further confirmed by the will of Thomas Crane of Habberley, who died in 1728, two years after John, and was probably Henry's brother. The value of Thomas' inventory was a little over £867, a very high figure by the standards of the time.

The rise of the independent yeoman had been facilitated by the replacement of the open fields by separate farms, each with its own hedged fields. By the start of the 18th century this gradual process was incomplete around Kidderminster. The final impetus for change was probably the desire of the Foley family to make the most efficient use of the agricultural land they had steadily acquired. In 1704 a survey of Lord Foley's land was undertaken and a map produced. Burton saw the map and was able to include an extract in his history of Kidderminster. He stated firmly that 'Lord Foley's estate in 1704 at Wribbenhall, Oldington, Hoarstone, High Habberley, and the Lea was divided into these half-acre strips'. Foley's survey was undertaken for a reason, and it must be likely that the arable strips were removed soon afterwards. It is possible also that this was the time of the demise of the 'hall' at Oldington, replaced by a farm occupied by one of the Cranes. At about this time Foley was making improvements to the farms on his estates to the east of Kidderminster by introducing an irrigation system. By this method various watercourses took water from the Wannerton Brook in sequence to the farms at Hurcott, Heathy, Dunclent and Wannerton. The land had been 'very poor arable', according to Pitt, but when the estates were auctioned in 1833 they were described as the 'pet estate of the county' and 'irrigated at pleasure'.[13]

Any surviving aspects of the open-field system in the borough itself were certainly dismantled between 1733 and 1753. In the former year Lord Foley purchased the Kidderminster manorial interests of Lord Abergavenny, and the 1753 Doharty plan shows hedged fields where the open fields once lay. Foley paid £10,000 for the two thirds of Kidderminster manor, which once had been known as Kidderminster Biset and Burnell, but now were Kidderminster Borough and Foreign.[14] The common field of Cursefield or Crossfield was being sold off in plots during the same period, leading to the building of the *Barley Mow* on Bewdley Road by 1746. This public house was an important landmark until its demolition for the ring road.[15]

## THE CLOTH INDUSTRY

The early 18th century was also a time of change for the cloth industry. In 1717 demand for Kidderminster's cloth collapsed. In his diary for July of that year Joseph Williams, then a young man, recorded that his father, a master weaver, sent for him and 'informed me of the state of his worldly affairs; and that, when everything he had, or was concerned in, was estimated, he should possess but a trifling remainder'.[16] A number of weavers went bankrupt before diversification ensured the industry's survival. In addition to rough woollen frieze, woven for the Dutch, finer cloths were turned out including figured starrets and barleycords for abroad. Also woven were cheyneys and harateens for bed furniture. One man who assisted the recovery was William Greaves of London, who settled in Kidderminster in 1717 and encouraged the manufacture of prunellas (strong woollen cloths for clergymen's gowns) and striped tammies.[17]

There was no longer any mention in documents of the Society of Weavers. This period opened a class difference between the clothiers and the weavers. The trend was for the clothiers to hold no looms of their own, but to sub-contract the weaving process to weavers. John Williams evidently had a loom shop, either in the house or adjacent to it, because his son Joseph was working there in 1707 and was disturbed because his mind was 'too much corrupted by the filthy conversation of the shop-men'. Yet Joseph himself did not appear to own looms when he later took on the trade. A clear indication of the class divide which was opening up is contained in Joseph's diary, where he refers to those who worked for him as 'servants'. He clearly was talking of his trade, not of domestic matters. He also rebukes himself for 'indecent sallies of passion'. One servant 'had been negligent, another had spoiled his work, a third had been dishonest; but what then? … ought I not to have suffered a little loss patiently, rather than ruffle my temper, and disturb the peace of my soul?'

Some of the clothiers were beginning to travel great distances to secure customers and were no longer relying upon merchants. Williams begins to refer to these journeys in 1726, when he went to London. He visited Lancashire twice in the next two years.[18] In her diaries Hannah Housman refers to her husband's visits to London in 1724 and 1731. The latter entry illustrates the dangers of such travel and the strength of her religious faith:

Through the mercy of God my dear spouse is returned safe from London … Many dangers he hath escaped … He escaped the hands of violent, wicked men, when others that lodged in the same inn the same night he did, fell into their hands, and were robbed and abused. How good is it to pray to God, and to put ourselves under his care![19]

Such risk and enterprise was required to survive in a changing industry. Hannah Jeavons and her brother, Abraham, operated their business from a large house in the Bull Ring. Hannah died in 1730, and she continued to deal with merchants until her death. In other ways their work was organised in the modern way. They did no spinning or weaving themselves, but put the work out to others. They did finish the cloth, and had a workshop for this purpose. The 1753 plan of the town indicates that large workshops were still exceptional. However, increased use of the area close to the Stour was being made. Across the bridge from the Bull Ring there was considerable development and it is likely that Pitts Lane had been constructed by the 1730s. Presumably, this area was named after one of the Pitt family, who had been weaving cloth for over a century.[20]

Still we have not entered a period when fortunes were being made in Kidderminster. Joseph Williams was one of the more prosperous clothiers, but there is little evidence of capital accumulation even in his case. The years 1717 to 1735 saw the cloth industry enjoy stability, apart from a crisis in 1725 brought about by the bankruptcy of a London merchant who owed money to many Kidderminster clothiers. It was a period when the industrious clothiers and weavers of the town sought new ways to diversify and survive. The most significant example of this was in 1735, when John Pearsall is widely regarded as having started Kidderminster's carpet industry. Before this time 'carpets' for wall hangings and furniture drapery had been made, but now Pearsall turned his attention to making floor coverings for people to walk on. There was no explosive start, and the true rise of the industry was to come nearly fifteen years later. At first carpets were just another variety of the fabrics being made in the town. Indeed, the cloth industry as a whole went into depression in 1735. In 1740 the clothiers of Kidderminster petitioned Parliament because their trade was being ruined by the export of wool.[21]

## DIVINE PROVIDENCE

From the perspective of our materialistic age, it is startling to reflect that three hundred years ago there existed a close-knit community in Kidderminster for whom religion and seriousness of purpose were central to their lives. Around Church Street, Mill Street, the Bull Ring and adjacent areas lived many committed dissenters. Virtually all the weavers or clothiers mentioned in this chapter are known to have been nonconformists. Religion, the legacy of Baxter, gave strength to their efforts to revive and maintain the staple industry of the town. The diaries of Joseph Williams and Hannah Housman give us a wonderful insight into the nature of those religious ideas. Many diaries were kept by Puritans for whom they were 'the reckoning books in which they checked the assets and liabilities of their souls in faith. When they opened these books, they set down lapses of morality with appropriate expressions

20. Joseph Williams
(1692-1755).

of repentance and balanced them against the evidences of faith'.[22]

Still, in the middle part of the 18th century, many of Kidderminster's nonconformists would have called themselves Calvinists, though as we shall see later there were important differences which would ultimately divide the congregation. At the heart of Calvinism was the idea that only a minority, the elect, would enjoy the salvation of their souls. God's power over the world was complete. Calvin's doctrine of providence held that not even a sparrow fell to the ground without God's decree. God's power was such that everyone was predestined either to salvation or to eternal damnation.

Some Calvinists liked nothing more than to tell others they were damned, while some delighted in the opposite. Most Calvinists were sorely troubled by the need to satisfy themselves of their own salvation. In many cases this provided the driving force for enterprise and industry. Some believed that their own worldly success was a sign of God's favour, although this was a matter of intense theological controversy for many years. On 1 January 1738 Joseph Williams wrote that it had been 'a year of prosperity: bad as trade is in general, God hath been pleased to bless my endeavours with good success: if not equal to some years, yet I am sure far beyond my deserts'. Yet Puritans would rarely allow themselves a moment's complacency. By 26 March he was warning himself against 'the remains of envy and discontent'. Discontent was 'not a likely means of obtaining the blessing of God'.[23]

When these diaries were being written, illness and death were never far away and it is possible to see the fortitude which deep religious conviction gave Joseph Williams and Hannah Housman. The former lost five children, including a daughter to smallpox in 1737, whilst the latter lost her first child in 1718. Hannah was a member of the Pearsall family, who had probably the most common name in the town at that time. She was the sister of Phebe Pearsall, wife of Joseph Williams. Hannah's diary was published in 1744 by her brother, the Rev. Richard Pearsall of Warminster and later of Taunton. In his introduction he spoke of her 'exemplary life' and 'triumphant death', and said that the diary gave 'fresh testimony to the admirable efficacy of the distinguishing Grace of God'. However, he alluded to what he perhaps saw as the diminishing religious fervour of the time by acknowledging that the diary's contents would be unacceptable to some who did not relish anything in so 'plain' or 'serious' a dress. In 1720 Hannah wrote about her dead child: 'It is two years since it pleased the infinitely wise and good God to remove my dear Joseph ... I hope I have been enabled to justify and acknowledge his sovereignty in all his dealings; and am not without hope that his dealings were mercy, love and faithfulness to me'. The diary concludes with an account by her servant of her death in October 1735 after five days of suffering from a sudden acute illness. Her last utterances included these words: 'These pains make me to love my Lord Jesus better ... It is true, I love my husband, I love my child, I love them dearly, and I love life; but I can cheerfully die and leave them all, to go and be with Christ, because it will be far better'.

Both diaries refer to the mysterious 'fever' which regularly struck Kidderminster. Writing many years later, Nash noted that the period 1727 to 1729 had seen the inhabitants 'terrified'. In November 1726 Joseph Williams wrote that there had been 20 deaths in one week and eight in one day. By the following June death 'again prevails amongst us'.[24] By then one of the victims had been the minister of the dissenting church, John Spilsbury. On 2 February 1727 Hannah Housman wrote that 'this day dear Mr Spilsbury was laid in the grave. The great God seems to have a controversy with us; he hath smitten the shepherd'. She suffered personally, with the death of her eldest brother in January of that year, and later that month she recorded the serious illness of her daughter: 'The child was almost free among the dead, had all the symptoms of death, and yet God said, *return and live*'. Two years later Hannah's entries for the spring of 1729 reveal a very troubled time. On 20 March she wrote: 'The late tidings of the losses which our friends and neighbours sustain give a large demonstration of the vanity of the world'. On 23 April she continued: 'I live when others die. I hear of two persons of note, that are thought dangerously ill; and the tolling of the bell gives me notice that another is dead'. Then on 13 May she had been visiting 'those that are sick and weak. One young person that seems near another world ... is lamenting the loss of precious time, and fearing to enter upon eternity. Oh my soul be awakened and quickened to be up and doing with all thy might'.

Hannah's reference to the 'vanity' of this world is a reminder that the nonconformist trading classes had not yet become used to enjoying worldly success. Joseph Williams' diary frequently touched upon this theme. His little sister, Abigail, had died in his thirteenth year, and this led him to muse on death and to form very lively convictions of the 'vanity of the world, and its insufficiency to my real happiness'. At the age of 18 he wondered how people could spend time in 'caring for things which they must quickly leave, while they neglected the salvation of their souls'. In 1735, as a mature man of 42 years, he railed against the 'pride, self-conceit, and self-confidence too generally prevalent in adult persons'. A year later he wrote: 'The getting of riches on earth is nothing to me in comparison with the laying up for myself "treasures in heaven" '. After a threat was made to his life he fell to wondering 'What preparation I have made for eternity'. At the time of depressed trade Williams had been involved in attempts to reduce the price of spinning. His efforts had been rewarded by 'a letter thrust in at my window last night, wherein my life is threatened'.[25]

## CARPETS AND CAPITAL

The time was coming when the nonconformists would grow accustomed to riches and the vanities of this world. We have already referred to the unusual wealth left by Thomas Crane of Habberley as revealed by his inventory of 1728. By then there was already evidence that the industrial classes of the town were capable of accumulating such an amount. In 1726 the clothier, Thomas Pearsall, left an inventory valued at £845, a sum described by Don Gilbert as 'staggering'.[26] Thomas was almost certainly the father of John Pearsall, the founder of the carpet industry. They were nonconformists, and the baptisms of four of John's children are recorded in the registers of Old Meeting. It is a major undertaking to construct a Pearsall family tree, but there are sufficient wills to establish with absolute certainty that Thomas and John were part of a different branch of the family from the Rev. Richard Pearsall and his sisters Hannah and Phebe. Thomas was probably second cousin to the three of them. In his turn, John would then have been third cousin to Nicholas Pearsall, the founder of New Meeting. The relationship was no closer than that, though it is sometimes suggested otherwise.

The wealth of Thomas Pearsall suggests that a capitalist class was about to emerge in Kidderminster. Instead of a gradual development of industry, there emerged the possibility of sudden growth due to substantial investment. One way in which this would become apparent was through the construction of industrial buildings. Doharty's plan of 1753 revealed Kidderminster as a town in the very early stages of its transformation into an industrial environment. There was none of the congestion which would disfigure the town a hundred years later. Behind most of the houses were gardens, which had not yet been covered with outbuildings and which in many cases gave way to fields. The plan showed that this might be about to change, with the streets envisaged by Lord Foley completely enclosing gardens. Gradually the fields and gardens would have workshops and factories built upon them. We know that the Housman family had a dyehouse, almost certainly in Church Street, and the Jeavons family had a workshop in the Bull Ring: but the 1753 plan showed that these were exceptions and much of the industrial endeavour of the inhabitants went on in the chambers, garrets and other rooms of their own homes. However, the plan showed the immensely significant beginnings of the factory system with the clear identification of two carpet halls, one on Mount Skipet above Park Lane and the other close to Pitts Lane. The first of these belonged to the great partnership of Pearsall and Broom, the pioneers of Kidderminster's carpet industry, who probably joined forces in 1749.[27] Although it was John Pearsall who began carpet production in the town, he is less well known than the legendary John Broom. Pearsall's role was perhaps more prosaic, providing much-needed capital to turn carpet manufacturing into something more than an arm of the cloth industry. Broom's role was more colourful and apparently involved bringing the secrets of the pile carpet to England.

## LEGENDS OF BRUSSELS CARPETS

It cannot be confidently said that Britain's carpet industry began in Kidderminster. Pearsall was a pioneer, but it is possible that carpets were being made in Scotland at Kilmarnock from around 1728. In fact, the 'Kidderminster' carpet made by Pearsall was also known as 'Scotch'. This type of carpet was made entirely of wool and was reversible, showing the same pattern on both sides. The yarn was dyed before weaving. This process was known as dying 'in the grain', and hence another name for such a carpet was 'Ingrain'. By contrast a Brussels carpet was one-sided, consisting of a woollen loop pile inserted into a linen base. In March 1749 Pearsall and Broom leased the land on which their carpet hall was to be built on Mount Skipet above Park Lane. It was 50 yards long, with ground and upper storeys, which could accommodate 32 carpet looms. It was here that Brussels carpets were first made in the town. Kidderminster lagged behind the Wiltshire town of Wilton, which had been producing such carpets with the aid of French weavers for several years. Somehow Kidderminster, through John Broom, acquired the secret, but there is uncertainty about how he managed to do it.

Legend has it that Broom, troubled by the competition from Wilton, travelled to Brussels and Tournai and returned with skilled weavers, who were set up in the Mount Skipet premises. Production began there in great secrecy, but another manufacturer engaged a man to spy on the weavers and so the new manufacturing process began to spread through the town. This story receives some corroboration from private papers held by the Lea family. According to these, in 1815 the carpet manufacturer Thomas Simcox Lea visited the factory of the Lefevre Brothers in Tournai, but was refused access on the grounds that a workman from their firm had taken the trade to England.[28] A story in the *Shuttle* in 1900 adds further substance to the tale. The first foreign workman 'brought over' apparently lived in a Mill Street court opposite the *Reindeer Inn*, and a woman who waited on him at his last illness would often talk of the deathbed scene of the 'old Huguenot'.[29]

The legend has, however, been doubted by two of Kidderminster's most distinguished local historians, A. J. Perrett and Don Gilbert. Their argument is that Broom might well have obtained his inspiration and his weavers from Wilton. By 1758 the partnership of Pearsall and Broom was being dissolved. Deeds were drawn up to split the carpet hall on Mount Skipet into two equal portions. Broom had the north-west half, and on his deed is a reference to two adjoining dwellings belonging to William Foster and John Tanner, which were probably cottages surviving on the site today. Perrett guessed that these men were weavers from Wilton brought to Kidderminster by Broom, because until then the two names were unknown locally. It is a theory which is as difficult to prove as the Broom legend. Don Gilbert, on the other hand, has put together previously unconsidered evidence that in fact the new type of carpet being made in Kidderminster at this time was not strictly a Brussels carpet, but was the type known as 'Wilton'. Brussels and Wilton carpets are closely related, so that today Brussels is really considered to be a type of Wilton carpet. Both are pile carpets woven on a strong base. The crucial difference is that the Brussels pile is looped and hard wearing, whereas the loops of the Wilton pile are cut by the weaver, and the erect ends of the tufts provide a softer velvet-like surface. A Wilton carpet has always been in the luxurious, expensive range of the market. When the traveller Richard Pococke visited the town in 1751, he saw carpets made 'the same as at Wilton'. Finally, found in a book in the old Kidderminster museum were these words written on the last page: 'Jno. Broom of Kidderminster, cut carpet weaver'.[30]

The truth lay perhaps in a combination of the legend of continental travels and the clear Wilton influence. What is certainly true is that by the 1750s Kidderminster was entering a period of confidence and growth, in line with a national trend. Undoubtedly the enterprise and initiative of Pearsall and Broom were significant factors in this expansion. Nevertheless, it was to be several decades before carpet manufacturing was to emerge above cloth production as the town's major industry.

# V

# *Industrialisation*

The foundations for Kidderminster as an industrial town were laid in the second half of the 18th century. During this period carpet manufacturing gradually overtook the cloth industry in economic importance. One of the effects of this transition was the steady development of various loom shops and other outbuildings, instead of the familiar pattern of weavers working in their attics on their own looms. The carpet industry required different organisation from the traditional cloth industry because of the size and cost of carpet looms. The independent skilled artisan with his own loom continued to have a place in the cloth industry, but carpet weavers worked in premises and on looms owned by the manufacturer.

For two decades Kidderminster was prosperous, and there was a surge in population after it had barely increased for a hundred years. Nash observed that by 1772 it had risen to over six thousand from the estimated four thousand in 1753. The silk and worsted industry was booming, with the number of looms in the town increasing from 1,000 to 1,700 in the same period. Among the products were half-yard-wide Spanish poplins as well as other stuffs a yard wide. The influx of people into the town created pressure on the housing supply. No book on Kidderminster's history has been complete without the claim that in 1753 Lord Foley arranged for the building of one hundred and fifty, or even three hundred, new houses.[1] Study of deeds for the suggested district show beyond doubt that few such houses were built under the supervision of Lord Foley.

## LORD FOLEY'S HOUSES

John Doharty Jnr's map of Kidderminster of 1753 has to be treated with great caution. It was not an accurate map of the existing streets and should really have no more status than an estate agent's plan. Doharty inserted new streets 'as intended to be built'. It is not easy to identify the new streets. We must assume they are the lightly shaded streets in the area formerly occupied by the manor house and the land still attached to it. These are Hall Street, Orchard

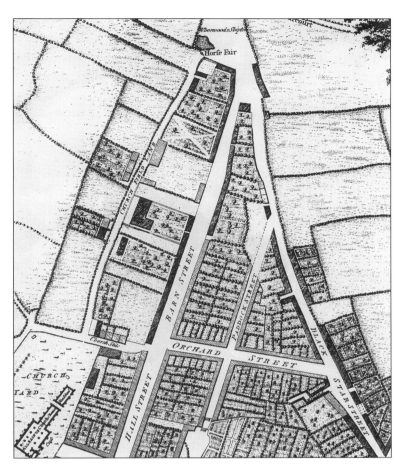

21. Section from Doharty's Plan 1753. The streets intended to be built by Lord Foley are presumably those lightly shaded.

Street, Paddock Street, the top of Church Street and the south-east side of Barn Street. This area was ripe for development. Lord Foley was based, of course, at Witley Court, and he had no children. He had no immediate use for the Kidderminster manor house, and so an obvious course of action was to pull it down in order to develop the entire area. Foley's plans were given some publicity apart from the publication of the map itself. In March 1753 *Berrow's Worcester Journal* reported that he had agreed with a builder 'to erect 150 new houses for the reception of such as, at this time, are obliged to live a considerable distance from their employments'. A year later the same newspaper described the houses as still 'intended to be built'.[2] No confirmation of the plans being put into effect was ever printed by the paper. The likelihood is that there was never any paternalistic involvement by Lord Foley to ensure that much-needed housing was provided, but that over the next fifty years or longer the land was gradually sold off to various builders and others in straightforward commercial transactions. In any case the capacity of the Lord Foley of 1753, who was High Steward of Kidderminster and had inherited the title Baron of Kidderminster from his father, to supervise the growth of the town was terminated by his death in 1766. His estate passed by will to Thomas Foley of Stoke Edith. The latter was soon to become preoccupied by the need to safeguard the family fortune from the gambling debts of his sons, as revealed by his will after his death in 1777. The best guess is that only Hall Street, part of Orchard Street and the top of Church Street were built soon after 1753, with no more than 40 or so houses.

In ring road development of the 1960s the identical houses on either side of Hall Street were pulled down. They were classic weavers' houses with attics and could well have dated from the 1750s. It is possible that the south-west side of Orchard Street was also developed, though the houses were of a different design and are likely to have been built much later. Some houses from the period at the upper end of Church Street still survive, occupied now by dentists among others, but they are of a superior type to homes likely to have been built for weavers. Even if we add these to the 27 houses in Hall Street, it does not begin to approach the 150 intended to have been built. Various deeds prove that at the start of the 19th century the south-east side of Barn Street and the north-east side of Orchard Street were still awaiting development. Paddock Street was never developed. The Foley family did not sell much of this area until 1805, when the conveyance of the area known as 'the Paddock' referred to 'several barns, storehouses, coach house, engine house, stables and buildings',

22. Hall Street. The south side pictured in 1965 prior to demolition.

but to no houses, even though the land was bounded by Barn Street and Orchard Street. This deed referred also to another part of the Paddock having 'lately been sold to Benjamin Grosvenor'.[3] He came to Kidderminster in 1790 to establish himself as a maker of ropes and cordage, used in the equipment of the harness looms for the carpet and other textile industries of the district. Far from a street called Paddock Street with weavers' cottages, there was a rope walk and the site was established for industrial use, which was to continue into the 20th century with the tannery of Columbus Smith.

In the absence of a comprehensive development of the manor house grounds in 1753 under the guidance of Lord Foley, we must look to later development in Churchfields and to a lesser degree along Bewdley Road for the accommodation of the growing population. Corroboration of this view is provided by Ebenezer Guest in his recollections when he referred to 'Hall Street having been built and part of Orchard Street by one of the Lord Foleys'.[4] Further corroboration can be taken to come from a Kidderminster doctor, James Johnstone M.D., who published: 'An Historical Dissertation concerning the Malignant Epidemic Fever of 1756'. In the course of this he wrote of the poor housing in the town, but he made no mention of any major recent development.

## JAMES JOHNSTONE

When Johnstone, a young Scottish physician, came to Kidderminster in 1751, his 21st year, he had just completed his degree of doctor of medicine. He acquired a great deal of celebrity by his successful treatment of the Kidderminster fever. He was a member of the nonconformist community and married Hannah Crane, daughter of the Church Street woolstapler, Henry Crane. He was listed among members of the breakaway New Meeting church who in 1782 unsuccessfully invited Samuel Fawcett to be their first minister. At some stage Johnstone moved to Worcester, where he died in 1802, but he was buried in Kidderminster churchyard. His treatise on the town's virulent fever contained these words:

> The inhabitants of this place are generally employed in the worsted and silk manufactory ... They are many of them lodged in small nasty houses, for the most part crowded with looms and other utensils. A considerable part of the town is built across some low marshy and boggy ground, which extends itself from north to south for several miles above and below the town ... The stagnating water ... rising into the air in putrid moist vapours ... cannot but co-operate with a long course of moist and rainy weather in producing putrid malignant disorders. In fact this place has been very remarkably liable to such disorders long before I became acquainted with it, as well as since.

The boom enjoyed by manufacturing at this time enabled rebuilding to take place in the streets occupied by the employers. The timber-framed houses started to disappear, and in Church Street and Mill Street the process was probably

23. Dr James Johnstone (1730-1802). This portrait now hangs in the canteen of the Charles Hastings Education Centre at Worcester Royal Hospital.

quite fast. For example, a deed of 1758 reveals that the silk and worsted weaver, Nicholas Penn, was about to pull down and rebuild his Church Street premises.[5] The wealth available to Kidderminster's businessmen during that decade illustrated by an entry made by Joseph Williams in his diary in 1753, when writing to his brother-in-law, Benjamin Watson. The latter's son, John, had been taken as an apprentice by Williams in 1740, and subsequently had become a partner. Williams wrote: 'Your son and I are getting money like dust'. His following words showed how the prosperous times had enabled them to fund the building of a new meeting house. He told Watson: 'I devoted, seven months ago, a hundred pounds, and your son thirty, towards building a house for God.' Any worries he harboured about whether he could afford it proved groundless as he examined his recent returns. 'Here is at least two hundred and fifty pounds more than our usual increase, which the Lord has already given us as bounty-money for the hundred and thirty pounds we lent him.'[6]

That the wealth coming into the town was not spread widely can perhaps be indicated by food riots in Kidderminster in 1766 and 1767 'when poor harvests had led to exceptionally high prices of basic foodstuffs'.[7] The improvement of their living conditions was the prerogative of the wealthy minority. These included the pioneers of the carpet industry, John Pearsall and John Broom, who began the trend for the manufacturers to move into the country air away from the unhealthy town streets. Broom was probably the first. He died in 1779 at his home in Blakebrook, which was later known as Blakebrook Cottage and then as the *Cedars Hotel*. We do not know when Broom built the house, but it is reasonable to suppose that it was in the 1750s or 1760s when his carpet trade was well established. John Pearsall built an extraordinary house of great character on the Stour flood plain at Puxton, probably around 1764 when he took a long lease on the land.[8]

## THE CLOTH INDUSTRY BOOM

Sheriff's map of 1780 showed where much-needed housing was being built to cater for the expanding population in the boom period prior to that year. The enclosure of Cussfield allowed development by builders. At the top of Park

24. The Guildhall. Built in 1760, it was redundant after the building of the Town Hall and was demolished in 1878.

Butts, whose north side was fully built up, was a courtyard known as the Square. This had been advertised in 1770 as 'newly erected leasehold tenements'.[9] Next to it was 'The Battery', described in the Broadfield directory of 1889 as a place where 'until a few years ago people lived in rooms or holes cut in the solid rock'. The most extensive development shown was around the Churchfield area, but it was clearly piecemeal and there was no sign of a planned project by Lord Foley or anybody else. Part of the lane, Churchfield, had itself been built on. Leading off it, Rackfield, Duke Street and Paradise Street were emerging, and here Rhodenhurst Bough, a builder, erected six houses around 1775.[10] The 1780 map showed that Queen Street and Back Queen Street were not yet fully formed and were probably built in haste. Much of this work was by builders or 'masons', such as Thomas Osborne and Thomas Fry, who provided houses with attics, where looms could be located, for silk and worsted weavers.[11]

The industrial age was accompanied by improvements in the transport network. In 1760 an Act of Parliament provided turnpike powers concerning the roads into Kidderminster. In 1771 the Staffordshire and Worcestershire Canal through the town was opened. Its construction created the town of Stourport at its junction with the Severn. Previously this sparsely populated

25. Canal and Wharf. This
photograph, taken in 1935, shows
the heavy industrialisation of the
area between Mill Street and the
canal.

26. Engraving of Kidderminster
*c.*1780. The skyline was then
dominated by smoke from a
pottery.

area was known as Mitton. Stourport quickly grew in importance, and by
1776 powers were being sought to extend the scope of the Turnpike Act to
cover roads at Kidderminster which connected with the new town. The canal
immediately changed the character of the area around St Mary's church. Its path
went straight through the almshouses provided by Sir Edward Blount's legacy
and by 1780 they were rebuilt at Churchfield, at the end of the embryonic
Rackfield, where they were to stay until demolition in the 1960s.

    In their place by the side of the canal wharf a pottery was built, but it was
a short-lived enterprise. In July 1776 a newspaper noted the bankruptcy of
Stephen Miles the elder of Kidderminster, 'goldsmith, grocer and potter'. The

notice referred to 'all that new established pottery or earthen manufactory very advantageously situated upon the banks of the River Stour within 30 yards of the Staffs. and Worcs. canal navigation'. Miles was followed by Nicholas Phipps, a potter from the Spitalfields area of London, but he was bankrupt by 1782. The partnership of Stanley and Turner took over in 1783, but by 1798 the pottery no longer functioned. In 1965 Ian Walker took the opportunity to examine an excavation at the site when the ring road was in preparation. He found saggars, kiln props and earthenware dating from around 1770-80. No pottery pieces marked from Kidderminster have ever been found.[12]

## THE DECLINE OF THE CLOTH INDUSTRY

The boom years gave way in the 1770s to a period when there were trade difficulties. In 1772 an Act of Parliament was obtained for the more easy and speedy recovery of small debts within the Borough and Foreign of Kidderminster. The preamble to the Act referred to the refusal of many debtors to pay up, who relied upon the reluctance of their creditors to incur the 'great expense' of recovery. Many prominent local people were appointed Commissioners 'to hear and determine all such causes and matters of debt'. These included the Bailiff, aldermen and Common Council, and a long list of named persons. The latter contained nonconformists such as the Pearsalls and the Brooms, who continued to be barred from serving in the government of the town, and important landowners and farmers, such as members of the Crane family and Henry Chellingworth of Trimpley. In the same year, according to Nash, there was a 'general decay of credit after Fordyce's bankruptcy ... a great number of workmen were dismissed from their looms and left the town and above 100 died of small pox'. Many unemployed weavers enlisted in the army during the American War of Independence. Between 1772 and 1784 Kidderminster's industry was undermined by competition from cotton cloth, and the number of looms in the town declined from 1,700 to a thousand or less. The number of cloth manufacturers was reduced from 30 to seven. Writing in 1780, Nash stated that the population was 'at least seven hundred less than it was in 1773'.[13]

The surviving manufacturers operated on a larger scale than before, with the average number under their control rising from 60 to 140 looms. One of them was Henry Lea, whose large business enabled him to resolve the shortage of spinners by employing agents in Black Country towns. Lea's expansion enabled him to set up a London warehouse fully to exploit the market there. Henry Lea was one of those to rebuild his timber-framed town house, which was in Mill Street and completed by the time of his marriage in 1774. We start to form an impression of the encroachment of small industrial buildings on to the gardens behind the houses. Lea's garden stretched down to the Stour and contained a warehouse, dyehouse and other outbuildings.[14] A similar picture is created by the advertisement in 1776 for the Mill Street home of the bankrupt silk and worsted manufacturer Joseph Bradley. This was newly built too, and the premises contained a shop, warehouse and garden 'particularly eligible for a Kidderminster manufacturer' with the Stour running 'by the side of the garden'.[15]

## THE STOUR

The river Stour enjoyed a good reputation in those days. In 1753 Doharty's plan claimed the water of the Stour was 'accounted equal to the Stroud water for dyeing colours in grain'. In 1780 Nash waxed lyrical about 'the fitness of the water of the Stour for scouring and striking the colour'. Apparently, the streets were well paved and kept free from rubbish, the principal sewers were carried underground and the Stour was cleared of obstructions. So successful was this work that a 1793 directory was able to claim that 'inundations of the lower part of the town are become less frequent' and so too were the diseases attendant on 'damp and filthy dwellings'. It was even said that 'nothing is at all omitted which can conduce to convenience or promote the interest of the inhabitants'.[16] This may have been an optimistic assessment of the quality of the environment, given the prevalence of vats and furnaces employed to eliminate the oil and gum used in the spinning of wool and silk respectively. The dyed yarn was hung out to dry in gardens. The novelist, Mrs Sherwood, wrote of her childhood in Kidderminster about 1788 and she was unimpressed. She spoke of 'the dirty environs of Kidderminster, where the very air is tainted with the odour of dyed worsteds … our romances, these harmless imaginations … saved us from much coarse contamination, for we often walked along those dirty suburbs without paying any attention to what we saw about us'.[17]

The troubles of the cloth industry were offset by the consolidation of the carpet industry. In 1776 numerous advertisements for information about frauds by workmen in the carpet trade revealed there were at least nine firms. The partnership of Pearsall and Broom had been severed in 1758. Whereas the Broom company was to grow in importance, trade directories ceased to list Pearsalls by the beginning of the 19th century. The name of Brinton first appeared in 1783 with the partnership of Richard Green and Samuel Brinton. This enterprise, however, was unsuccessful, ending in 1790 with the bankruptcy of both men. The cloth industry itself received a final boost with the introduction of the manufacture of bombazine from 1779 onwards. Bombazine was a very fine silk and worsted fabric used for clothing. One of the driving forces behind the new product was a London trader named Proby, who came to Kidderminster in 1780. Other prominent bombazine manufacturers were members of the nonconformist Penn family, based in Church Street. They built Milk Street off Churchfield, probably in the late 19th century. It was an unusual development because each of the tenements contained bombazine shops, mostly for four looms. Possibly the new bombazine manufacturers were seeking to exercise the same sort of control over the weaving process as the carpet manufacturers. Of course, in many instances manufacturers were operating in both industries, as indeed were the Penn family.[18]

## THE WEALTH OF THE FEW

In the late 18th century there arose a wealthy middle class among the manufacturers. One man to emerge with considerable wealth was Henry Crane, the woolstapler of Church Street, who died in 1775. The financial bequests amount to the extraordinary sum of £2,700.[19] In 1779 John Broom I died at his home in Blakebrook, with bequests amounting to £1,150. This made him, in the words of Don Gilbert, a 'rich man'.[20] His erstwhile partner, John Pearsall, had means enough to retire to Nottingham where he died in 1794. In the previous year he had been listed by the *Universal British Directory* under the gentry of that town as John Pearsall Esq. Like Broom, he called himself 'gentleman' in his will, which carried bequests of £1,175. However, the wealth of these men paled into insignificance beside that of the Church Street silk and worsted manufacturer, Joseph Lea, whose money bequests alone came to over £11,000.[21]

The town elite included the millers and two families, both belonging to the dissenting congregation, were prominent. The Best family occupied the historic Caldwall mill located just downstream from Caldwall Hall. Francis Best's life was ended by his horrific murder in a field on a Saturday morning in June 1771. At the age of 67 he was taking his regular walk to Bewdley Market when he was attacked from behind with an oak bludgeon as he approached Bewdley Hill. He struggled until his throat was cut and £12 was removed from his pockets. The murderer, John Child, was soon apprehended, and after trial he was hanged at Worcester admitting to the crime.[22] Francis' grandson, William Butler Best, was to achieve great standing in the 19th century as Mayor, woolstapler and landowner.

The Jefferys family leased the Town Mills in Mill Street from Lord Foley. Three generations would play a leading role in the town until they departed for London in 1833. They were in Kidderminster by February 1740, when the baptism of Matthew, son of John Jefferys, was recorded in the Old Meeting lists. In 1769 John purchased Franche Hall, one of the finest houses in the countryside round the town. Matthew quickly became a very wealthy man, so that the family relinquished their interest in the mills before his death in

27. Matthew Jefferys. A portrait in pastel by John Russell, 1775.

1815, and his own son, John, never had to work for his living. Matthew was a considerable landowner. In 1777 the estate of Anthony Deane, who had inherited Caldwall and other lands of the Clare family, was formally purchased by Matthew and his brother, Thomas, for just over £19,000. The money paid was all Matthew's, and in the following year the lands were vested solely in him. The property included the manors of Caldwall, with its mill occupied by Daniel Best, and also those of Over Mitton, Trimpley and Habberley. In his will of 1813 he was able to leave £18,000 to his daughter.[23] His home at Blakebrook House, which he built around 1785, was one of the finest and largest seen in Kidderminster. Its demolition in approximately 1950 was one of the town's most serious acts of architectural vandalism. This colourful family included the map engraver Thomas, Matthew's uncle, who was appointed Geographer to George III in 1760 and whose work included the engraving of Doharty's 1753 plan of Kidderminster. Matthew's brother, also Thomas, was for many years from 1765 onwards a goldsmith and jeweller in Cockspur Street, London, and from 1783 partner in a firm which won appointments as goldsmith to the King.

## ENCLOSURE AND COUNTRY HOUSES

Virtually all the houses in the countryside around Kidderminster at this time were farmhouses. Even the grander ones, such as at Park Attwood and Low Habberley, were occupied by farming families like the Chellingworths and Cranes. One exception was Franche Hall, which may have been a gentleman's home before John Jefferys bought it in 1769. Matthew Jefferys' home at Blakebrook was one of the earliest examples of country houses built for townspeople or gentlemen. Fine farmhouses continued to be built during the late 18th century, including those at High Habberley and Grey Green. Those at the Lea, Sutton and Oldington occupied medieval hamlet sites, but the farmhouses may have been built shortly after Lord Foley's survey of his land in 1704 and a subsequent enclosure of arable strips. By 1774 these three farms sat between the common at Blakebrook and the huge swathe of heathland on the west stretching from Wassell Hill down towards the Stour north of where Stourport was about to grow. In that year most of this land was to be enclosed by an Act of Parliament, although Habberley Valley was untouched and so

too was Burlish Common, which was eventually to be enclosed in 1822. The precise details were contained in the award of 1775, when the land was divided between those with interests in it. The enclosure award provided the potential for carving out estates for new country houses on this land. There is a tradition that the whole point of the Act was to allow Samuel Skey, a prosperous Bewdley grocer and banker, to build himself a country

28. **Blakebrook House, built by Matthew Jefferys c.1785.**

seat. Indeed, Lord Foley duly sold land awarded to him, to Skey in 1775, and Spring Grove was built in 1787. This land included the pools known as the Slashes.[24] Also enclosed was Blakebrook Common, making possible the erection of Summerhill on Bewdley Hill by 1787, and it was leased by Lord Foley to a series of manufacturers from the town. Nothing was ever done with a considerable portion of this poor-quality land, some of which now forms the two nature reserves, Devil's Spittleful and Rifle Range.

Writing of her childhood many years later, Martha Sherwood's recollection was that there were no 'little elegant country houses in the neighbourhood of Kidderminster'. This was not entirely accurate, but it was close to the truth. The trend started by John Pearsall and John Broom began to gather pace well before the end of the century. Mrs Sherwood arrived in Kidderminster in 1788, by which time the Shrubbery had certainly been built in Birmingham Road by William Lea, the son of Joseph. Further out near Blakedown on the same road stood Park Hall, which by 1774 was the home of Abraham Turner. The fine Woodfield House, which still stands in Bewdley Road, was erected in 1784 by Doctor Abraham Wilkinson, husband of Rebecca Crane.[25] Gradually the wealth created in the dirty town was enabling a few to adopt a more genteel lifestyle in the country air. Martha Sherwood noted that once 'people lived where their business was'. Having subsequently left Kidderminster, she was aware of the 'constant abandonment of the place by such families as have made their fortunes'.

## OLD AND NEW MEETING

Mrs Sherwood's father, George Butt, had moved to the town to take up the position of vicar. She commented on his friendly relations with the other congregations, and added that 'certainly we found that the dissenting portion of the society at Kidderminster was the best educated'.[26] By the time of their arrival in town, the dissenters had split into two main groups. During the 18th century many factors combined to erode the old Calvinist certainties. The educated members of congregations began to question dogmas, and the wealthier among them no longer felt the need to subscribe to ideas better attuned to a persecuted sect. The splits in the dissenters' congregation were described by Thomas Wright Hill, father of Rowland. 'A considerable number, among whom were my mother and her nearest relations, were Calvinists; a considerable number, of whom my father was one, were Arminians. My father too, and some of the Arminians were likewise Arians, and among those was even the Minister himself, though he managed so far to conceal his opinions as to be very popular with his hearers.'[27]

Arminians disputed the Calvinist doctrine of predestination and believed that men and women were free to achieve their own salvation by finding a true faith. The minister mentioned by Thomas Hill was Benjamin Fawcett. Also among his congregation were people who looked beyond their own number to the saving of souls. This evangelical tendency was encouraged by the Countess of Huntingdon, and Joseph Williams had himself been a minor figure in this movement. Fawcett managed to hold the dissenters together from 1745 until his death in 1780. The split came immediately afterwards. Those who broke away to form New Meeting questioned much more than the Calvinist view of salvation. Many were Arians who doubted the divinity of Christ and did not believe that he was of the same substance as God. Some were prepared to believe that Christ was created as an instrument of God, but others moved further towards Unitarianism, which sought to break down any idea offensive to rational thought and saw Christ simply as a religious leader. These doctrinal niceties were to cause divisions among New Meeting even after the secession. The most important founder member of the breakaway group was Nicholas Pearsall. He was a strict Unitarian and his commitment to the cause enabled New Meeting chapel to be built and ready by October 1782.[28]

A new chapel had been necessary because the orthodox Calvinists, who became known as Old Meeting, retained the meeting house, whilst the free-thinking secessionists took the minister's house on Church Street, which was known as the Parsonage House and had been built in 1732 by the trustees of the Rev. Spilsbury. Nicholas Pearsall owned the property next door to the Parsonage House, the Corner House, and also the land behind both properties. These he donated, enabling first the erection of the chapel, which then stood

29. New
Meeting School
before 1865.

discretely behind the Parsonage House and Corner House, but now has an
open frontage following their demolition in the 1920s. By 1786 both a Sunday
School and a Day School had been built adjacent to the chapel at Pearsall's
own expense. The latter was for the basic education of 100 poor boys and girls
in reading, writing and accounts. It was funded thereafter by collections from
the congregation and various trusts. In 1795 Pearsall founded a Grammar
School on the same site, and in this case its continued funding was by means
of an endowment made by him.[29]

The ability of Nicholas Pearsall to finance all this was a further indication
of the increased wealth and standing of Kidderminster's manufacturing classes.
In one respect the source of his wealth is clear. By marrying Ann Fincher of
Shell, near Droitwich, he acquired substantial lands which she had inherited.
The manor and lands were disposed of in Pearsall's will and helped to fund
the considerable legacies. Yet such a marriage was likely only if Pearsall had
already become a man of substance. His manufacturing background is not
completely clear. It is certain he was involved in weaving, but the evidence for
the claim that he was a carpet manufacturer is lacking. Such a claim is probably
made because Nicholas shared his surname with the founder of the industry,
but as we have seen they were almost certainly only third cousins. The wealth
made by weaving must have been substantial, because the extraordinary list
of legacies in Nicholas' will after his death in 1798 goes way beyond his wife's
obvious inheritance. The financial gifts amounted to over £4,500.[30]

## THE THEATRE

One aspect of Kidderminster's social life which was testing the dissenters'
capacity for free thinking was the theatre. Puritans had traditionally been

hostile to this form of entertainment, which was certainly being provided in the town at this time. An undated report has recorded the protest of a Mr Watson, upon 'a set of itinerants being tolerably well received at Kidderminster'. He nailed a card on the door of the barn, 'which was dignified with the name of *The Summer Royal Theatre*'. It contained the words:

> How art thou fallen, Oh! Kidderminster;
> When every spulster, spinner, spinster,
> Whose fathers lived in Baxter's prayers,
> Are now run gadding after players.
> Oh! Richard, coulds't thou take a survey
> Of this vile place, for sin so scurvy,
> Thy pious shade, enraged, would scold then
> And make the barn too hot to hold them.[31]

The writer seemed to sense that the old Puritan values were breaking down in Kidderminster, and perhaps the secession of New Meeting should be seen in that light. It is likely that the author was John Watson, nephew and partner of Joseph Williams. He is not known to have joined New Meeting and an obituary of 1804 reflected upon his conservative opinions. He held to the classic Calvinist doctrine of 'justification by faith only, regarding good works not as the condition of salvation, but as the necessary fruits of a true and lively faith'. Interestingly, he apparently regarded the monarchy as the 'friends and protectors of civil and religious liberty'.[32]

The theatre is thought to have been sited since about 1780 at the foot of Comberton Hill, where the Playhouse would later emerge. Certainly in 1792 Mr J. Eyeley and Company expressed gratitude for the 'liberal support' received from the Ladies and Gentlemen of Kidderminster and hoped for their continued 'kind patronage'. Three old deeds held by the Nonentities today suggest that the theatre was indeed set up at this site during this period. The land concerned was near Worcester Cross 'near a comon style there leading into Leswell field'. The deeds extended to 1770 and made no mention of a theatre, which was presumably established later.[33]

## SEDITION

For many nonconformists political thought was linked to their religion, which barred them from public office and from attending the two English universities. The French Revolution of 1789, in which the monarchy was overthrown, drew attention to the limitations of Britain's parliamentary democracy. The polarisation of opinion was most extreme in Birmingham, where many nonconformists were sympathetic to the aspirations of the revolution. A 'Church and King' mob appeared on the streets on 14 July 1791 and proceeded to burn meeting houses and the private houses of leading nonconformists. One of the first victims was Joseph Priestley, Unitarian minister and the discoverer of oxygen. His work destroyed, he fled and was in London by 19 July. One account has it that Priestley met a member of his congregation, Thomas Ryland, in Kidderminster, but was advised that there was much ill-feeling

30. John Broom II (1735-1811). He lived at Spennells House and was probably responsible for setting up the family's spinning mill nearby.

against him and it would be wise to change into non-clerical garb for his flight to London. He was sheltered briefly by John Broom at Spennells House. Ryland and Priestley then took a coach to Worcester, and the driver said afterwards that 'had he known who they really were he would have turned over the chaise and broken their necks.'[34]

The repressive times must have persuaded some to drop any sympathy for democratic reforms. It would be interesting to know whether John Watson had been such a staunch monarchist in 1791 as he was at his death in 1804. The Birmingham riots were just the beginning, for in the following year the phenomenal success of Thomas Paine's *Rights of Man* provoked the English government into further political repression. Paine's book was

31. Spennells House. By 1803, when he wrote his will, John Broom was living at Spennells, and it must be likely that this house was built in the 1780s.

KIDDERMINSTER.

December 10th, 1792.

TO
ROBERT SHIRLEY and JOSHUA MORETON, Esqrs.
High Bailiff, and Justice of Kidderminster.

WHEREAS it appears that several persons have been industrious in circulating seditious publications, tending to subvert our established and happy constitution—And that endeavours have been made to instil various seditious tenets and opinions into the minds of the lower class of men—And whereas ASSOCIATIONS, for preserving LIBERTY and PROPERTY against Republicans and Levellers, have been formed by a set of respectable gentlemen at the Crown and Anchor Tavern, London, and by the most respectable Merchants, Bankers, and Traders in the city of London, at Merchant-Taylor's Hall, as well as at Birmingham, and other respectable places in this kingdom;

We, whose names are hereunto subscribed, impressed with a due regard for our laws and constitution, and sensible of the happiness and liberty we enjoy under the same; and with the patriotism of the before-mentioned several Societies, and being convinced of the necessity of opposing the further progress of sedition, do request you to call a Meeting of the friends of the Constitution and Government in this town and neighbourhood, to consider of the propriety of establishing a similar Association.

| | |
|---|---|
| George Butt, Vicar, | John Newcomb, jun. |
| Richard Colley, | Abraham Turner, |
| John Newcomb, | Henry Perrin, |
| Joseph Pardoe, | William Wheeler, |
| James Pinches, | George Colley, |
| Herbert Bury, | Edward Barber, |
| James Hooman, | James Hawker, |
| George Gower, | George Hallen, |
| Joseph Crane, | Thomas Pratt, |
| Thomas Wells, | William Hickman, |
| Richard Morris, | Gervase Wheeler, |
| Edward Moore, | John Powell, |
| William Perry, | John Lavender, |
| George Robinson, | Alexander Patrick, |
| Peter Hughes, | George Gorton, |
| Henry Bird, | John Crane, |
| William Lea, | John Mainwaring, |
| Josiah Lea, | John Hillman, |
| William Thorn, | Joseph Turner, |
| Thomas Roofe, | William Callow, Curate |
| Thomas Griffin, | of Kidderminster, |
| John Woodward, | Henry Chellingworth, |
| William Lea, | John Morris, |
| Edward Baynham, | Walter Dickins, |
| Thomas Mole, | Richard Colley, jun. |
| Edmund Walker, | John Jones, |
| Jacob Turner, | Joseph Clymer, |
| John Steward, | John Barnett, jun, |
| Thomas Morris, | Stephen Miles, |
| Samuel Wright, | Rev. T. Morgan, |
| Charles Wright, | Benjamin Pearce. |
| Thomas Williams, | |

In compliance with the above requisition, we appoint a GENERAL MEETING of the inhabitants of the town and neighbourhood, at the Great Room at the Lion Inn, on Saturday the 22d instant, precisely at eleven o'clock in the forenoon.

ROBERT SHIRLEY.
JOSHUA MORETON.

32. 1792 anti-sedition notice.

written in support of the ideals of the French Revolution. It was revolutionary in democratic terms and showed scant respect for the monarchy. In a population of ten million it sold perhaps a quarter of a million copies in two years. Paine was indicted for seditious libel and was forced to flee the country. We can take it that *Rights of Man* was being read in Kidderminster, particularly in the light of the formation of an association by the town's loyal subjects against 'republicans and levellers' in December 1792. It was alleged that 'several persons have been industrious in circulating seditious publications' among the lower class of men. The list of supporters is a guide to the Anglican establishment governing the town at that time. No leading nonconformists included their names, not even John Watson, although Nicholas Pearsall was subsequently to become a member of their committee. In the circumstances most nonconformists probably decided to keep their heads down and get on with their business. During this difficult international period Kidderminster's trade was steady and the borough's population in 1801 was 6,110. The silk and worsted industry suffered little decline, but in 1805 Holden's *Triennial Directory* became the first to recognise that carpet manufacturing was more important.

# VI

# *A Carpet Town*

Now that Kidderminster was established as being primarily a carpet town, its weavers were having to get used to the reduced status which went with the developing capitalist system. They were no longer independent artisans working at home with their own loom, but the employees of manufacturers with the resources to supply them with the loom and a factory to work in. The potential for class conflict was eventually to be realised with the great strike of 1828. In fact, the insistence of the male weavers that they represented a skilled tradition, both necessary to the carpet industry and deserving of dignity, was to lead to further disputes in the latter part of the century. Meanwhile, Kidderminster was very definitely an industrial town, and in the period up to about 1825 its main industry would grow considerably. During this time the town started to extend outwards at a greater rate than before, and the older parts became more congested as every bit of land was built on. Kidderminster was no longer a town with extensive gardens behind the house frontages, and no parks or other recreational areas had been created to compensate. To an extent the authorities took steps to deal with the worst effects of industrialisation, but their efforts were feeble.

An industrial town was rarely a pretty town, and at the turn of the century Kidderminster had probably improved little since James Johnstone referred to its nasty little houses. This is suggested by a letter written in 1803 to a future Lord Chancellor by the literary figure Matthew Gregory Lewis, who was forced to spend a night in the town, though he may have exaggerated a little:

> I do warn you, Lord Henry Petty, in order that you may warn all other Lord Henry Petties even unto the fiftieth generation, not to suffer any human considerations, neither interest, flattery, nor force, to entice you into the limbo of Kidderminster. Do you happen to have heard of any enormous crime committed by the inhabitants? For that the place is accursed of heaven is past a doubt. The roads are all sand; the hills are all brick-dust colour; the houses are all dirty; the children are all ugly; the men are all stupid; and I do verily believe in my conscience that all the women are born old … Had I possessed the wand of a sorcerer, I should certainly have ordered the ground to open and swallow up this detestable town.[1]

Those with money evidently shared these sentiments, for the trend was to set fine houses in the countryside outside town. John Broom II was well-established at Spennells House. In 1802 John Lea built the Lakes, a mansion on Franche Road. Lea was one of the silk and worsted manufacturers who were switching production to carpets. One of the grandest mansions built by the carpet manufacturers was Broomfield House, the home of John Broom III, which was also erected on Franche Road. On the other side of town Greenhill was built by Lord Foley, overlooking Broadwaters, and it was let to George Talbot in 1802, until he purchased the house some years later. In 1810 his brother and partner, Henry, purchased nearby land, where he built Oaklands.[2] George and Henry were also stuffs manufacturers making the transition to carpets. Further out, the farming community of Trimpley was being transformed by the wealth of the Chellingworth family, who held both Park Attwood and Holt Castle. The elegant farmhouses, Trimpley House and Holbeache House, originate from the early years of the century, and provided homes for the growing number of males in the family.[3]

## BOMBAZINE AND CARPETS

In the years leading up to the end of the French wars in 1815 there were only five stuffs manufacturers left in the town, but three of them were also making carpets and it was clear that there was a feeling that the silk and worsted trade would never recover its previous importance. The only cloth made in any significant quantity by then was bombazine. The industry would hold its own for a little longer, before falling into decline in the 1820s. By contrast the carpet industry continued to expand. Capital was needed to buy the looms and set them up in shops or factories, and it was often provided from outsiders. These included James Cole, who switched from the building trade and was making carpets by 1798. Another to put capital into the trade was the bookseller and printer, George Gower, who joined forces with Charles Wright and John Gough in 1807. The partnership of Woodward and Morton was formed in 1809. John Woodward's origins are not clear, but his partner, James Morton, was the son of a wealthy Worcester cabinet maker. Despite this growth, there was a period of great hardship up to 1812. The British and French governments were trying to damage each other's sea trade. In the case of Britain this was done by means of Orders-in-Council, and in May 1812 a Parliamentary committee took evidence about their effect. In Kidderminster, where the population had reached 8,038, there had evidently been a petition expressing concern about the impact on the town's trade. Richard Watson was interviewed, and he claimed that the number employed in the carpet industry had been reduced by half to 1,200 people, half of whom were women and children. The questioner was clearly sceptical of the claims.

33. Handloom Carpet Shop with an adjoining dye house, thought to have been near New Road.

Nevertheless, there is other evidence of hard times from 1810 to 1817. A series of arson attacks affected the millers, Jefferys and Wagstaff, in 1810. Matthew Jefferys was in the twilight of his career as a miller, with his lease on the town mills expiring in 1813. He died in January 1814, aged 74, and his obituary referred to the esteem in which he was held for the 'benevolence of his heart' and his 'extensive charity'.[4] However, it was evident those qualities were not uppermost in the minds of the townspeople in 1810, when many were presumably starving and not appreciative of the price of bread. In the course of twelve months there were four attacks, beginning with a fire at Jefferys and Wagstaff's barn opposite Woodfield House. Three months later their 'barns, cottages, cowhouses and winnowing machine, on that side of the canal opposite to the mill, were completely destroyed, everything uninsured'. In June 1810 the barn in Barn Street, occupied by Daniel Wagstaff, was set alight and 'in a moment both side of the street were in one general blaze. The scene was truly horrible and terrific; in a few hours seven barns, three stables, three dwelling houses and a large manufactory belonging to Lea and Newcomb were completely destroyed'. Finally there was a repeat of the attack upon the barn opposite Woodfield.[5]

The ending of the French wars in 1815 did not have an immediately beneficial effect. There was a depression, which by January 1817 was causing much distress. The main casualty of this period was William Penn who was made bankrupt in 1816. The real heyday of the carpet trade began in 1817 and extended to 1825, but it is by no means clear that the great profits made were widely shared.[6] A sign that all was not well in the town was the destruction in November 1817 of a spinning mill belonging to Pardoe, Hooman and Pardoe in an arson attack. By this time spinning was no longer a domestic industry and this mill was a large one. This catastrophic fire put 400 people out of work. The

34. Handloom Carpet Shops. This pair survive today in Long Acre, and both once accommodated two handlooms on each floor.

35. Cemetery Cottage. Built by Matthew Jefferys, as a boathouse by the pool he created when landscaping the Caldwall estate, it was pulled down in the late 19th century.

background to the attack was the wage disputes between journeymen carpet weavers and their employers. Their requests not having been met, the weavers 'generally entered into unlawful combinations to enforce their demands, and a number of them turned out, or struck: they frequently assembled in different places in great numbers, to consult together: thus things went on for some weeks.'[7] It is clear that the class lines, which were to emerge so dramatically in

1828, were already drawn by 1817. George Hallen, Town Clerk, advised the Home Secretary that the weavers were using sick clubs as a front to fund their action.[8]

## COOPER AND BRINTON

Another company to cease trading at this time was the partnership between John Cooper, his nephew William Cooper, and William Brinton, bombazine and carpet manufacturers. John Cooper was undoubtedly a very substantial figure. He purchased the magnificent Woodfield House in 1800 for £1,780. By this time he was a carpet manufacturer, and like most of them he was a nonconformist, who married Hannah, the daughter of John Watson. Like Watson, he probably remained loyal to the Old Meeting congregation. The extent of his wealth can be gauged by a codicil to his will dated 1810, in which he left £10,000 to his sister Phebe.[9] The partnership with William Brinton may have been made possible by their Old Meeting connections. Brinton was a leading figure there, and he was for many years from 1807 the respected superintendent of the Sunday School, which had been built in Fish Street.[10]

The partnership was dissolved in December 1816, but apparently for reasons unconnected with the depression. Cooper was the senior partner, who had been growing rich and took William Brinton into partnership probably between 1811 and 1814. Cooper, who had no children, also took his nephew into the partnership, but William Cooper was apparently jealous of the good prospects his uncle held out for Brinton and his sons. This is what ruined the partnership, with the nephew inflicting 'great injuries' on Brinton and his family by 'depriving him of his uncle's good intentions'. Brinton received only £250 as his share from the dissolved partnership and went to work as manager of Thomas Lea's spinning mill, where he remained for more than ten years. His son, Henry, also went to work with Lea as a traveller, and it was he who was to set up the famous family firm of Brintons, probably between 1819 and 1821. It is clear that the bicentenary celebrated by Brintons Ltd in 1983 should in fact be planned for around 2020.[11]

## PAVING COMMISSIONERS

The charter, which provided for the government of the town by the High Bailiff and burgesses, was approaching its 200th anniversary. Yet industrialisation and an expanding population were beginning to pose problems beyond anything dreamed of in 1636. Moreover, nonconformists were still excluded from the undemocratic self-perpetuating oligarchy formed by the burgesses, and so many of the town's most wealthy and influential inhabitants, as well as the

poorest, played no part in municipal affairs. For example, a deed of 1822 listed
16 of the burgesses, only one of whom, the Anglican Joseph Newcombe, was
a carpet manufacturer. The rest comprised three drapers, two gentlemen, two
grocers, two bakers, a woolstapler, an innkeeper, a builder, a bookseller, a miller
and a clockmaker.[12] The system was outdated and required new powers to
deal with the growing filth and congestion. Many towns paid for their own
'Improvement Act' to be passed by Parliament granting them the necessary
powers. Kidderminster was slow in this respect.[13] However, the poor conditions
experienced in the depressed years 1810-12 prodded the townspeople into
action and in 1813 royal assent was given to an Act for 'Paving, Cleansing,
Lighting, Watching, and otherwise improving the Streets, and other public
Passages and Places in Kidderminster'.

The Act created a body of people known as the Paving Commissioners,
including not only the Bailiff and burgesses, but also a long list of over fifty
prominent people in the town. The commissioners were empowered to raise
money by borrowing or levying a rate. The first project involved work to
prevent the Stour flooding. This included the deepening of the river by six
inches and a new course and weir at Caldwall. The lowest tender of £478 was
accepted and the work was finished by October 1813, but the weir had to be
rebuilt with its height raised in 1815. In the same year the Daddle Brook was
cleansed. In July 1813 six watchmen were appointed at a wage of 12 shillings
per week. This system, a precursor of the police force, was ineffective and
had to be reorganised in 1823, when 'each watchman was assigned a beat and
equipped with a lantern, short staff and a large rattle'. There seems to have been
little improvement because between 1823 and 1835 half of the 46 watchmen
employed were dismissed for drunkenness or other offences. Also in 1813 a
contract was awarded by the commissioners to the enterprising Blankley Perrins
Willis, who we shall soon meet again in other contexts, for the erection of 350
oil lamps, which he was to light 140 nights a year for two years. A further 100
lamps were erected in 1816.

The lighting arrangements were not satisfactory, and in 1818 another
local Act of Parliament was passed to complement the 1813 Act. This was 'an
Act for lighting the Borough of Kidderminster in the County of Worcester
with Gas'. It created a corporate body, the Kidderminster and Gas Light and
Coke Company, whose purpose was to produce 'inflammable Air, carburetted
Hydrogen, Coal Gas, Coke, Oil, Tar, Pitch'. This company was empowered to
enter into contracts with the Paving Commissioners for putting into effect the
lighting purposes of the 1813 Act. Most of the members of the new company
were also Paving Commissioners, but it was still deemed proper for a contract
between the two bodies to be agreed in August 1819 for the lighting of the
town with gas and oil for £283 per annum.

Under the 1813 Act the Commissioners had certain powers concerning sanitation. They could appoint somebody to cleanse the streets or take away dirt and soil. They could also dig drains and sewers across courts, yards, gardens and alleys, provided they agreed recompense with the owners. As the years went by sanitation was to be a major failing, but from 1821 to 1826 some work was done. During that time culverts were either built or improved in Vicar Street, Barn Street, Bird Lane, Hall Street, Queen Street, Oxford Street, Broad Street, the Square, Park Butts and the Horsefair. Other work carried out included the laying of footpaths with proper kerb stones in Barn Street and Fish Street between 1821 and 1823. Another major project was the replacement of Callows Bridge.[14] Perhaps this early flurry of activity in good economic conditions just about kept Kidderminster in good order. Thus in 1820 one observer was able to report on the town in reasonably favourable terms. He referred to the 'ranges of new streets for the workmen, and the number of small, yet elegant villas in the vicinity. Kidderminster was 'flourishing' as a trading place 'principally owing to the industry, frugality, and simplicity of the manners of its inhabitants.'[15]

## EXPANSION

Some of the new streets mentioned by Laird would have been designed to accommodate the flourishing bombazine industry, but most of these are likely to have been established by the turn of the century and probably no later than 1810, when it was clear the industry was no longer advancing. A possible late development is the complex of streets off the top end of Blackwell Street, comprising Union Street, Silver Street and the beginning of Waterloo Street. It is by no means certain when they were laid down, but the Baptist church in Silver Street was built in 1813. The interesting feature of Silver Street was that six of the properties had attics capable of taking six bombazine looms.[16] The space required was not great. Bombazine was a light material, and the loom was also light and quite small. It is likely that some weavers still could not afford the relatively inexpensive bombazine loom, and this encouraged some weavers to accumulate a number of looms which they hired out to their neighbours.[17]

Most of the expansion was due to the growth of the carpet industry. The population of the borough nearly doubled in 20 years from just over 8,000 in 1811 to 14,981 in 1831. It is likely that most of this increase had already occurred by 1825, when the boom was over. The early 1820s was a time of considerable development. A new workhouse had been erected in 1816 in Broad Street, and in 1821 houses were built at the lower end of the street, so the houses were set amidst open fields. The name of the street probably referred to the powers of the Paving Commissioners to insist that new main streets should be at least fourteen yards wide. For a time the inhabitants of Broad Street were

36. South Street. These houses may have been back-to-backs. Photographed here in 1969, they were ready for demolition. In the background is St George's Junior School, which was also pulled down.

'comfortably off, in better positions, and cleaner and tidier' than they were to be in later years, according to Ebenezer Guest.[18] Also in 1821 Lord Foley's agents were seeing to a congested development of Lion Field above and behind the *Lion Hotel*. Three streets ran from north to south (these being Bromsgrove Street, Cross Street and George Street), and three ran from west to east (Lion Street, Fair Street and South Street). In years to come Bromsgrove Street and George Street were to be extended across to Comberton Hill, and in modern times the ring road has been driven right through the centre of the area.[19]

Later in the decade the willingness of John Jefferys to start breaking up the Caldwall estate enabled building to take place on the south side of Bewdley Street on what was known as the Gravel Pit Field. For a while the only building on this land had been a carpet factory built around 1800 by John Lea.[20] In 1824 land adjacent to this factory was sold by Jefferys to a new carpet manufacturer, John Sutton Barber of Walsall, who had formed a partnership with his brother-in-law, James Cole. The deeds refer to intended new streets with a width of 14 yards. Barber and Cole's factory was to front Park Street and run between Hill Street and Brussels Street.[21] These streets are shown on the 1835 Broadfield map of the town, as are Wood Street and Chapel Street. The development was confined to an area extending no more than perhaps a hundred yards from

Bewdley Street. Many years later Wood Street and Park Street were to be extended to their current length.

A major and lasting change to the town centre took place in the 1820s, when Oxford Street was developed into an important commercial part of the town centre. According to Ebenezer Guest, it was all due to the 'prudence and foresight of one man', Blankley Perrins Willis. In 1824 he purchased the land on the south side of Oxford Street down to the river extending all the way from what is now Bank Buildings up to Worcester Cross. Up to that time only the north side of the road was built upon and even that was

37. *The Tap House*, Blakebrook. This fine pub stood with its back to the workhouse near the Sutton Road corner. It is photographed here a few years before demolition in 1889.

'practically the back part of Worcester Street'. The town finished there. The area known as Vicar's Meadows was 'swamp in some parts', though until 1816 it had contained the workhouse in Caldwall Row, which was later to become Market Street.[22] By 1830 the transformation of the district was ensured by the Turnpike Trustees building New Road through Willis' land. This road replaced Park Lane as the main road to Stourport.

During these years the grand residences of Blakebrook were built, just over the borough boundary, on land taken from the common by the Enclosure Award of 1775. Much of this land had been granted to Lord Foley, who sold the first plot to Thomas Crowther, and the adjoining second plot, in 1821, to the versatile Blankley Perrins Willis. By the end of that year four houses (now numbers 18-21) were completed. Such building was simply an investment for men with money. Willis paid Foley £180 for the land and three years later he sold the houses for £1,060 to Abel Lea, the bombazine manufacturer who was also looking for another way of using his money. Lea was already busy building more houses on the land next to the north side of Willis' plot. By 1825 two more grand houses were being assessed for the poor rates. These were the present-day Brookdale Nursing Home and its adjoining house. Lea bought the Crowther houses and by 1832 he had added the three-storey house, which is now number 22, so that he owned a row of seven houses on the east side of the road, which he rented out to carpet manufacturers and other members of the growing middle class.[23] Henry Brinton was listed as a tenant of number 21 from 1830 until 1846. The Brintons had lived for some time in Mill Street and it would seem that Henry maintained a residence there until at least August 1830, when the house was attacked by rioters. It is possible that the Blakebrook house at first functioned as his 'country' residence and an escape from the increasingly polluted conditions of industrial Kidderminster. Abel Lea himself was one who apparently maintained both a town and country residence. He lived in Mill Street too, but he was at his 'summer residence' in Blakeshill (sic) when he died in 1838.[24] Lea's tenant at number 22 for a time was the Rev. Robert Ross, who had moved from Edinburgh in 1827 to become Minister of Old Meeting. He had a sympathetic landlord. Abel Lea was a leading member and one of the principal subscribers to the new and larger meeting house, which was built in 1824 and still stands behind the Baxter Church in the Bull Ring.

## MORE CHURCHES

During the first three decades of the 19th century many chapels and churches were built in Kidderminster. There seems to have been great competition between the different denominations to capture the growing working class. As we have suggested, the Calvinist congregation in the town had for over 200 years been the obvious refuge for the weaving community who now formed the aspiring middle class. As some of them became wealthy employers and others became poor employees, it was not clear that the latter belonged there any longer. In addition, the influx into the town of people looking for work brought an increasing number of those with other religious loyalties.

The Baptist church was establishing itself at this time, having opened the Silver Street chapel in March 1813. The early evangelical fervour of the supporters of the Countess of Huntingdon had not been very successful. They had been able to build a chapel at the bottom of Mill Street, but after the Countess' death in 1791 they had to sell the chapel to the Methodists. In due course their group revived and in 1819 a new chapel was built in Barn Street. It was known as the Ebenezer Chapel and was financed by four members, including William Binnian, a builder who lived in Broad Street.[25] It was built on a patch of ground near Grosvenor's rope walk, in the area which Lord Foley had supposedly planned to develop in 1753. Like all the dissenters' meeting houses, it was set back from the road with a little lawn on each side of the entrance. Unfortunately there were financial problems, and the land at the front was sold for houses, which spoilt the approach to the chapel. The great John Wesley had stayed with the Rev. Fawcett in 1771, but it was to be some time

38. Old Meeting House, Bull Ring. Built in 1824, it was pulled down after only 60 years and the current Baxter Church opened in 1885. The 18th-century meeting house can be seen behind, where it still stands today.

before the Methodists gained a foothold in Kidderminster. Having purchased the chapel in Mill Street, they demolished it to build their own in 1803. They were able to enlarge it in 1821. They too suffered from divisions among themselves, and in 1824 a small chapel was built by the Primitive Methodists in the new Lion Field development at Cross Street. The building of religious houses was reaching its peak, and in 1824 a large new Old Meeting House was built between the old one and the Bull Ring.

The established church was becoming alert to the advances being made by the dissenting chapels. In 1818 Parliament, in what was known as the 'Million Pound Act', voted money to ensure that Anglican churches had an increased capacity to absorb new members. In the following year a committee was formed in Kidderminster, with Thomas Hallen as secretary, to plan the building of a new church. This resulted in the consecration of St George's church in April 1824. It was located just beyond the streets amid the first fields, but ideally positioned for those from the growing working-class areas on the east side of town. It was built on an impressive scale, seating 2,000 people and having a tall spire. The cost was nearly £20,000, of which £17,047 was granted by the new fund, the third largest award for any church outside London.[26]

## CONFLICT AND DEPRESSION

The role of the churches doubtless included trying to reconcile the working classes to their reduced status. The carpet industry might have been highly profitable in the period up to 1825, but that does not mean that Kidderminster's streets were full of contented weavers. Indeed, the arson attack of 1817 was not an isolated incident. Such antagonism had been growing for many years. In 1820 George Hallen had again written to the Home Secretary to say there had been a number of buildings 'maliciously set on fire'. He had quoted a letter read to a crowd in the street and addressed to the magistrate William Boycot, who had been 'very forward upon all occasions' to suppress disorder. This letter threatened to burn his house down and warned that 'the rich shall be mede poor and the poor shall be med rich'.[27] This house was almost certainly the beautiful Hill Grove, which Boycot occupied by 1823 and now forms part of King Charles I School. The tension in the town reflected the bitterness caused by years of repression. The industrialisation of British society had been accompanied by the banning of trade unions under the Combination Acts of 1799 and 1800. To protect their interests the weavers had no choice but to resort to secret activity.

Despite the generally healthy state of the carpet industry, the years 1823/24 were calamitous for the Wagstaff family. Like others, they had transferred their capital from another business, that of flour milling. In 1823 both Daniel and Samuel Wagstaff were bankrupt. The reason for their trouble is unclear, but their bankruptcy encompassed Daniel's son, John Hill Wagstaff, who was based in London. In March 1824 John was charged with forging a cheque for £250. Having found him guilty, the harsh English criminal law showed him no mercy, and he was hanged at Newgate in June after an 'agonizing' parting from his family.[28] From then on the Wagstaff family, so firmly rooted in the town's nonconformist community, disappeared from Kidderminster life. The name was to survive only with the future miller, Daniel Wagstaff Goodwin, whose mother was John's sister. The demise of the family's carpet interests was a sign that too many had entered the industry and that there was trouble ahead. In December 1825 there was a financial crash which had a serious effect on the national economy. Kidderminster's trade entered a depression which lasted into 1827. The heyday of the carpet industry was over. The decline in the manufacture of bombazine must have become more severe, but it was still a significant occupation in the town. Abel Lea's will, dated 1827, referred to his brother, Henry, as a 'dealer in carpeting and bombazine' and was signed by Henry Woodward, 'bombazine manufacturer'.

## THE GREAT STRIKE

The prosperity of Kidderminster now depended almost entirely on making carpets, and in particular the town specialised in the production of Brussels carpets. Scotland was a competitor in the manufacture of 'Kidderminster' or 'Scotch' carpets, but Kidderminster was dominating the Brussels trade. In 1828 concern grew that northern towns were entering the field, and that they were able to undercut Kidderminster trade by paying less to their Brussels weavers. In March of that year the manufacturers gave notice, without any consultation whatsoever, that the rate of pay for Brussels was to be reduced from one shilling a yard to ten pence. The reaction of the weavers was swift. On 17 March a meeting of 2,000 men resolved to strike.

The strike was to last five months and the uncompromising approach of both sides was extraordinary, showing that Kidderminster was barely a community any more. The weavers were confronted by the iron law of capitalism: that

39. Henry Brinton (1796-1857), founder of Brintons c.1820. He took a harsh line during the 1828 strike, but later his reputation was to soften considerably.

wages had to be reduced to what was being paid elsewhere. Henry Brinton was prominent in maintaining this principle. They also found themselves dealing with employers who at times showed they no longer had anything in common with their workers. *The Times*, which reported the strike throughout, put the manufacturers' case that for weavers to earn more than was required was a 'temptation to idleness and drunkedness'. Joseph Bowyer was particularly fond of this argument. Over three months were to pass before there was any sign of concession from the employers. On 28 June a 'moderate' group made an improved offer. In July one employer offered a compromise eleven pence a yard. Both these offers were rejected by the weavers, despite the suffering that was already taking place. There is no evidence the union was able to use funds of their own to support their striking members. By June the condition of strikers was appalling and financial support was only just beginning to come from elsewhere. The strike was coordinated by a committee, but the slightest false move was going to be pounced upon by the authorities. Although the Combination Acts were repealed in 1824, more or less any pressure brought to bear by unions on non-members remained illegal.[29] By the end of April George Hallen, who by now was both High Bailiff and Chief Magistrate, was seeking to arrest weavers as

# Carpet Weavers

## OF

# KIDDERMINSTER.

AS your Chief Magistrate, seeing that you are upon the brink of ruin, I cannot refrain from writing these few lines, which contain my sentiments relative to the unhappy dispute between you and your Masters. The last time I addressed you was verbally on your turn-out. I wish, for your sakes, the advice I then gave had been attended to, namely, for a few of you to wait upon your Masters, and respectfully submit to them your grievances; instead of which you have relied upon your Committee, whose avowed object has been the ruin of the Masters and of the Town. But, as these are evils which are passed, and therefore cannot be remedied, look at your present situation, and see what steps might be taken to prevent troubles which are fast coming upon you. Your late employers are applying elsewhere for hands; some have arrived; and as many as are wanted are desirous of coming. Those men must be employed; and will always, as long as their behaviour merits, be properly treated, and kept in employment. The Masters also will be induced to take Apprentices, who will soon be enabled to weave Carpets, as is now the case at Bewdley. When these things are effected, how much the value of your labour will be reduced! Your Committee will tell you the parish must maintain you; so it must,—but not without work: and should you unfortunately be compelled to apply for relief, the Parish Officers will be obliged to rent or build Shopping, and provide Looms, and you must weave therein, and perform as much work, and in as good a manner, as you can, but receive no wages; for the Parish Officers will receive those, and you must be inhabitants of the Poor House. Should these plans unhappily be resorted to, the Manufacturers will be benefited, by having their Carpets wove probably at two pence or three pence per yard under what they now offer you; the Scotch trade brought back; and the general interests of the Town advanced.—Your late Masters, you may depend upon it, will not let their large capitals, embarked in Buildings, Machinery, &c. lie idle they will exert themselves to get the same brought into action. The respectable part of the Weavers, many of whom I have long known, and whose conduct I have always admired, and to whom I particularly address myself, let me entreat you seriously to consider this statement of probable results which appear to me may be reasonably expected, and see how your ruin might be prevented. My advice to you is, to return to your work at the proffered wages, and thereby prevent any further introduction of strangers. Your Masters will receive and treat you kindly, if they find that your conduct towards them is respectful; and those grievances which may have existed in the trade to your injury I have no doubt will be remedied. These are, in my opinion, the only means that can avert the ruin which threatens you and your families.

I am,

Your sincere friend and well-wisher,

**GEO. HALLEN,**

*High Bailiff.*

Kidderminster, July 17th, 1828.

40.  George Hallen's address.

vagrants for begging in the streets. On 17 May Hallen was able to summon troops from Birmingham after a rare violent incident in which a weaver who wished to return to work was pelted with stones and mud. Hallen believed that 'many men would go in to their work if protected'.[30]

George Hallen was an important figure in the strike. Together with his son Thomas, the Town Clerk, he represented the established order seen by the weavers as taking the side of the employers. On 17 July he issued a written address to the weavers as their 'sincere friend' warning them that they faced 'ruin' and urging them to accept the offered wages. Two days later a press advertisement gave the weavers further cause to doubt the impartiality of the town's authorities. The Constable, who was appointed by the Paving Commissioners to supervise the watchmen, advertised for apprentices on behalf of the carpet manufacturers. The gulf between the two sides was illustrated by a letter delivered to Henry Brinton, in which he was told 'you shall lose your life you need not have another suit of clothes made for the next you have shall be your shroud'.[31]

It is incredible that the conflict dragged on for five months with the town watching its own destruction. In 56 pages of his ground-breaking book, Len Smith is unable to record a single significant intervention from any impartial leading local person to try to settle the dispute. Given the increase in the number of churches which we have remarked upon, it is particularly surprising that religious leaders were making no obvious contribution to getting an agreement as the suffering went on. Their silence is all the more astonishing when we consider the intervention of an outsider, the Reverend Humphrey Price.

## THE REVEREND HUMPHREY PRICE

Humphrey Price was a parson at Christ's Church, Needwood, near Lichfield, but had been born in Kidderminster in 1775. His mother lived at Summer Place, which was built in 1822, at the time of the strike, but she also owned the fine house at Hall Street, which later became the Savings Bank and in which she kept a day and boarding school.[32] Price had attended the Grammar School, where his fellow pupils included future carpet manufacturers such as John Woodward and Herbert Broom. Yet his intervention in the strike was firmly on the side of the weavers. He produced a series of leaflets and other written contributions, including personal letters to the employers. He placed the onus firmly on them to settle the dispute and invited them to visit the abodes of weavers, whose accumulated debt would press them down for the rest of their lives, and to see their famished offspring.[33] One manufacturer, James Hooman, was conciliatory and wanted Price to act as a mediator, but others were enraged by some of his writings, which at first were anonymous. Two poems published

# THE REV. MR. PRICE'S

# PARTING ADDRESS,

## TO THE

## KIDDERMINSTER CARPET WEAVERS.

My beloved friends. I leave you with extreme reluctance; but the same sense of duty which brought me here takes me back again. Your conduct excites the admiration of your nobler, and the malice of your meaner foes. It is an impenetrable shield over you and your cause; behind which both are safe. In the rigid execution of his office a Magistrate may be unwisely bent upon fines and imprisonments. . In his hands a neglected Clause may be used as a trap for the unwary, a sword against the innocent—and the extremity of Justice may thus become the extremity of Injury, dismay may seize the heart and sorrow-cloud the countenance; yet, let the impenetrable shield of an upright conduct be still sustained, and though some one or more of the members may perish the main body will be secure. In Righteous Law there is sometimes a Recoil which is as terrible to the Magistrate as it is consolatory to the People.

The only Petition I ever presented to your Magistrates was denied. The only Request I ever made of you will, I hope, be granted. The Petition was, " *that I might be allowed to attend at the Town-Hall as the Advocate of those poor men who might be summoned in order to be fined.*" The Request was, " *that in standing up for what you deemed your just and necessary dues, you would prove to all the world by your conduct that you feared God and honoured the King.*

Once more then, beloved friends, let me say to you " Fear God and honour the King." If you should still think it right and be determined to persevere; you must prevail. But it is the most severe Contest I ever beheld of weakness against strength, poverty against wealth, and almost universal desertion against almost universal opinion! And yet, I say, if you persevere, and your aids continue increasing as of late, and the Operatives in your own line remain faithful to you, you *must* prevail.

Once more, look to your Conduct. The loss of your Shield would be Ruin.

FAREWELL.

HENRY DEIGHTON, PRINTER, CHURCH-STREET, KIDDERMINSTER.

41. The Rev. Price's parting address prior to leaving the town on 8 August 1828.

in late April and early May were particularly provocative. *The Complaint of a Kidderminster Weaver's Wife to her Infant* was about a family who were starving, due to the tyranny of the masters. *A Kidderminster Weaver's Wife's Dream* referred to the 'oppressor's rich abode' enclosed in cedar and painted in vermilion, which everybody knew to be the home of John Broom III.[34]

The time came for Price's authorship to be revealed. He published a scathing reply to Hallen's 'sincere friend' address, but the handbill was printed without a printer's name contrary to legal requirements. The furious Hallen immediately began enquiries, which resulted in Price acknowledging all his work. Hallen began to prepare for libel action and the end of the strike was in sight. William Charlton was prosecuted for his role in the affair. On 15 August he appeared in court with Hallen presiding, and he was fined £200, with an alternative of five years' imprisonment. This harsh punishment was a manoeuvre designed to break the strike. The weavers were told the proceedings would be quashed if they broke up their strike committee. They agreed, and the return to work followed on the next day. For the weavers, it was a total defeat with nothing to show for their efforts.[35] Whatever clubs and committees might exist over the next few decades, it was to be 1866 before a genuine trade union was to be created.

Justice for Humphrey Price was delayed a while, before the full might of English law was brought to bear. In March 1829 he was tried at Hereford Assizes and found guilty, and the judge refused the jury the right to qualify that verdict with 'not with an intent to injure'. To the weavers Price was a hero and a body of them had marched the 45 miles to Hereford to support him. There is no record of any support at all from Kidderminster's middle classes. In June he was sentenced to one year in Stafford Jail, after the Attorney General had argued that Price's publications were not merely libellous, but contained incitements to sedition and the demolition of property.[36] After serving his sentence Price was to prove that his involvement in the dispute had not been a passing whim. He continued to communicate with the weavers on political matters and in 1838 was encouraging them to become Chartists. The Great Strike of Kidderminster's carpet weavers was a major event in the nation's industrial history. Yet many of today's inhabitants of the town know little or nothing about it. We should be ashamed that there is no museum to show the sacrifices made as Kidderminster became one of the world's most important carpet towns. The suffering during the strike was immense and, as we shall see, the damaging effects were to be felt for three decades or more.

# VII

# *Hard Times*

T he low point of Kidderminster's history may well have been the period from 1828 extending into the 1860s. Their defeat in the strike had left the weavers bereft of resources and saddled with debt. In the 1830s there was no sustained recovery to alleviate the sense of hopelessness. Much of the evidence suggests that both material and moral standards were low. The following decade was a period of even greater hardship, the 'hungry forties', which Kidderminster shared with the nation. It also shared the dreadful insanitary conditions of other industrial towns, which reacted too slowly to rapidly growing populations. It is even possible that the town's suffering was greater than most. In 1849 a London reporter wrote that 'in all England it would be difficult to find a more thoroughly disagreeable town'.[1] Worse was to come. The local carpet manufacturers were slow to see the possibilities of steam power and allowed Halifax to take full advantage. Between 1851 and 1861, whilst Victorian Britain was booming, Kidderminster's population fell by a quarter.

The vengeful prosecution of the Rev. Price had shown that there was to be no spirit of reconciliation. It was not to be long before serious conflict arose again, but this time it was of a violent nature. In August 1830 riots took place after wage cuts were announced by William Cooper. Lamp-posts were smashed, paving stones removed and Cooper's house was attacked. Damage was caused to other buildings belonging to the strongest supporters of the employers during the strike. These included the homes of carpet manufacturers Henry Brinton, Thomas Simcox Lea, James Dobson and John Gough Snr and the offices of George Hallen. The Town Clerk, Thomas Hallen, attempted to read the Riot Act, but he was forced to run for refuge in the *Black Horse Inn*, which was then seriously damaged by missiles. The cavalry arrived to keep order the following day, and the quartering of the military in the town was to be a regular feature until another strike in 1836. In 1833 Thomas Hallen asked the Home Office if a permanent barracks might be erected. It was as if the manufacturing class and its employees were at war during this period. Indeed, a visitor from

Bewdley after the 1830 riot observed 'perfect hatred' between them.[2] Caught in the midst of all these troubles were the shopkeepers and small traders of the town. Many must have been in serious difficulty due to the poverty of their customers. One casualty was a Bull Ring hatter, Thomas Whitcombe, who suffered bankruptcy. His misfortune was hastened by his support for the weavers in the 1828 strike. He was fined heavily for displaying their leaflets in his window when they had no printer's name.[3]

Generally the accumulated wealth of the manufacturers sustained them in difficult times, but there were several bankruptcies. The most disastrous was that of John Broom, whose demise in 1832 meant the laying idle of 200 looms and spinning mills at Hoo Brook and Spennells. Much of his property was concentrated in Mill Street, where he had a spinning mill and carpet factory built across the Stour meadows near the canal. At the upper end of the street, probably underneath the rock which now carries Mill Lane, he owned 36 tenements with gardens and the Primrose Hill and Lockett's factories.[4]

From the 1830s concern was growing about the working conditions in factories. Various government commissions showed that the character of Kidderminster was akin to that of northern industrial towns. A Yorkshire land agent, Richard Oastler, had denounced the 'slavery' endured by children in the woollen mills. Such campaigning produced the Ten Hours Bill, which became the Factory Act 1833. Many in Kidderminster were interviewed about the bill at that time. Their contributions showed concern, but much complacency. It was perceived that the bill would apply only to the three larger spinning mills and perhaps to two large carpet factories. The rest of the carpet industry was housed in small workplaces scattered through the town and regular working hours could not be enforced easily. Indeed, the Act was to prove ineffective, partly because only four inspectors were appointed nationally. Among its provisions, which applied to textile factories, was the banning of night work for children, the banning of work for children under nine and the limiting of the working day to nine hours for children under fourteen. The reports of the commissions revealed how relevant this was to Kidderminster.

The carpet industry was heavily dependent upon the labour of children, many under ten years of age. Each carpet weaver had a child assisting him continuously. So if the weaver worked extremely long hours, perhaps well into the night, to finish his piece, so did the draw-boy or girl. In any case the standard working day was very long, beginning at six in the morning and continuing until eight or nine in the evening, usually for six days a week. The conclusion of the commissioners was that the average work of the drawers was not injurious to their health. They found them to be 'stout, healthy-looking children, well clothed, and apparently well-fed'. This was the view of most manufacturers, including Henry Brinton. An exception was George Hooman, who said that his firm had wanted to forward a petition in support of the bill, but had dropped the matter due to strong political feeling. Brinton did admit that the children stood at their work nearly all the time. A local doctor, George Jotham, had 'frequently seen distortions of the ankle joints, apparently produced by standing at their work a number of hours, and also yielding of knee joints.' He added that the weavers were 'decidedly inferior in strength and fullness of growth to the rural population around Kidderminster'. Another doctor, Thomas Thursfield, confirmed that weavers were less healthy than other artisans, because they lived in 'confined air' and had 'more debauched habits'.

Several contributors spoke of a decline in moral conduct since the strike of 1828. There had been a great falling off in church attendance and an increase in drunkenness and prostitution. There was special concern for children working away from their parents and learning all sorts of vices. It was suggested that many parents fully co-operated in the exploitation of their children. The former manager of John Broom's yarn manufactory at Spennells, Charles Farrer, revealed that their normal working week was seven days and many parents grumbled when it was reduced to six days in a 'slack' period. Clearly there was a divided working class. Joel Viney, a weaver, spoke of the children being 'very much exhausted, beyond what I could express'. He said that the 'thinking part' of the weavers was in favour of reduced hours. Another weaver, William Gowen, agreed, saying 'it would be best for body and soul'.[5]

## EDUCATION

For some the answer lay in expanding opportunities for educating young people. One carpet manufacturer, Thomas Simcox Lea, spoke of the rivalry between churches to educate the greatest number of children. This was put in perspective by the Rev. Robert Ross, minister at Old Meeting, who agreed that the facilities were there, but that children were deprived of these advantages by going to work so early. The daily school attached to his chapel offered schooling for 2d. per week, but sixty or seventy out of every one hundred left before their education was half complete.

In 1840 another government commission of enquiry, this time into the conditions of hand-loom weavers, showed the state of play in this competition between churches. A total of 1,113 children were receiving daily education in these schools. There were 381 at the 'Old Church School' with a further 50 and 34 respectively at its branches at Park Place and Mill Street. St George's School took 258 pupils. Therefore, the Church of England schools had nearly two-thirds of the total. At Old Meeting School in Fish Street there were 187 pupils. The Ebenezer School in Hall Street, which belonged to the Countess of Huntingdon's Connexion, had 126 scholars. Finally, there were 77 children attending New Meeting school in Church Street. Many children received their only education at Sunday school. A total of 2,952 children received Sunday instruction, of whom only 1,169 attended the established church's provision.[6] Most of these children were working-class. The middle classes sought their education at the many private schools which sprang up in the early 19th century. These included Townshend School at Proud Cross, where the carpet manufacturer Michael Tomkinson was educated. John Brinton, born in 1827, went to school in Birmingham.

At this time the King Charles I Grammar School may not have been seen as relevant for a modern industrial society. Like many such schools, it was saddled with a charter emphasising a classical education, limited to 40 sons of members of the Church of England. This ruled out the sons of many of the manufacturing families who continued to be nonconformists. Controversy dogged the Grammar School for a time during the late 1840s. The school left the chantry next to St Mary's church to move to new premises, built in the old style, in Bewdley Road in 1848. The mansion next door, Woodfield House, was acquired by the headmaster, the Rev. W. Cockin, to accommodate boarders. Local discontentment was growing that boarders were displacing Kidderminster boys. The row was further fuelled by those who suggested that since the school was a 'Free Grammar School', according to its charter, its provision should be free of expense. The outrage was such that a town meeting was held in December 1848. The objectors proceeded to the Court of Chancery. The case was weak, as the charter specified that the only provision which should be free was Latin Grammar. In 1851 judgment was given against the petitioners, except that it was declared that sons of Dissenters should be admitted in future. The decision did nothing to halt the decline of the Grammar School, which in 1867 had only four day-pupils and two boarders.[7]

## POVERTY AND POLITICS

Widespread poverty and unemployment were constant sources of anxiety to ratepayers. In order to curb spending, the system based upon out-relief for the poor was abolished and replaced in 1834 by one based on entry into the hated workhouse. A new Union Workhouse was built in 1837 to serve the parishes of both Kidderminster Borough and the Foreign. Designed by local architects Knight and Nettleship, it was erected at Blakebrook.[8] Families were refused parish relief unless they entered the workhouse to labour at stone breaking. After the failure of industrial action in 1828, some of the intelligent working men of Kidderminster began to look to political action as a means of raising their lives above permanent struggle. Led by a carpet weaver, William Charlton, they subscribed to the Chartist principles, including universal suffrage, developed by the London Working Men's Association. In August 1838 they organised a meeting to be held in the Lion Field. The speakers were leaders of the Birmingham Political Union, which had been calling for democratic reform for some years and was by then working with the Chartists. The events of that day showed their weakness and the nature of the forces opposing them. The meeting was broken up by a crowd led by prominent Tories, including a local draper, Joseph Boycot, who was a great favourite with the mob. Boycot and others took over proceedings and the Chartists withdrew. Although violence did not take place, the potential for it was clearly there. This was shown by the reports in the Kidderminster newspaper, the *Ten Towns Messenger*, which was strongly pro-Tory.

### TO THE
# INHABITANTS
### OF
# KIDDERMINSTER.

FELLOW TOWNSMEN,

It is reported and generally believed, that " I sold the late Election, in league with Mr. Best's Party ; that I had Voters in my house, and prevented them from going to the Poll to record their Votes in favor of Mr. Gisborne;" in confirmation of this it is asserted " that I was seen at Mr. Best's, at Blakebrook, on the evening previous to the Election ;" which assertions I declare positively to be without the slightest foundation.

I now state that I have never on any occasion, directly or indirectly, had any communication with Mr. Best or his Party, in reference to the late Election, and I defy any Person or Persons to prove to the contrary.

I have considered it my duty to contradict statements so devoid of truth, and so highly prejudicial to my character and interests.

I remain,
Fellow Townsmen,
Your obedient and humble Servant,

## JOSEPH BOYCOT.

Kidderminster, Sept. 15. 1849.

G. FRIEND, PRINTER, BULL-RING, KIDDERMINSTER.

42. Joseph Boycot's address, whatever the truth in this particular instance, is illustrative of democratic standards expected at the time.

A few days before the meeting it printed an inflammatory piece on the Birmingham Political Union, who were coming even though they had been told 'they dared not show their face in Kidderminster'. One of the proposed speakers, Mr Muntz, was

> a perfect savage in his appearance, and wears a beard which would shame the Pacha of Egypt himself … Why they should bring this man to dictate to the inhabitants of Kidderminster is to us a mystery … As for Salt, he appears an absolute lunatic whilst addressing the people.

A week later the paper expressed satisfaction that 'the great dragon of Birmingham has fallen … defeated, scorned and scouted by the loyal operatives of Kidderminster'. It reflected with pride that 'Kidderminster to its honour has long been celebrated for the constitutional feeling of its inhabitants'. Clearly many of the crowd which stood on Lion Field that day were unimpressed by the willingness of their Birmingham visitors to support their right to a vote. On the contrary, one of the Tories who invaded the hustings, Tuck, was able to assure his audience that he had never advocated universal suffrage. Boycot was indeed the favourite, presenting himself 'ready at all times to support the views of the working classes'. His motion called for Queen Victoria to dismiss her present advisers and enact laws for 'the amelioration of the suffering conditions of the labouring classes'.[9] In the months which followed the Lion Field meeting, the *Messenger* promoted the growth of the Kidderminster Operative Conservatives. This group endeavoured to recruit working-class men to the Tory cause and by March 1839 claimed 600 members. In his final intervention in the political life of the town, the Rev. Humphrey Price urged working men to unite behind Chartism.[10]

A more amusing example of the town's resistance to progress was provided in the same year by Isaac Heath, a Blackwell Street maltster, who persistently tried to frustrate the efforts of the Paving Commissioners to paint the name of the street on his house. Heath was an interesting character. After his death an auction in 1861 purported to offer for sale his collection of oil paintings, including works by masters such as Rembrandt, Tintoretto, van Dyck, Poussin and Correggio.[11]

## ROWLAND HILL (1795-1879)

William Charlton and his colleagues must have wondered if there was ever to be progress for ordinary working people. His despair led him to emigrate to the United States a few years later. As for the Birmingham Political Union, its experience of meetings such as the one in Kidderminster contributed to its disintegration soon afterwards. However, one of the town's most famous sons was about to achieve lasting fame with a proposal which very definitely enhanced the lives of all classes of people. Rowland Hill was born in Blackwell Street, an event commemorated by a stone in the building which now stands on the site. His father, Thomas, was a stuffs manufacturer, and they left Kidderminster when Rowland was five after the business collapsed. Thomas, who had been influenced by Joseph Priestley's ideas on education, founded a school at Hill Top, Birmingham, and in 1807 Rowland became a teacher-pupil there. In 1819 Rowland established a new school, Hazelwood, in Edgbaston and in 1827 he removed his school to Tottenham in London.

In a pamphlet published in 1837 Rowland Hill proposed a low and uniform rate of postage, which was pre-paid by means of a stamp. He won widespread support and, despite opposition from within the civil service, the penny post was introduced in 1840. Until his reform the postal system was based upon a heavy charge to the person receiving the package. Much time and effort was wasted returning items which were refused. Hill saw that a low pre-paid charge would be possible because this inefficiency would be eliminated and there would be

massively increased usage. The potential benefits to commercial activity were
obvious and businessmen were prominent among Hill's backers. Yet poor
people were also to gain enormously. Previously, they had been unable to keep
in touch with friends and family at home when they moved to find work. Hill
was given a temporary position in the Treasury to supervise the introduction
of his reforms. However, he was dismissed in 1842 by Sir Robert Peel's Tory
government. When the Whigs under Lord Melbourne were returned in 1846,
Hill was appointed secretary to the Postmaster General. He was knighted in
1860. His statue outside the town hall was erected in 1881, two years after his
death.

## RELIGION

The nonconformists had been strong among the manufacturing classes in the
18th century and continued to be well represented in the 19th century. This
does not mean that the town was a stronghold for progressive ideas, and in
religion a conservative tradition remained strong. Loyalty to the Protestant
religion was shown by the survival of an Orange Lodge in Kidderminster until
1836. Annual marches to St Mary's Church took place. The statement issued in
March 1836 by the lodge upon its enforced dissolution stated that they 'cherish
the name of William III, Prince of Orange'. The principles of the Orangemen
were 'to preserve the rights of the Crown and not to subvert them'. It was a
sign of the times 'when religion and loyalty are considered as crimes.' Until this
time Catholicism had been inconspicuous in the town, although nuns had been
established in the convent on Birmingham Road since the 17th century.[12] Now
it was gaining strength. In 1834 a chapel was built in Birmingham Road. This
was replaced in 1858 by the church of St Ambrose.

In the succeeding decades mainstream Anglicanism was to be given fresh
life and a forward-looking approach by the appointment of the Rev. Thomas
Legh Claughton as Vicar of Kidderminster in 1841. He was an adherent of
the Oxford Movement, which sought to stir the Church of England from its
comfortable living and take the message to the poor. In his first year the Rev.
Claughton instigated the plans for the town's third Anglican Church, St John's,
to be built in Bewdley Road. It was completed in 1843 and could seat 1,255
people. Like St George's, it was built with the aid of a grant under the 1818
Act, but this time the grant was minimal. St John's was built on the cheap for
£4,075, with only five per cent covered by the grant. Its tower and spire were
half the height of St George's, and the main body of the new building was also
much lower. Designed by the obscure Gordon Alexander, it was built in drab
blue engineer's brick with minimal stone dressings. It took only twelve months
to build, whereas St George's had taken four years. Inevitably the building soon
came to be seen as inadequate. Between 1892 and 1904 it was rebuilt, retaining

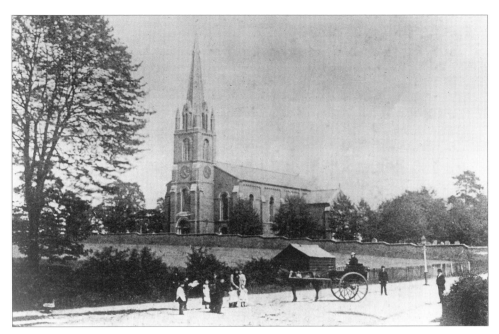

43. St John's Church. The original Black Church, built 1842-3 and shown here in the 1880s.

44. The Nonconformist Cemetery 1844: a lithograph by W.L. Walton.

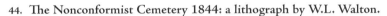

only the tower and spire. The new church included a long and lofty chancel.[13] The original building had a stained glass window commemorating one of its major benefactors, the carpet manufacturer John Woodward of Summerhill. This was not incorporated in the new plans and was lost without trace.

The strength of feeling still excited by religion was shown by a dispute in 1842 over the burial arrangements for the New Meeting minister, Richard Fry. Up to then the interring of nonconformists in St Mary's churchyard had not been a matter for controversy. This all changed with the intervention, in the absence of the vicar, of the curate, the Rev. S. Waller. He insisted that the proposed burial would be a 'tacit acknowledgment' that Fry was no longer a dissenter. The immediate result was that Fry was buried in front of the New Meeting chapel in the vault of Nicholas Pearsall. A further consequence was the creation of the nonconformist cemetery on the edge of town. The land chosen was on the west side of Park Lane and had been part of the Caldwall Estate, until sold by the Jefferys family. It is thought that the first person to be buried there was Charles Talbot, carpet manufacturer and a former mayor, who died in 1844. A cenotaph was erected there to the memory of the Rev. Fry.[14]

## HUNGRY FORTIES

Undoubtedly a significant factor in the decline of the town during these years was the demise of the historic cloth industry. By 1840 its disappearance was imminent. There were only 70 bombazine looms left in the town. Weekly wages averaged no more than 7s. for this work, which was usually performed by women and aged persons as it was comparatively light. In its latter days the trade was based around the area of Queen Street and Paradise Row, and its decline seems to have been the origin of long-term impoverishment of the district. Ebenezer Guest vividly recalled aspects of the industry. Many men obtained young female apprentices from other parishes to do the weaving. They boarded with the men's families and, when they left off weaving, nursed the children, and did the washing and all the housework. Their masters and their wives were tyrannical and exacting. The only recognised holidays were Christmas Day and Mothering Sunday and the young women had to be back at their looms by nine the following morning. They came from places such as Rock and Cleobury Mortimer, and if they were late they might be met by their irate master with his 'bombazine rod'. Guest had seen the beaten girls with blood about their face and ears rushing down Jerusalem Walk sobbing. No one would interfere.[15]

Another factor in the decline of Kidderminster was the concentration on Brussels production at a time when there was growing demand for Tapestry carpeting. Patented by Richard Whytock in 1832, Tapestry involved a simplified weaving process, during which there was no need to select the yarn colours because the yarn had been printed with the pattern beforehand. Not for the last time Crossleys of Halifax stole a march on their Kidderminster counterparts by acquiring the patent rights in August 1846. They became the biggest carpet firm in the country. Three Kidderminster firms were licensed to help Crossleys meet the middle-class demand for this cheaper alternative to Brussels. They were Henry Brinton & Sons, James Holmes, and Pardoe, Hooman and Pardoe.

In 1840 William Charlton told the government enquiry that the weavers dated their reduced condition from the strike of 1828. He spoke of the poorer condition of the town and the depreciation of the houses. An enormous amount of rent was due and this was unlikely to decrease. Charlton had difficulty in preserving his niece and nephews from the vicious example and loose habits of boys and girls around them. The vulnerability of children was further exposed by the Children's Employment Commission of 1843. The children's statements showed that nothing had changed and the carpet industry remained as dependent as ever upon their long labouring hours. Mary Ann Smith, aged 12, said:

> I have been a drawer twelve months … I went to day-school at Ebenezer Chapel, and go there to Sunday School now. I can read, but cannot write … I go to work at six o'clock in the morning, and leave at nine at night … I have never played a great deal; I generally work six days out of seven. I am very tired when I go home; when I get home I read the bible sometimes … I would rather work from six to six than keep on till nine. I should get the same wages. If I did not I would rather work up to nine for the sake of my mother. I give all my wages to her.

Mary Ann Cadogan, aged 18, said:

> I have been a draw girl six years this summer, but I worked in Mr Butcher Lea's spinning mill before that for four years … I go to work at five or half-past in the morning, and leave it at eight, nine, or ten … None of us like these long hours, men or drawers; if so be we could be regular from six to six we should like it a deal better … I should not have to stand so long all day, and that would be better for my legs. I suffer so much in them; they swell so much at night; we should know something more about domestic comfort, which we have none of now; but I am afraid if our hours were shortened that the masters would drop our wages … I have never attended a day-school since I was seven years old … I can read pretty well, but cannot write; very few girls in the town can, and many can do neither … Certainly our boys and girls are brought up in great wickedness; 'tis true many go to Sunday schools and great pains are taken with them, but when they come away they forget what they have heard … [16]

In the same year, 1843, Kidderminster was visited by one of the members of the Health of Towns Commission, R.A. Slaney. This was to be the start of an extraordinary period during which the ratepayers were to resist taking action to address the dangerously insanitary state of the town. Despite the efforts of local medical practitioners such as William Roden, three decades were to elapse before serious measures were undertaken. Yet the picture drawn by Slaney was already bleak. He drew attention to the lack of arrangements for carrying away filth. There were many open privies and cesspools. Although there were some sewers, such as in Church Street and Hall Street, there was no systematic drainage in the town. Slaney said that the streets of the richer classes were 'open and well drained'. The water supply was from various wells and was generally good and plentiful. However, some were in danger of contamination. At the Square in Bewdley Road at the top of Park Butts the well was between full 'muck holes'. This area was clearly one of the worst. Slaney referred to Cussfield (now Mill Lane) and The Battery having a 'nasty open gutter'. Very bad open privies were noted in courts off Mill Street, and there were similar problems in the area of Queen Street and Jerusalem Walk. These primitive conditions existed even in schools. Only New Meeting had a covered privy. It was noted that at St George's National School the stench was 'dreadful' in hot weather due to the open privy.[17]

There was no sense of urgency. William Talbot, solicitor, told Slaney that the 1813 Act had been obtained at great expense, met by granting annuities. Unfortunately the recipients were all still alive, but he assured Slaney that at their death the funds would be diverted to the improvement of the town. Four years later, when Dr Roden brought the forthcoming Health of Towns Bill to the attention of the local council, Alderman Best provoked much laughter by suggesting that Dr Roden was talking shop. The council solemnly concluded that compulsory measures were 'at all times extremely distasteful to the British People'. This was 1847, and the town was experiencing a severe downturn in the carpet trade. At the beginning of that year a public meeting had been held to consider the terrible poverty in the town. Henry Talbot Snr, the carpet manufacturer, said that he had never before witnessed such distress. It was agreed to raise funds for the distribution of soup and coal.[18]

Cholera had struck Kidderminster in 1832 and there were fears of a further outbreak. In 1848 another local surgeon, Henry Homfray of Broadwaters House, warned against the complacency of the authorities who had again adjourned action. Instead of tackling the water supply, they chose to 'levy war upon the cottager's pig'. He called for the free supply of pure water, proper drainage and sewage, the frequent cleansing of the streets and the removal of all open cesspools. He described the 'imperfectly formed' streets at his 'entrance to the town', presumably those off the Stourbridge Road. They were intersected with the decaying remains of old posts and trees, luxuriating in the filth of ages. The drainage from houses and privies had no escape but on to the streets.[19] Homfray's warning went unheeded. The government's legislation was not compulsory, and the town does not appear to have adopted the 1848

Act. Various clean-up operations were carried out, but they could not prevent an outbreak of cholera in 1849. It was to be many years before major work on the water supply would be considered. The one major improvement was the building of public baths in 1855 in Mill Street, but even this failed to carry conviction. The council initially postponed the adoption of the Baths and Washhouses Act due to a reluctance to burden ratepayers, and by 1861 they wanted to sell off the baths.[20]

Unsurprisingly, during the 1830s and 1840s there was little change in the built environment of Kidderminster. Cushioned by their accumulated capital the manufacturers continued to live well in the bad times, but the erection of mansions slowed down almost to a standstill. The last great estate to be built during this time appears to have been Greatfield Hall, built on Bewdley Hill opposite Summerhill in 1838 to a design by local architects, Knight and Nettleship. This was the home of George Crump, carpet manufacturer. Other carpet barons started to look well away from the grim conditions of the town for their new home. For example, in 1842 Thomas Simcox Lea purchased Astley Hall for £3,000. There was little new street building during this period. One very interesting development was a group of small terraced houses called Cemetery Row built around 1852 by Frederick Talbot. Situated opposite the cemetery near Caldwall Tower, they survive today and form the lower end of Park Street. At about the same time the network of streets off Mill Lane (then Cussfield) began to take shape. By 1859 St John's Street, Woodfield Street and Habberley Street were shown on Broadfield's map of Kidderminster.

45.  Dr William Roden
1814-84.

Also shown in the early stages of development was Lark Hill, which adjoined the Queen Street area. The decline in weaving, particularly bombazine weaving, was offset on that side of town by the success of the iron and tin-plate works of Morgan, Banks and Morgan at the Stack Pool site. This was flourishing in 1845 and continued to operate until nearly the end of the century. Despite the poverty often reported in that locality, the proprietors built houses there. One of these was the fine Springfield House close to the *Old Bear* pub, probably built by Thomas Morgan Jnr, whose son William was living there in 1861. This house survives unobtrusively today, with its back to the Stourbridge Road.

House building was boosted by the construction of the railway. The Stourbridge to Evesham stretch was opened in May 1852, and it passed through

46. Railway Station. This fine black-and-white entrance hall was built to a design originally intended for Stratford-upon-Avon, probably post-1863. It was demolished in haste in 1968 owing to dry rot.

Kidderminster. By 1859 many houses had been built around the station area and the new streets included Farfield. Houses had begun to be built along the section of Chester Lane near the station. There was still open land on either side of Comberton Hill going towards town. A few old cottages had hindered the extension of Bromsgrove Street and George Street across to Comberton Hill. One of the last residents was the noted Kidderminster sorceress, Rebecca Swan, who died having fallen on her fire at her cottage in 1850. She had made her reputation when she appeared before a magistrate and told him he would die before she left prison. He died a few days later.

Another boost to house building was the formation of Land Clubs. The early 1850s was a peak period for this kind of initiative. The Kidderminster Freehold Land Society purchased an estate at Greenhill on the north side of Hurcott Road, which was to become Turton Street and Batham Street. The plots were balloted for in 1851, and by 1859 some houses had been built. Their second purchase was land south of Blakebrook, laid out as Franchise Street, Hume Street, Holman Street and Talbot Street. Again a few houses had been built by 1859. The club's third purchase was the west side of Wood Street; it is shown neatly laid out in plots in 1859, but only a few had been built upon. Finally, in 1851 they bought land near the planned railway line at

St George's Fields. This was laid out and a few houses built by 1859, and the streets were to become Lorne Street and Villiers Street. The growth of these land clubs has been linked to the demise of the Chartist campaign for universal suffrage. Supporters of the Liberal party sought to create new householders and freeholders who would be entitled to a vote under the limited franchise extension of the Reform Act 1832. It is not clear how successful their efforts would have been, but just a few new Liberal voters could have been critical in a town where parliamentary election results were usually on a knife edge. This was understood by the Tory mayor in 1851, William Boycot, whose brother Joseph had seen off the Chartists in 1838. He warned working men against building societies which were 'practically the very reverse' of being in their interest.[21]

There is no doubt that politics was a deadly serious business at that time. In 1857 the Liberal MP Robert Lowe was nearly killed by a Kidderminster mob. He had been the member since 1852, and this time he was opposed by William Boycot. On election day a polling booth was set up at Blakebrook and a crowd of three to four thousand gathered to hear the result. Lowe's triumph by 234 votes to 147 was not to their liking. He and his friends were trapped in the booth as the hostile crowd outside gathered stones. In the neighbouring street, The Battery, more of the bloodthirsty inhabitants prepared cauldrons of boiling water and various filthy liquids. Eventually the terrified group tried to make their escape amidst a hail of stones. They ran the gauntlet for 250 yards and those who fell were savagely kicked. One of the small police force trying to hold back the crowd, John Jukes, died from his injuries a few days later. They were rescued by the headmaster of the Grammar School, the Rev. Sheppard, who managed to get them safely inside Woodfield House after a struggle.

50. Robert Lowe,
Kidderminster MP (1852-9).

Lowe had suffered a skull fracture and was weak from loss of blood. For several hours rioting continued outside before the military arrived from Birmingham. Perhaps Lowe was thinking of this traumatic event when in 1866 he voted with the Conservatives to defeat his own party's bill to widen the franchise. He attacked the working class as 'unfit to have the vote'.

Lowe's unpopularity may have derived from his refusal to be the mouthpiece of the brewers. He had been very concerned about the trade getting into fewer hands. Furthermore, he had consistently refused to continue the tradition of corruption in Kidderminster, whereby the candidates sought to buy votes and political support by lavishing large sums of money on beer. Lowe's stance upset the town's 84 publicans and 60 beer-shop keepers and their customers. He had become the Liberal candidate through the patronage of Lord Ward, and his victories had been unusually decisive because he had the support also of some Conservatives. However, in 1859 his canvass showed him that he had lost that support, so he withdrew from the contest rather than resort to bribery.[22]

## STEAM POWER

In 1851 the American inventor, Erasmus Bigelow, set up his steam-powered loom at Hoobrook spinning mill. Unfortunately, the Kidderminster manufacturers missed their chance and Bigelow concluded a deal with Crossleys of Halifax. The days of the handloom were numbered, but the lack of foresight of the local carpet barons meant that for the time being Kidderminster would not be sharing in the Victorian boom years. Steam power did come to the town, under licence from Crossleys, and in two cases the transition was perhaps eased by prudent marriages entered into by two of the principal carpet families. John Brinton's sister, Martha, married Francis Crossley, and in 1858 their nephew John Lewis became a partner of John Brinton. Until 1870 the firm was Brinton and Lewis. In this way the medium-sized firm built by the careful Henry Brinton was to grow into the biggest company in the town. The other significant marriage was in 1855 between John Humphries and Hannah Collier, daughter of George Collier of Crossleys and a pioneer of the application of steam power to textile manufacturing. In 1853 James Humphries & Co. were the first company to commence steam-powered production in Kidderminster.

Other companies required the intervention of Lord Ward to give them the stimulus they needed. Two manufacturers, Joseph Kiteley and William Grosvenor, encouraged him to build a factory to house steam-powered looms to be let to local firms. It became known as 'Lord Ward's Shed'. The office building still stands at the top of Green Street, and its fine brickwork has ensured that it is listed. The project enabled some companies to make the transition into the power-loom era. Nevertheless there were significant casualties, the biggest being Pardoe, Hooman and Pardoe, who went bankrupt in 1857. They had converted to Tapestry power looms, as had James Holmes who also closed down in 1857. Many weavers were forced to seek work elsewhere and it is possible that several thousand emigrated. Between 1851 and 1861 the population of the town fell from 21,000 to 15,400. The poverty and the deteriorating environment must have seriously affected the health of townspeople. In 1850 the facilities at St Mary's Street dispensary were expanded. For the first time inpatients were to be taken. A third storey was added to the premises, to accommodate 12 beds, and the dispensary became the infirmary.

Amidst the terrible hardship there was still money in the town. In 1852 the Rev. Claughton bemoaned the lack of a suitable room for musical gatherings and the matter was taken in hand by the Mayor, Joseph Kiteley. A company was formed and the foundation stone was laid later in the year by Lord Ward. The Music Hall and Corn Exchange, which now form part of the Town Hall complex, were opened in Easter 1855. Yet this must have seemed to be an exceptional example of progress, as Kidderminster's environment continued to degenerate. It has been suggested that by the early 1860s whole streets were empty. This is not quite confirmed by the 1861 census, but many streets had a substantial number of empty houses. There were 16 in Blackwell

48. Joseph Kiteley (1807-80).

Street, for example. The area around Clensmore and Broad Street was badly affected. Paradise Row, Pleasant Row and Broad Street itself each had 11 vacant houses. It is possible that many more houses were vacated if the crisis deepened further as the decade progressed. Arthur Marsh suggested that the

49. The Music Hall and Corn Exchange: a collotype by Oliver Ayliffe.

'economic storm' lasted until 1863.[23] Four years later continuing bad trade was mentioned in newspaper correspondence from angry Kidderminster ratepayers, who were opposed to spending on improved drainage for the town.

## DEATH NESTS

The long-running sanitation saga was to approach a ludicrous conclusion. By this time it was the town council who were at centre stage, the Paving Commissioners having been wound up in 1856. They were not to cover themselves in glory, preferring to procrastinate if possible. Their helplessness was shown in an encounter with the spinner, Thomas Lea. In 1864 he erected the Slingfield Mill, which today is a listed building and is magnificent, but it was built without proper drainage. The soap suds formed in the process of washing the wool flooded the meadows and eventually created a stench unbearable to people living nearby. Mr Lea, as a good ratepayer, refused to take action. The council meekly proposed to meet half the cost, knowing that part of the problem was the lack of a comprehensive system for the town. The state of the streets was so bad that Alderman Jeffries suggested that when residents of other towns saw some one walking in the middle of the road, they said, 'That is a Kidderminster man.' Finally in 1866 they decided to form a Sanitary Committee. The situation was becoming urgent and tenders were requested for both a drainage system and a water supply. That from Mr Fairbank was provisionally accepted. Action had become essential because the volume of sewage in the Stour was such that flooding was a permanent threat. Furthermore, the filth was causing reduced power from the flow of the river, and legal action was threatened by the mill owner Daniel Wagstaff Goodwin.[24] Ironically, just at the moment when the town's leading citizens seemed reconciled to the expense, the plans were thrown into disarray by the outrage of the newly enfranchised (under the Reform Act 1867) working-class householders. In the council elections of the autumn of that year 'anti-drainage' candidates swept the board. The ratepayers were not prepared to foot the bill for a healthier town.[25]

In December 1868, in a report headed 'Kidderminster and its Death Nests', the *Brierley Hill Advertiser* claimed that the death rate was reported to be higher than any town in the country. The area around Lark Hill was particularly bad.[26] In January 1869 a desperate Dr William Roden urged the council to adopt government legislation regarding public health. Later in the year the Board of Guardians requested that a government inspector be sent to the town. Mr Arnold Taylor ordered the council to take action within one month by accepting the Fairbank plan. Finally, in October 1870 the first sod for a new waterworks was turned.

VIII

# Renewal

Recovery was probably well underway by December 1865, when it was reported that the unemployment of the former handloom weavers was nearly absorbed. In 1873 the *Littlebury Trade Directory* was able to state that 'the trade, commerce and population of Kidderminster have increased during the last ten years in a remarkable manner.' The manufacturers who led the transfer to steam power were clearly prospering. By 1867 John Brinton was the owner of Moor Hall in Stourport. At about this time John Humphries purchased Blakebrook House, with its 13 bedrooms. The new vitality in the town produced two weekly newspapers. The *Kidderminster Times* began in 1867 and the *Shuttle* in February 1870. The latter paper reported that a golden age ceased around the spring of 1871. The barons 'grew rich beyond their avaricious dreams', but the demand for Brussels carpets fell away because of the high cost of raw materials.[1] Nevertheless, Kidderminster had re-established itself as a major centre of carpet production. In 1878 the further expansion of the town was secured by Michael Tomkinson's purchase of the British rights to the Axminster power loom.

## CONSTRUCTION

Symbolic of Kidderminster's efforts to leave darker times behind was the departure of the Baptist church from their chapel in Silver Street to new premises in Church Street, which opened in 1868 at a cost of £2,700. Their services had previously suffered interruptions from noisy neighbours. The district had been of a mixed nature for some years, according to Ebenezer Guest, with brothels and tidy houses existing side by side. At Silver Hill decent folk had once woven bombazine in their garrets. The Baptists, who included the iron founder George Turton among their number, suffered derision and other inconveniences when attending their church. Efforts were made to clean up the area with some success, but it continued to bear a bad character.[2] In later years it was an Irish quarter, and in 1887 the Tory MP, Sir Frederick Godson, spoke of 'agita-

50. **Church Street Baptist Church, built in 1868 and photographed here c.1890.**

tors from Silver Street' causing disturbance on the Home Rule question.[3] Religion was still vitally important to many people and another church was soon built in the neighbourhood of the Horsefair. This was St James', erected in 1872 in Jerusalem Walk as a chapel-of-ease to St Mary's. It was paid for by the Rev. Hugh John Fortescue, a curate of the parish church. He was an unusually wealthy curate, who in 1871 with his three sisters had funded another chapel-at ease, St Barnabas' in Franche, at a cost of £3,010.

A major construction project at this time was the building of the infirmary at the top of Mill Street. While the authorities hesitated about taking preventive health measures concerning the water supply and drainage, it was decided in 1868 to seek a healthier site for the hospital. Built by Messrs J. Binnian & Son to a design by the architect Mr Bland of Birmingham, it cost £10,700, and was opened on 13 October 1871. The capital was raised by public subscription, including donations of £1,000 each from Thomas Lea and the Earl of Dudley. The running costs of such a large undertaking were to require a permanent struggle against debt until the creation of the national health service. Funds came partly from subscribers, who had rights to nominate both outpatients and inpatients. Other income came from street and workplace collections. The Saturday Collection movement had begun in 1864, when contributions were received from the workers of Watson & Naylor, and workers in other companies had followed their example. This was utterly appropriate, because the infirmary was really for them. It was a classic example of Victorian charity, directed at the 'deserving' poor. The rich paid for treatment at home or at more prestigious hospitals, while the destitute poor were treated in a special ward at the Blakebrook workhouse. Kidderminster declined to implement the power given by the Poor Law Amendment Act of 1868 to create infirmaries for the destitute sick. Access to the infirmary was controlled by the requirement that users should have a letter or 'ticket' of

51. The Infirmary, Mill Street. After over a century as a hospital, it has been converted into apartments in the last decade.

recommendation from a subscriber. A ticket would permit a patient to stay for a maximum of six weeks and could also be exchanged for an appliance. Thus a crutch required two tickets. The rules of the infirmary excluded those suffering from smallpox, cholera or any other infectious or contagious disease. The new hospital was not set up to deal with chronic or incurable conditions. There was a pragmatic side to the apparent philanthropic purpose. The infirmary was clearly designed to keep the workforce of an expanding carpet industry as fit as possible.[4]

## SCHOOL BOARD

The 1870s saw a substantial advance in the educational opportunities for children. There was a loosening of the control exercised by religious bodies over public education. Locally elected School Boards were created by the Education Act 1870, which empowered them to build schools where religious education would be undenominational and based on simple bible teaching. Schooling was still not necessarily compulsory or free, but the School Boards were given the option to enforce school attendance. The first two Board Schools were in Coventry Street (1873) and Hume Street (1877), and the Kidderminster School Board made school attendance compulsory for children under the age of thirteen. There was concern that some parents were falsifying the ages of their children in order to send them to work prematurely. An advertisement by the Board in 1878 asserted that it would not sanction attendance at a 'Dame or Adventure' school by any child over five years of age. At the same time it was revealed that the new Hume Street Infant School would charge 2d. a week.[5]

The School Boards represented an extension of democracy. Members were elected every three years and women were allowed to vote and to stand for election, although by 1880 only one woman, Mrs Sarah Talbot, was a member. The early years of the Board's activity were marked by consensus. The nine members were re-elected en bloc in 1874 and 1877 and the competition in 1880 seems to have been an occasion of some regret. There is little evidence of working-class representation on the board. It was a mixture of manufacturers, such as Edward Morton, Henry Willis and Michael Tomkinson, and religious representatives, notably the Rev. Boyle, Vicar of Kidderminster, and the Rev. Torond of the Catholic church. Edward Parry, editor of the *Kidderminster Shuttle*, added a nonconformist presence. The Board appeared to succeed in making its schools genuinely undenominational, so much so that in 1878 one of the

52. Sarah Talbot, known as 'Citizen Sarah' because of her commitment to women's rights. She was the first, and possibly the only, female member of the School Board. She was married to William Talbot, solicitor, and they lived at Whitville, Franche Road.

Coventry Street teachers, W. Wilkinson, was provoked into writing to the *Shuttle* to defend the Board Schools against the charge that they did not teach religion at all. His letter suggested that they took children of poor families which the voluntary schools 'hesitated to admit'. The strained resources of the Board Schools were obvious, because Mr Wilkinson's own class numbered 100. The Board had to endure sniping about extravagance at the ratepayers' expense, so class size was one way of keeping costs low. In 1880 the Rev. Boyle was able to claim that one of the Board Schools, presumably Coventry Street, was 'almost self-supporting and cost the ratepayers very little indeed'. School Board schools were often labelled 'nonconformist' by their critics, and the vexed question of religion was to cause tension until the Boards were abolished in 1902.[6]

1874 was an eventful year in the town. The parliamentary election of that year showed that the Reform Act, which in Kidderminster had resulted in about 3,000 voting rather than 400 or so, had done little to cure the corrupt nature of political life in the town. It also illustrated the weakness of working-class support for Thomas Lea, the sitting Liberal MP, whose Slingfield Mill had polluted the neighbourhood some years previously.[7] The Tory candidate was Baron Albert Grant, who had been MP for the town from 1865 to 1869. He campaigned for only two days, but succeeded in defeating Lea by 111 votes. His methods included promising two days' entertainment for his supporters if he was victorious. After his triumph 5,000 dinners and large quantities of free drink at public houses were duly supplied. Complaints were made, and a hearing declared the election null and void. This did the Liberals no good, however, because the Tory candidate, Sir W. A. Fraser, won the second contest of the year by over 300 votes.

Working-class organisation was growing substantially. The Kidderminster Industrial Co-operative Society had been formed in 1865 by 112 men who paid one shilling capital each. Premises were soon established in Worcester Street for the stock of groceries and provisions, and the first branch shop was to open in Cookley in 1876. At the end of 1865, over a decade since any handloom weavers' organisation had expired, the Power Loom Weavers Association had been formed. By the autumn of 1874 the new union was ready to respond to the poor economic conditions by entering a dispute with Brintons. This was provoked by John Brinton's attempt to compensate for the stagnation of the Brussels trade by introducing Tapestry looms, on which he proposed to employ women. This was opposed by the weavers' union, which was an exclusively male organisation at that time. They pointed out that hundreds of male weavers were on short time, with no more than three days' work each week. At first they demanded that the new looms should be given to males. Brinton refused and there was a strike. The union was widely criticised for its contempt for the rights of women and eventually accepted the principle of female labour provided they were paid the same as males. John Brinton was not interested and removed his tapestry looms to Leeds.

The strike was preceded by the publication by the weavers' union of a manifesto called 'Capital v. Labour'. This referred to the injustice of employing women at wages set at only 40 per cent of those earned by men. It described the employers as 'inhuman', and crushing weavers out of the trade by reducing their wages to 'starvation point'. The weavers sought to prevent the 'ever-grasping

53. John Brinton
(1827-1914).

hand of Capital from crushing us into mere machines'. It is tempting to conclude that some of the weavers had absorbed the language of Karl Marx, whose *Das Kapital* had been published in 1867. It is certainly clear from reports of well-attended union meetings of this period that a substantial number of weavers were well aware of the reality of class conflict. On the other hand many of their fellow union members did believe it was possible to co-operate with Brinton and obviously formed a majority of the committee responsible for union affairs. They privately wrote a grovelling letter to Brinton begging him to bring back the tapestry looms. They apologised for the things that had been said by their members arising from their 'want of education', but their efforts were in vain. Brinton replied that he would bring back the looms only if the union recognised his right to employ whoever he liked. When the contents of this correspondence was revealed to the wider membership, there was uproar and the committee was rebuked.[8]

One of the weavers' leaders during the dispute was the articulate Noah Cooke, a poet whose work had been published regularly by the *Shuttle*. Cooke regarded John Brinton as a 'despotic Whig manufacturer'. The dignity of labour was a recurring theme of his poetry:

> Though I yield myself to labour,
> Subject to a master's plan,
> By that act I do not forfeit
> Right and freedom as a man;

Cooke's only volume of verse was published in 1876 by subscription. One of the subscribers to *Wild Warblings* was John Brinton.[9]

It is worth pausing at this point, as the male weavers sought to perpetuate their standing as inheritors of a skilled tradition, to remember that there were still handloom weavers in the town, and Tomkinson & Adam were to retain a section into the 1920s. There was even, three or four decades after the demise of bombazine, one family continuing to weave silk. Thomas Paget was a silk weaver and publican in 1861. He had opened the *Grand Turk* pub in Sutton Road around 1855 and subsequently built a row of houses behind there called Grand Turk Place. In the 1891 census his son, also Thomas, was the only silk weaver in Kidderminster.[10]

## CIVIC DEVELOPMENT 1875-94

Although the first sod had been turned for the new waterworks in 1870, there was to be no quick solution to the insanitary state of the town. The grim saga was to continue into the mid-1880s, with the name of the scheme's engineer, Fairbank, becoming a term of abuse. His plan involved a water supply near to the Stourport Road, where a well was sunk and water pumped into an open reservoir. In addition sewage disposal was managed by works built at the bottom of Green Street. Here the waste was collected in tanks, before being pumped to a sewage farm at Oldington on the Birchen Coppice side of the Stourport Road. Opened in 1874, the new facilities continued to be a source of great anguish to ratepayers because of the cost. A map in the possession of the author reveals that the council borrowed £23,400 to finance the work. One estimate has the initial cost as £99,519, although in 1887 a letter to the *Shuttle* suggested that the cost, which still rankled, was as high as £140,000.[11] Worse still, the scheme was to prove ineffective. It is clear the fault lay at least partly with the council, because there is no doubt that the construction of the works was not according to plan. Another problem was that use of the water supply and the sewage scheme was voluntary. Water was still obtainable from wells and it was even suggested that Alderman Jefferies, carpet manufacturer and keen supporter of the improvements, carried on discharging waste from his works directly into the Stour.[12]

In 1875 a newspaper article vividly described the sanitary state of Kidderminster. The Stour was 'simply an uncovered sewer'. From the bridge in Mill Street the reporters were able to look up and down the river to see a series of sewer-openings and waste pipes. They noted the state of the middens in the town. 'No Corporation carts are provided. Private persons, at their own expense, have to convey their excrementitious and other refuse away'. Inadequacies in the new sewage system were already apparent. The receiving tanks were too near the town and represented a danger if they were to be overtaken by development within a few years. The sewers were a great nuisance at night, with powerful stenches rising from the gratings. It was thought that this problem might have been alleviated by persuading more of the inhabitants to cease using polluted well water and convert to tap water. The reporters suggested the price of the water was too high at 10d. per 1,000 gallons, producing an annual cost for one modest householder whom they consulted of £13 per annum.[13]

Nevertheless during this period Kidderminster's landscape grew in a way which reflected its standing as the preeminent carpet town. In 1875 a statue of Richard Baxter was erected in the Bull Ring. Six years later that of Rowland Hill was built in front of the new town hall complex. The council had purchased the music hall and corn exchange, which had been erected by private

54. Baxter Statue, Bull Ring, in its original place. This photograph was taken *c*.1910.

subscription, and added a new extension, built to a design by J.T. Meredith, at a cost of £8,000. This was opened in 1877. The redundant Guildhall at the bottom of the High Street was demolished in 1878 by the building contractor George Law for £75.[14]

The area's status as the focus of civic and cultural affairs was enhanced by the development of nearby Caldwall Row. This became Market Street with the opening of the cattle market there in 1871. Although the market was to move to Comberton Hill in 1959, the original entrance lodge, built in the 'Elizabethan style', still remains.[15] Market Street went from strength to strength, based on land on the corner of Exchange Street donated by the miller Daniel Wagstaff Goodwin. The School of Art was opened there in 1879, followed by the School of Science in 1887 and the Free Library in 1894. The latter was funded by public subscription, the collection being organised by Michael Tomkinson. Opposite them a new post office was built in 1885. These buildings in Market Street have all been demolished in recent years.

55. Cattle Market, Market Street, founded in 1871. This picture from 1902 shows the unusual entrance lodge which survives today on New Road. In the background are the Pike Mills.

Two significant land developments took the town westwards. By 1872 the parish churchyard at St Mary's had to be closed. In 1878 the new cemetery was opened next to the nonconformist cemetery. The plot comprised part of the old Caldwall Estate, which for many decades had gradually been broken up and sold off. This area formed a sharp dip in the landscape through which the Black Brook flowed. It had been landscaped by the Jefferys family, who had made a series of pools and built a thatched cottage there which served as a boathouse. The pools were apparently filled in with rubble from the construction work on the indoor market at the end of the 19th century.[16] In 1887 Brinton Park was opened, taking the town right to the edge of the borough boundary. The next step would be the development of Foley Park.

56. Daniel Wagstaff Goodwin (1821-90), Mayor in 1883.

The streets of Kidderminster were beginning to reach out and to take a shape which would be recognisable to residents a century later. On the higher ground, to both the west and east, are now many houses with date stones from the 1870s onwards. Yet at the time the growth was seen as spasmodic and uncertain. In 1888 the *Shuttle* cited Crane Street as 'one of those uncompleted purposes of which there are so many in Kidderminster'.[17] Yet there was growth on both sides of Bewdley Street. Another Board School was opened in Bennett Street in 1884. This street was itself a recent addition to the network of streets which had emerged largely in the 1850s, and it contained a row of ten cottages, Alma Terrace, built in 1879, which has survived the ravages of the ring road and is intact today. The Wood Street area was extended down to the cemetery. Today the west side of that street contains an assortment of houses, possibly indicative of a piecemeal allocation of plots by a land club. Many are built directly on to the pavement. One row of terraced houses just below Plimsoll Street is set back and presents a tidy contrast. Date stones suggest that the middle parts of both sides were built around 1878, but the lower part of the east side was not developed until 1898. Park Street's growth was also piecemeal, with houses going up in the early 1880s in a scattered fashion. Spaces were filled later over a period of more than twenty years including, in 1899, a tidy terraced row, Carlton Cottages, with a fine frontage built right against the pavement. The area was undoubtedly a respectable working-class neighbourhood. We know that a number of the weavers' leaders lived in this network of streets. Tom

Rowe lived for some years at 6 Plimsoll Street, John Poutney lived in Chapel Street and Albert Moule lived in Liddon Cottage, Park Street. This growing community included a public house, the *Unity*, whose opening in 1891 was apparently controversial, possibly because of the presence of a strong teetotal lobby, among whom were both Rowe and Moule.[18] Directly opposite the *Unity* was built a new church for the Countess of Huntingdon's Connexion, opened in 1896.

The changes on the east side of town were reflected in the renaming of Bird Lane in 1871 and Love Lane in 1886 to Hurcott Road and Offmore Road respectively.[19] Building was particularly heavy east of George Street. In the 1850s Love Lane and Comberton Hill had continued to pass through fields where stood just a few cottages, but extensive building, stimulated by the railway, carried on, and by the end of the century houses covered the area. The pioneering development in the Villiers Street locality was eventually extended down to Comberton Hill, and Lorne Street was fully formed. Date stones suggest this happened 1870-86. In the same period Lea Street was built, and the School Board opened their school in 1883. Offmore Road was built up on

57. Josiah Mason's birthplace, Mill Street, demolished in 1883. A house built there afterwards carries a plaque, but it simply marks the site. Mason (1795-1881) was a Kidderminster carpet weaver, who left for Birmingham as a young man. He made a fortune as a pen manufacturer and was a major benefactor of the city. He founded the Scientific College.

both sides in the 1880s. Once cottages in the way could be removed, George Street was extended into Comberton Hill. This enabled Cherry Orchard to be constructed off George Street. The expanding population required extra churches. The Baptist Church, Milton Hall, completed the development of Lorne Street in 1890. It was a chapel-of-ease to the church in Church Street, seating 350, and was the gift of the seed merchant J.P. Harvey. It had three classrooms on either side. In 1902 another church was erected, showing the continuing strength of religion in Kidderminster. This was built by the Primitive Methodists on the corner of Leswell Lane and George Street, accommodating 300 people and, like Milton Hall, containing six classrooms. In 1905 the main body of Methodists built a large church seating 500 people on Birmingham Road. Perhaps the most striking addition was the arrival in Kidderminster of yet another movement, that of the followers of an 18th-century Swedish theologian, Emanuel Swedenborg. In 1909 they built a grand church at the corner of George Street and Comberton Hill. It was to be yet another example of the terrible waste of bricks in the town, only surviving until 1963, and now the site is occupied by a video store.[20]

## FOLEY PARK

Foley Park was to grow very slowly, even though by 1884 many of the main streets were laid out, named after those who, centuries ago, used to lord it over Kidderminster. The Ordnance Survey map shows Northumberland Avenue, Neville Avenue, Blount Terrace, Beauchamp Avenue and Lisle Terrace, tree-lined but virtually devoid of houses. A terrace of 12 cottages was built on the south side of Northumberland Avenue close to the Stourport Road. There were seven houses on Neville Avenue and just one on Blount Terrace. Twenty years later there had been some growth, but still there were large empty spaces. Beauchamp Avenue had one, solitary, house, as did Lisle Terrace.

The key to this slow expansion is that Foley Park seems to have been conceived as an area of higher standing than the typical working-class streets being built at the time. In 1884 an advertisement was directed at potential freeholders, offering this land at 1s. 6d. per square yard. 'The roads (42 feet wide) are made and sewered.' In order to tempt purchasers it was noted that Foley Park was just outside the borough boundary and exempt from the town rates. From 1892 to 1895 attempts were made by the Larches Land Club to develop part of Sir Thomas Lea's estate, extending south to the north side of Northumberland Avenue. Subscriptions were paid during that period by 20 members, but the failure to attract more interested parties resulted in the winding up of the club and the abandonment of the proposed purchase. By 1901 some advance had been made and a fine terraced row with attics had been built at the east end of Northumberland Avenue looking across at the still open ground of the Larches. In 1905 a further attempt was made to sell the vacant land south of Northumberland Avenue, when groups of plots were offered as distinct lots. Being outside the borough, the estate was not connected to the nearby sewer taking the town's waste along the Stourport Road to the sewage farm. Instead drainage was into a tank situated on the land sloping down to the canal on the east side of the estate. From this tank the waste was distributed 'thus forming irrigated land adapted and now partly used for garden purposes and allotments.'[21]

The community of Foley Park did start to take shape. The Primitive Methodists erected a small chapel on the Stourport Road. The school in Northumberland Avenue opened in 1894. The Kidderminster to Bewdley railway line, built in 1878, passed nearby and eventually a little station was added at Foley Halt. Industry, too, came to the area in about 1912, when a carpet factory was built by Thomas Griffin for his firm, the Empire Carpet Company. The full development of Foley Park was to wait until after the First World War, by which time it had been taken into the Borough.


## AXMINSTER

Kidderminster's expansion during these decades was due to the lead it established by developing the new Axminster technology. Brussels trade was sluggish, and there was a crisis in the Tapestry trade, with the demise of two firms, Crabtree Bros. and Isaac Hampton, in the late 1870s. The former had occupied Spennells Mill, which had for so long been used by the Broom family for spinning. The history of this rural location as a centre of industry was brought dramatically to an end with the destruction, by fire, of the five-storey mill in 1880.[22] Meanwhile, the enterprising partnership of Tomkinson & Adam broke with the hesitant example set by earlier Kidderminster manufacturers and acquired the British rights to an American invention. In 1878 Michael Tomkinson sailed to New York, where he purchased the rights to the power loom designed by Halcyon Skinner. This inventor had been working since 1855 on ways of reproducing the type of hand-knotted carpet made famous in Axminster, England. Tomkinson, the master salesman, returned with the rights, and by September 1878 the company of Tomkinson & Adam were weaving the new product, which they called Royal Axminster. Their expansion was rapid.[23] The new looms were light, allowing the company to exploit further the cheaper female labour they had used right from the beginning. There was no limit to the number of colours in the pattern, so the pressure on manufacturers of other types of carpet was to increase. Other Kidderminster firms would follow Crabtree Brothers and Isaac Hampton out of business. For the time being a

58. Charles and Sarah Payne. Charles Payne (1821-1909) is reputed to have been a Chartist. He lived at Hope Cottage, Cherry Orchard.

59. William Payne. Son of Charles, his sacking for trade union activity by Henry Dixon Jnr was a prelude to the violent strike at that firm in 1884. William went on to be president of the carpet weavers' union in 1914.

limited number of companies attempted to secure their future by acquiring licences from Tomkinson & Adam to produce Royal Axminster. These included two Kidderminster firms at first, H. J. Dixon & Sons and Morton & Sons, and later, in 1883, Woodward Grosvenor & Co. joined them.

The prominence of drysalters and chemical manufacturers is noteworthy at this time. The dyes needed by the carpet industry were so vital that in 1903 the *Shuttle* commented that 'chemistry has become its most potent handmaid'. Robert Chadwick was one such manufacturer, who by 1875 was occupying the grand Consterdine House at the bottom of Franche Road. His business was in Church Street, as was that of George Holdsworth, who started on his own in 1876 and whose private residence became Springfield House in Stourbridge Road. B. Hepworth & Co. was a Yorkshire company, which was established in Kidderminster in 1881, first in Callows Lane, then for many years in Coventry Street. These were the new generation. The old was represented by John Watson, who was still operating from 29 Church Street in 1884. He had supplied vegetable dyes, but the discovery of aniline colours, based on coal tar, reduced demand to a minimum. Watson retired and lived in style at Waresley Court near Hartlebury, where he bred race horses and died in 1893.[24]

Life was not so easy for the companies who had to pay for the privilege of producing Royal Axminster. This was shown by the extraordinary dispute in 1884 at one of the licensees, Dixon's. It was a repeat of all the arguments over female labour. The trouble started because Dixon was unable to obtain enough work to keep his Tapestry looms running. He adapted some of them for the weaving of a new curtain material. His intention was to employ only women on them. This enraged the weavers' union, which remained an exclusively male organisation. In the face of a strike threat Dixon bade a theatrical farewell to all his weavers on the day before the strike was to begin and immediately brought in non-union labour to carry on production. Dixon refused to engage in further talks, while a bitter and violent strike continued for seven weeks. There was a settlement only when MP John Brinton intervened to salvage Kidderminster's reputation, which was suffering because of the daily reporting of large demonstrations and fighting on the streets of the town.[25]

These events were of great significance. The reaction of the union showed their fear that male weavers faced a very uncertain future. Whereas in the Brinton's dispute they had accepted female labour, provided it was paid at the same rate as for males, this time the union completely opposed the principle of females on the looms. Their desperation was further shown by their preparedness to accept female rates of pay if Dixon would employ males. Clearly the rise of Tomkinson & Adam with their Axminster looms was turning Kidderminster into a town characterised by employment opportunities for women and low pay. The serious conflict of these weeks exposed the continuing class divide which had been obvious in 1828.

## HEALTH AND SANITATION

Despite the wealth flowing into Kidderminster life remained hard for working people in 1884. In October of that year Dr William Roden died. He had fought a long and sometimes lonely struggle to create a healthy environment for the town's inhabitants. At least he lived to witness the gradual emergence of improved terraced housing, but he would have been saddened that his last months saw a further crisis concerning the town's susceptibility to disease. Smallpox broke out at the end of 1883 in Bromsgrove Street. At first the strategy was to isolate the affected cottages, but after one death the Town Council decided to erect an Infectious Diseases Hospital, a step which had previously been urged upon them on more than one occasion. They had staved off such a decision on the grounds of economy.[26] The new isolation hospital was built quickly on a site adjacent to the Stourport Road north of the Bewdley railway line. It was ready by the middle of January 1884, but by the end of the epidemic in March 10 people had died.

In the latter part of 1884 there was a very serious outbreak of enteric fever, or typhoid. This epidemic was investigated by a government inspector, Dr Parsons, whose report revealed that by 14 November there had been 1,200 cases with 89 deaths. It was preceded by a fortnight of diarrhoea, during which 55 died. Kidderminster was liable to this 'summer diarrhoea' every year, but this number of deaths was the highest on record. Dr Parsons revealed the inadequacy of the Fairbank water supply and drainage scheme constructed over a decade previously. He noted that 'in the construction of the sewers considerable deviations were made from the plans as sanctioned by the Local Government Board, and that much of the work was badly executed'. Some sewers were actually laid with a reverse fall. Pipes were too narrow and there was inadequate ventilation. Foul gases accumulated and escaped where they could, often ascending to the higher levels of town. During the summer of 1884 sewer smells had been frequent and overpowering. Although he recognised, as had Dr Slaney forty years before, that many of the houses of the poorer

60. This picture taken in the 1880s, looking down on Swan Street and High Street, gives a vivid impression of the congested nature of the town centre.

61. Somerleyton House, a fine late 19th-century house, which stood at the corner of Somerleyton Avenue and the Bromsgrove Road. It was one of the many such houses to be lost in the modern period as the wealthier classes left Kidderminster.

classes were in poor condition with little space around them and filth lying in the courtyards, the inspector pointed out that the disease was not particularly concentrated there. Indeed, the streets which suffered most were comparatively new ones in elevated situations in which respectable artisans lived. Here Dr Parsons was probably referring to areas such as Wood Street and St John's Street. The water supply was failing at these higher levels and so the sewers were not being flushed properly, allowing blockages to accumulate.[27]

There was also concern about the possibility that the water supply from the Green Street well, which had been brought into use 'temporarily' in 1879, was being contaminated by a dangerously close sewer pipe. There was concern also about the continued existence of many middens, which were still not being cleared systematically. This terrible epidemic was a further incentive for the provision of water closets for each home. The most immediate impact was the building of a new reservoir at a higher position, off what is now the top end of Sutton Park Road. The new reservoir, this time covered, was opened in September 1886. It has supplied water to the town up to the present day, in conjunction with a new well sunk at Green Street in 1898.

## SPLIT IN LIBERAL PARTY

John Brinton had been elected as Liberal MP for the town in March 1880. His victory was marred by a threat from the Tories to have the poll declared void because he employed as his agent the colourful local solicitor, Miller Corbet, who had been reported for bribery during the 1874 municipal elections. To avoid the controversy of an enquiry, Brinton took the 'Chiltern Hundreds' so that a second election was needed, in which he was returned unopposed. It was not an auspicious start, and considering the bitter dispute of 1874 it is not surprising that his selection as the Liberal candidate was attended by some criticism. Nevertheless, he had the backing of several working-class leaders, including the president of the weavers' union, Joseph Cooke, a future president, Tom Rowe, and the former Chartist weaver, Alderman George Holloway. For a while Brinton's election was probably attended by some optimism based on the belief that workers and employers had a common interest in the health of their industry. At this time other leading manufacturers were at the head of progressive Liberal opinion. Michael Tomkinson, for example, led a massive demonstration in 1884 in favour of the Reform Bill. However, another leading Liberal was Henry Dixon, and the violent dispute at his firm earlier in the same year must have shaken confidence. In 1885 Brinton was re-elected, but Parnell's Irish Home Rule Party held the balance of power and Gladstone moved to come to terms with them. This split the Liberal party, with Brinton and Tomkinson among those who opposed Gladstone. Brinton thus ruled himself out as the candidate in the election which followed in 1886. The Liberals lost to the Conservative, Sir Frederick Godson, who held the seat for 20 years. There was some bitterness at Brinton's abandonment of the cause. In 1887, at a meeting held to discuss Irish policy, Tom Rowe commented that after working men had worked 'as hard as they could at Mr Brinton's last election, they were not only not thanked for their services, but they were actually snubbed because the majority was a reduced one'. The issue dogged the Liberal party for many years as the unionists worked with the Tory party. In 1892 the *Shuttle* criticised Brinton and Sir Thomas Lea for sharing a Tory platform. It commented that the 'poor little Irish colony of Kidderminster' used to wear the green and look to them for justice in Ireland.[28]

## HABBERLEY VALLEY

When Burton published his *History of Kidderminster* in 1888, he noted that the lord of the manor of Habberley, John Henry Crane, had made arrangements to transfer Habberley Valley to the Borough Council. In fact, although the gift was initially accepted, it was eventually refused by the council in March 1891 after protracted negotiations. There were fears that the character of the

Valley would be damaged by certain conditions attached to the transfer. These involved the erection of fences and a reduction in the area open to the public. Much of the controversy surrounded the intentions of the new owner of the *Yew Tree* public house, Mr W.H. Anderson. It was feared that his premises would become 'a kind of Continental Beer Hall, to which thousands from the Black Country will be attracted, for whom the Valley pure and simple has no charms, but who for the sake of the liquor and the humours of a perennial wake, will not object to the scenery'.

The valley comprised a surviving area of the open heath and common land which had extended across the west side of Kidderminster as far as the Stourport Road until the Enclosure Award of 1775. Probably since then it had been a focal point for the recreation of the townspeople. Shepherds and agricultural labourers lived there. The land was grazed by sheep and there were far fewer trees than today. The *Shuttle* waxed lyrical about this 'Garden of Eden', the thought of which made the heart soften and the eyes moisten for any native of Kidderminster. A little beerhouse had long existed there, but in anticipation of the transfer it was developing into a 'garish drinking shop'. The decision by the Town Council to decline the gift seems to have been uncontroversial, but the inevitable commercialisation of the valley was merely delayed.[29]

## HUSTLERS

It was a case of the survival of the fittest in the carpet industry during the final two decades of the century. The closures included two of the Woodward family's companies in the early 1880s, which were followed by the bankruptcy of C.E. & H. Jefferies in 1887. Later losses were J. Bennie & Co. in 1892, Potter & Lewis in the same year, W. Green in 1896 and H.R. Willis & Co. in 1897. Henry Dixon's troubled firm ceased production in 1895. This was in part due to customer preference for Axminster carpets, but by the 1890s it was due also to unfavourable economic conditions which were to continue up to the First World War. The growth in the home market was slow and exports fell away from their peak in the 1880s.[30] It was just as well that the town possessed inherent vigour, as noted in 1891 by the *Textile Mercury*, which compared Kidderminster favourably with northern towns:

> Kidderminster is a bright exception in what is otherwise an almost uniformly dull region. The town bubbles over with life, and many of its inhabitants are what Americans would term "hustlers" of the first water. It is this which has enabled the town to maintain its pre-eminence in a trade that is more keenly competed for every year.[31]

It is a paradox that the carpet weavers' union engaged in serious industrial action against Brintons and Dixons over female labour, but at the same time they left alone the firm of Tomkinson & Adam who, from its formation in 1869, concentrated upon the use of women. Probably the union did not at first treat them as a serious force and believed in the ultimate superiority of the Brussels and Wilton product, woven by males on heavier looms. The potential of Axminster was enormous, however, being unlimited as to colours, whereas Brussels and Wilton were limited to five or six colours. Furthermore, Axminster had a softer tread than the loop pile of a Brussels carpet. By 1895, faced with heavy unemployment, the union could no longer ignore Tomkinsons. In March of that year a conference was held at the union's request between them and the Axminster producers. The weavers' representatives drew attention to the widespread unemployment of their members and begged the employers, led by Michael Tomkinson, to start to employ males on their looms. Although the meeting was amicable, no concession was made by the manufacturers. The tone of the union's submissions was distinctly humble and it was clear they were struggling to hold on to pride in their craft.[32]

The unemployment of union members was eased eventually by Brintons' response to the Axminster challenge. John Brinton refused to take a licence from Tomkinson & Adam, and his firm developed its own technology for reproducing the Axminster effect. In 1890 they patented the Brinton Jacquard Gripper loom, based on the work of Albert Dangerfield and Thomas Greenwood. This allowed them to lay the foundation for their re-emergence as Kidderminster's foremost carpet firm and their survival throughout the 20th century. However, for the time being it is probable that they lagged just behind Tomkinson & Adam in terms of numbers employed.[33] In 1899 a further boost to employment was given by the relocation to the town of the Victoria Carpet Company, who were previously based at Kirkcaldy in Scotland, where they had been held back by a shortage of skilled labour.[34] They were Tapestry specialists and were obviously attracted by the available workforce in Kidderminster after the closure of so much of that branch of the trade. Edward Hughes was probably the only significant local Tapestry producer left. Victoria took over the Green Street works of one of the failed firms, William Green, and today they occupy premises in Worcester Road.

## IX

# *War and Empire*

The early weeks of the Boer War, which broke out in October 1899, showed that in Kidderminster there was complete confidence in the British Empire. Local Liberals pushed aside their doubts and supported the war entered into by a Conservative government. The weavers' union and church leaders joined in the patriotic support for the nation's troops, which included men from the town. No dissenting voices were heard to say that the Boers of Transvaal, having made their trek into the interior in the 1830s, might have had a right to independence. No voices were heard to say that the fight might have had something to do with the massive wealth at stake from the gold discovered there in 1886. On the contrary, the general opinion was that right was on the British side, which was fighting for justice not only for the many thousands of British 'Uitlanders' in Transvaal but also for the native peoples.[1]

62. Park Attwood, 1899. The heyday of gentlemen farmers was over. The Chellingworths had departed and the historic property was owned briefly by the carpet manufacturer, William Green, before being put up for sale again.

There was also complete confidence that the war would be won easily and quickly. The carpet manufacturers, far from fearing disruption of their trade, were looking forward to an expansion of their export markets. Travellers from the Carpet Manufacturing Company usually went into Transvaal and the Orange Free State at the turn of the year, but they had done badly for a long time because of the disturbed state of the area. The firm's chairman, W.H. Smith, spoke of his hope for a settled government with progressive ideas which encouraged the flow of capital. He believed that the war would secure such conditions. Gilbert Henderson, a Director at Brintons, also looked forward to a new 'enlightened government' allowing money to flow in and out of the country. Club and hotel life would quickly develop, luxuries would be demanded and the well-to-do people would naturally look to carpet as a warm floor covering.[2]

## EDWARD PARRY

The Liberals were in control of the town council during the years around the turn of the century. The Mayor at the start of the Boer War was Edward Parry and his attitude to the conflict was probably typical of many in his party. Born in Stratford-on-Avon in 1828, he came to Kidderminster in 1855 to be minister at New Meeting. He resigned in 1869 and founded the *Kidderminster Shuttle*. He was thereafter at the forefront of progressive thinking, and yet he was able to greet the outbreak of the war by unashamedly subscribing to the political ideals and principles which it was the British Empire's 'privilege and glory' to maintain. These included political freedom, and civil and religious liberty. He described the Boers as an ignorant, obstinate race of peasants. Early in November, at a meeting held to raise funds for the families of those men who had gone away to fight, Parry admitted that he had thought that the negotiations preceding the war had been conducted in 'not too friendly a spirit'. However, he swept aside his doubts and it was their duty to close ranks and stand up for 'the integrity and honour of the Empire'.[3]

It was clear that many believed that such was the might of the British Empire that victory would be immediate. On 21 October the *Shuttle* warned those people that they might have to wait for five or six weeks. Despite its backing of the conflict the *Shuttle* vividly described the agony of wives as eight reservists were sent off from the railway station the following morning. A great crowd marched to the station and overcame efforts to limit access to the platform to friends and relatives. It was mob rule. The greatest enthusiasm was displayed, but it was a selfish and somewhat brutal crowd.

Wives and families left behind received a small allowance from the Government, but they were still dependent upon fund-raising by the local community. A few months into the war there was concern expressed at the 'almost niggardly way the funds were being distributed'. A meeting of the weavers' union also expressed disappointment that no working men were serving on the committee, but there was no doubt that the weavers supported the war effort. Gradually it was realised that the Boers were not going to be a pushover. The Mayor expressed indignation at the November meeting that the Boers had shown that they had prepared for the war. He also expressed 'exasperation' at the capture of 1,800 British troops at Ladysmith. This did not dim the patriotism of the townspeople. Later in the month a crowded and enthusiastic meeting packed the Town Hall to confirm their backing for the war. Those present included

63. Edward Parry
(1828-1926).

the Vicar of Kidderminster, S. Phillips, and various other ministers of the church. Wherever the British flag went, it was said, it carried with it 'liberty, freedom, self-government and toleration'.[4]

In January 1901 the Victoria Cross was awarded to Sergeant Thomas Lawrence, son of a Kidderminster timber merchant. The war was not to be won easily. The small Boer army denied Britain an early victory by forming commando groups, which used the speed of horseback. The British lacked cavalry and were forced to call upon the part-time Yeomanry Cavalry who had seen little active service. Many volunteered to go and, after frantic preparations, the first contingent arrived in South Africa in March 1900. A further contingent followed in April 1901. The British forces were not well prepared or supplied. In the Worcestershire Regiment three times as many died from disease as were killed in action. Eventually the length and severity of the struggle were to dent seriously the confidence of the British Empire. With no end to the war in sight the relief of the siege of Mafeking was greeted with hysterical enthusiasm, particularly in London, giving rise to a new word: to 'maffick', meaning to 'exult riotously'. The celebrations in Kidderminster spread over several days.[5]

The inevitable surrender of the Boers did not come until May 1902, by which time 22,000 British soldiers had died. It is uncertain how many of them were from Kidderminster. Four men are amongst those commemorated by a white marble tablet at the west end of the north aisle in St Mary's church. L/Corp. Ralph Douglas Jones and Privates Arthur Handley, Bill Perks and Charles Rowe were volunteers among a group of 106 from the town and district, who joined either the Service Company of the Worcestershire Regiment or the Imperial Yeomanry. Rowe was the son of Thomas Rowe, who had for many years been prominent among the carpet weavers' union leadership. Rowe died, not in action, but of typhoid in May 1900 at Bloemfontein, where he was buried. A photographic portrait of him was displayed in the St John's Institute in Crowther Street.

In the cemetery there is a memorial to three men of the Worcestershire Imperial Yeomanry who died at Kleinfontein in October 1901. One is the same Ralph Douglas Jones, aged 21, but the other names are different: Frederick Hall and Walter James Maunder, both aged 19. This stone, unveiled in April 1902, was the idea of Alderman Pensotti and paid for by some friends. At a memorial service by the monument later that year, Pensotti referred to those others who had died:

> He was sorry that the names of those since fallen could not be put upon the tablet … but he hoped the names of the others would be added, because the compliment was not intended for the three only, but for all who had fought and died for their country … Passing through his mind at that moment were the names of other young men who fought in the war, Troopers Horace, Wyre, Handley, Harding, Cox and others, whose names would be remembered.[6]

## RICHARD EVE

In June 1902, shortly after the end of the Boer War, a drinking fountain was unveiled in Brinton Park to the memory of Richard Eve. There it continues to stand today, albeit in need of some refurbishment. It is nearly thirty feet high and was built to the design of Joseph Pritchard, head of the firm of architects Meredith and Pritchard of Bank Buildings, Kidderminster. On its south side is a medallion bust of Eve, which was the work of a sculptor named Broad, a native of Chaddesley Corbett. An inscription reads: 'Chivalrous by nature and fired with the enthusiasm of humanity, he resisted oppression and did battle of the right.' Yet it is a perplexing matter that he should have been honoured in this way, for his deeds on behalf of Kidderminster were not outstanding. Chas Townley has made a study of the monument and has concluded that it represented some kind of political statement.[7]

Eve's main contribution to town life was to lose two general election contests in 1892 and 1895. On both occasions he stood as the Liberal candidate opposed to the Conservative, Frederick Godson. Eve was born in Kidderminster, the son of a foreman at Pardoe, Hooman and Pardoe's spinning department. At the age of 15 he left the town to pursue a legal career and eventually established a solicitor's practice in Aldershot, which was his home until his death. His failure to beat Godson meant that the Tory held the Kidderminster seat from 1886 until 1906. The Liberals must have been frustrated by these defeats, because at the turn of the century they were the dominant force on the town council. From 1898 until 1904 all of the town's mayors were Liberals, namely Edward Parry (twice), Peter Adam (twice), George Holdsworth, William Talbot and William Adam. In 1900-1 they held 17 council seats to seven of the unionists. Perhaps the erection of the fountain in memory of Eve, who died in 1900 aged 68, was a way of giving expression to their values. Yet Tories also had a fond regard for Eve. Sir Frederick Godson himself spoke at the unveiling ceremony, where he revealed that he and Eve had been private friends for many years before their political contests because of their membership of the Freemasons. If the monument was a political statement, then it was one on which both Liberals and Tories could agree, perhaps with an uneasy eye on the rising Labour Party. Eve was perhaps an acceptable alternative to socialism, being

64. Richard Eve Monument pictured in 2001, badly in need of restoration.

a Radical, who in his 1892 campaign urged Kidderminster workers to secure their own representatives in Parliament in future so that they might 'have none of these laws made by landlord law makers'. The drawn out struggle of the Boer War had sapped the confidence of the British establishment, and men like Eve were perhaps seen as being capable of guiding the forces of labour. Certainly in Kidderminster the forces of Liberalism were nearly spent and the monument symbolised the coming end of that era. In 1906, as Liberalism benefited from a nonconformist reaction to the unpopular measure of abolishing school boards, Kidderminster elected its last Liberal MP, Sir E.F. Barnard, but the Tories won in 1910 and were to hold the seat until 1945.

## WORKING-CLASS CONDITIONS 1908

In 1908 an enquiry was published by the Board of Trade into the cost of living of the working classes. Kidderminster was revealed as a town whose main industry was, at best, steady, but not advancing. The population had remained static at just over 24,000 from 1881 to 1901, despite an excess of births over deaths, because many workers had emigrated. The report mentions the change of public taste from heavier Brussels to the lighter Axminster and the consequent increase in female employment. Total employment figures in the town for men and women over 10 years old were 4,304 and 4,127. However, women were in the majority in carpet manufacturing by 2,740 to 2,247. The employment of children was still commonplace, despite the efforts of the school authorities. Indeed, of children aged over 10 and under 14, 19.7 per cent of boys and 13.1 per cent of girls were 'occupied'. They probably had to be because of the lower wages commanded by women. The report commented:

> Much of the work formerly performed by men has been now taken over by women and girls. On the other hand, it is probable that this change has not always resulted in a reduction of the family earnings, since many female workers earn a guinea a week, and several women of the same family are often out at work.

Despite the lack of growth in the population between 1881 and 1901 the number of houses had increased by about three hundred to a total of 5,503. Many of these were of a more recent, improved standard of a 'five-roomed' type, with a living room and a kitchen downstairs, two bedrooms and an attic, all in the main body of the house. At the back each had a scullery built near the house with 'covered communication', and a coalhouse, water closet and ashpit adjoining. Most of these houses were supplied with water. They were occupied by artisans, usually weavers, which the report distinguishes from the 'labouring class'. However, there were 1,840 of an older 'four-roomed' type. These contained a living room and kitchen downstairs and two rooms upstairs. Both downstairs rooms as a rule had a tiled floor. They contained no gardens at the rear, only small paved yards. Here there were common washhouses, water closets and ashpits, usually one for every three houses. There was one tap for a supply of water to the whole row. These houses were generally inhabited by the labouring class, as were a variety of terraces and back-to-backs in the old courts which continued to survive in the older parts of town. There were 211 and 453 two-roomed and three-roomed tenements respectively. The report noted that the courts were 'periodically swept', which suggested that the filth was still being allowed to accumulate for a time in these areas where the poorest people lived.

Kidderminster was a working-class town where the vast majority of houses were privately rented. Many of the landlords were people who had made money elsewhere and decided to invest some of it in housing to provide themselves with a steady income. They were not necessarily willing or able to maintain those properties properly. This is reflected in the low rents in the town as revealed by the 1908 report, which compared the rents of 73 towns with those of London. Only three towns had lower rents than those in Kidderminster, which were 43 per cent of those in London.[8]

## HERBERT SMITH

The hopes expressed by carpet manufacturers about the expansion of markets at the outset of the Boer War were not to be realised. In the period leading up to the First World War, exports never returned to the levels achieved in the 1880s.[9] One major company to fail was Barton & Sons, of Vicar Street, who were descended from a firm founded in 1807 by Charles Wright, George Gower and John Gough. Wright's nephew, George Crump, had taken over and for a time the company was Crump and Crane. In 1872 fine office buildings fronting Vicar Street had been built. When business ceased in 1905, Vicar Street's character as an industrial street changed. Shop frontages were inserted and today these premises are occupied by W.H. Smith and others.[10]

Another company which encountered difficulty was the well-established concern of James Humphries & Sons Ltd. John Humphries had died in 1901, by which time the firm had been struggling for some years. They had been slow to gain a foothold in the Axminster trade. His three sons were unable to make the company profitable. In 1906 they appointed one of their designers, Herbert Smith, as General Manager. By all accounts he embarked upon a 'ruthless' reorganisation programme and a profit was recorded for the first time in 13 years. In 1910 his offer to buy out the three brothers was accepted and he began a meteoric rise, which would lead to a knighthood and a home at Witley Court. Smith appears to have been alone among Kidderminster's carpet barons in acquiring such an unqualified reputation for ruthlessness. Perhaps he caused resentment among the established carpet families as he rose quickly from a relatively obscure background, basing his success not upon technical innovation, but on reorganisation. Yet he had artistic taste, which he perhaps acquired from his father, Horatio Smith, a carpet designer. Herbert excelled in reproductions of old Persian carpets and many of his designs were bestsellers. As a carpet craftsman he was a 'genius'. He was a capable violinist, but he had a 'philistine way of dealing with ineptitude'. One of the stories about him is that he once boasted that he would one day own both the Humphries' business and the family home. This he achieved in 1911 when he purchased Blakebrook House from Sydney Humphries.[11]

Smith was instantly recognisable by his shaven head. It is thought he may have adopted this style in the mistaken hope that it would reduce the chances of catching anthrax, which had begun to appear in English industrial towns in the late 19th century due to the importation of contaminated Persian wool. The worst year for Kidderminster was 1903, when three deaths were

65. Edward Hughes (d.1902), the carpet manufacturer, and his wife Anne lived at the Woodlands in Low Habberley.

recorded. Whatever the truth about Smith's own concern about the disease, there was little public discussion about a matter which today might cause something close to panic. Anthrax did continue to affect the town, and its last victim may have been a carpet weaver who died from the disease in 1965.[12]

During these early years of the new century other companies continued to develop their technology. An engineer from the firm of Edward Hughes, William Youngjohns, invented the first power loom to weave the *Ghiordes* knot. This enabled them to produce by machine a type of carpet which had previously been possible only by expensive hand weaving. At the time of Hughes' death in 1902 his firm employed 100 weavers on these looms, which produced carpets characteristic of the East, particularly

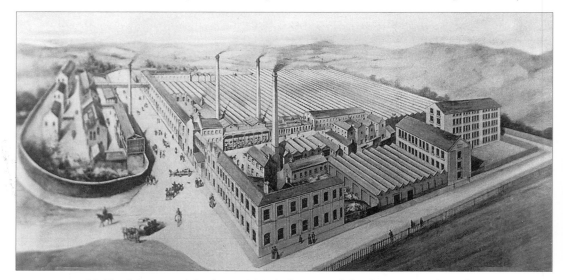

66. Tomkinson & Adam's in 1904. A drawing of the factory complex taken from a company price list.

67. Michael Tomkinson
(1841-1921).

of Turkey. In 1904 Cecil Brinton, who was chairman of his company, took charge of the project to bring Brinton's abreast of the trend for broad looms. Until then their looms were no wider than 4½ feet. On 14 November 1905 their new 15-foot-wide loom 'The Majestic' commenced production. In 1910 Tomkinson & Adam maintained their reputation for enterprise by securing the patent rights for a French loom which wove a perfect *Ghiordes* knot. This was to serve them well for many years, weaving carpets that were often taken for the genuine Turkish or Persian article. The looms operated on the Jacquard principle and were up to 16½ feet wide.[13]

## PROGRESS

The Infirmary had gradually expanded over the years, with separate facilities for children introduced in 1886, subject to the letter system. The William Adam ward was added in 1902/3, and a neighbouring school was to be converted into a nurses' home in 1913. There was concern for the future because of the Liberal government's Insurance Act of 1911 whereby workers made weekly contributions, as did the employers and the state, towards the funding of benefits and pensions. It was feared that workers would be less inclined to contribute to hospital funds. However, the fears proved groundless, and the workers of one firm voted by eight to one to re-instate contributions after they had briefly been abandoned.[14]

In 1912 Kidderminster saw something of the agitation for change in regard to women's rights. On Wednesday evening, 24 January, a crowded Town Hall heard a speech from the leader of the militant suffragettes, Mrs Emmeline Pankhurst. She had addressed a meeting earlier in the evening and motored to Kidderminster, arriving at half-past eight. She spoke for an hour and a quarter, and her audience listened attentively although many were not in sympathy with the methods of the Women's Social and Political Union. The meeting was chaired by Reginald S. Brinton, who explained his support for Women's Suffrage as defined in the Conciliation Bill and the granting of the franchise to women on the same terms as it is to men. He went on to say:

> One of my friends wrote to me the other day as follows – 'I trust Mrs Pankhurst will spare your windows. I hear it is one of her maxims that "nothing is really achieved in this world without taking panes"' ... I would like to say ... In the first place, these ladies who deliberately transgress the law do so with their eyes wide open, and they

are fully prepared to take the consequences ... A second point is that the methods of
the Society have been effective ... Those who are ready to accuse W.S.P.U. of violence
should remember that the extension of the franchise has on nearly every occasion
been accompanied by violence.[15]

The strength of Brinton's support was striking, and there is ample evidence
of a family commitment to the advancement of women. Also present at the
meeting were Miss Brinton (Cheltenham), Mrs Brinton and the Misses
Brinton. The daughter of Roland Brinton, Reginald's cousin and a London
doctor, was Mary Stocks, champion of women's rights and a pioneer of birth
control clinics. Born in 1891, she became a Labour Life Peer at the age of 75.

There was a local branch of the Non-Militant Society for promoting the
vote for women. At a meeting in October 1912 in Kingsley Hall the speaker
revealed that the Tory MP for Kidderminster, Major Knight, had promised to
support an amendment to the Franchise Bill then before Parliament to include
women in the franchise. Local speakers included Mrs Anton, Mrs Ellis Talbot
and the Rev. J.E. Stronge, who was thoroughly sympathetic to the object of
the society. Also present was the carpet weaver, Tom Rowe, who had been
prominent in the leadership of his trade union for well over two decades. He
said he had always been in favour of women's suffrage. However, there was
local opposition to female suffrage. In March 1912 a meeting in the Town Hall
was organised by those against the movement. The chairman was Rowland
Hill, the High Sheriff-Elect of Worcestershire. Also on the platform were Miss
Gladys Pott and Ald. E.J. Morton. It is hard to gauge the strength and character
of this opposition, but the name of Morton represents one of Kidderminster's
foremost Tory and Church of England carpet families, by contrast with the
tradition of Liberal nonconformity in the Brinton family.[16]

The debate at these Kidderminster meetings was being conducted between
the middle classes, but at the same time agitation of a different kind was
affecting working-class women in the carpet industry. In September 1912
the Town Hall was the forum for another speech by a woman of national
standing. The speaker was one of the great leaders of the women's labour
movement, Mary Macarthur, general secretary of the National Federation of
Women Workers. Born in 1880, she was an inspirational organiser and was
revered throughout the Black Country after she led the women chain-makers
of Cradley Heath in a successful campaign for improved pay. She turned her
attention to Kidderminster, where about one thousand women workers had
joined the local branch of the union prior to her visit. They had been provoked
into strike action the previous July when certain employers tried to cut their
wages in order to pass on the extra costs resulting from the National Insurance
Act 1911. In her speech Macarthur explained the objects of the Federation
by describing the badge which members were expected to wear. The bundle

of sticks represented the strength which unity gave to the members who were bound together to defend their interests. The clasped hands of the man and woman indicated the friendship which existed between the two classes of workers. She was delighted that the male workers of the town had come to the assistance of the women, and a considerable number of the Carpet Weavers' Association was present at the meeting. Macarthur joked that she knew that sometimes women's heads were full of other unions than trade organisations, but she urged her listeners to work to give 'the opportunity to all to enjoy brighter conditions, new joys, and higher conceptions of human life'.[17]

## DEVELOPMENT

In 1912 the need for Borough expansion was met by the bringing of Comberton, Foley Park, Franche and Broadwaters within its boundaries. Some of these parts were reached by the tram service set up in 1898. They ran from Oxford Street in one direction up Comberton Hill to Somerleyton, and in the other direction through Foley Park to Stourport. Cultural opportunities were enhanced in 1903 by the building of the Opera House on Comberton Hill. In 1910 the first two cinemas opened in Mill Street. The Electric Theatre was to become the Grand and enjoy a long life as a cinema. The Bijou Theatre, on the other hand, closed in 1912, but was to enjoy considerable success as Frank Freeman's in later years.

68. The Playhouse, formerly the Opera House.

## FIRST WORLD WAR

The extent of the hardship in Kidderminster during the war years was considerable. The war memorial in front of St Mary's church records the loss of 661 men. To this terrible toll must be added the economic hardship. The town was dependent on a 'luxury' industry, which was subject to inevitable decline in time of war. House building ceased, further depressing the demand for carpets. One estimate is that factories had sufficient orders for about one-third of normal production. The effect of the war was immediate and local manufacturers declared a three-day week. It was reported that large sums of money were locked up in German debt to the local carpet industry. Most designing establishments closed down. They had close links with French and German manufacturers, who generally made their purchases in September. A Relief Fund was established in the early part of the war by the Mayor, Reginald Brinton. This time workers' representatives were on the administering committee, but again, just as in the Boer War, the carpet weavers' union felt that ungenerous poor-law attitudes prevailed. Concerned for the dignity of their members, the union reached an agreement with the fund committee, whereby they received £500 for distribution by themselves to their members.[18]

For a brief period the full horror of what was in store was not apparent. In September a packed meeting at the Town Hall displayed the 'utmost enthusiasm' for the war effort. All party politics were put aside and the prospective Liberal candidate, Sylvain Mayer, supported the town's MP, Major Knight. The *Shuttle* ran a series, 'In The Firing Line', featuring the direct observations of local men at the front. Private Edmund Tandy of Park Street, who had been invalided home, had some 'thrilling experiences' at the front, as did his neighbour, Driver Arthur Oliver, also of Park Street.[19] Headlines emphasised German losses, and in November, with regard to the struggle at Ypres in Belgium, it was claimed that 'the battlefield is strewn with German dead'. Sadly, it was to become evident that some of those victims were Kidderminster men. On 31 October the 2nd Battalion of the Worcestershire Regiment had become involved in desperate fighting amongst the trees at a village called Gheluvelt near Ypres. Bayonets were used in a battle so confused that the Worcestershire men tried to identify themselves by cheering as they fought, and many were killed by 'friendly fire'. Their bravery succeeded in halting the German advance for a time and may have saved the British army from defeat, but a third of the battalion's strength were killed or wounded.[20] After the war their sacrifice was commemorated by the naming of a new street in Kidderminster, Gheluvelt Avenue.

By late November 1914 a sober realisation of the dreadful nature of the war was already dawning. Even though the losses at Gheluvelt had not been reported as such, a growing number of individual deaths were being recorded every week

**69.** *Roebuck Hotel*, Oxford Street 1913.

in the *Shuttle*. These included Private William Hobson of Bewdley Street, who had once been heavyweight boxing champion of the Midlands and was the former manager of the defunct Bijou Theatre in Mill Street. The column 'In The Firing Line' began to drop its tendency to romanticise and instead revealed the grim reality. Private William Rollings of Clarence Street wrote that 'the fighting is terrible where we are'. The following week he repeated the message and showed readers that trench warfare was already becoming established. 'It is terrible in the trenches now, some three or four inches in water'.[21]

## ENTERTAINMENT

Life had to go on and the places of entertainment continued to operate during the war years. There were three main venues which offered both films and live acts. Before the war the Picture House in Vicar Street, which later became the Futurist Cinema, secured 'at great expense' a film called 'The Wreck', which invited the public to see a sensational picture depicting two trains crashing into each other. At the same time it was putting on such attractions as the Glenroy Troupe of dancers in their 'phenomenal success', 'The 17th Lancers'. The Electric Theatre presented a similar mixture of films and performers, such as 'The Whirlwind Demons' who were held to be 'the most sensational gymnastic act in the world'. It was refurbished as the Grand in December 1915. The Opera House on Comberton Hill was the third major centre for welcome distraction from the anxiety and grief of war.

One man, Herbert Smith, dominated these war years. Again he showed himself to be a different breed from his fellow carpet manufacturers. Whilst they carried on business as usual as far as was possible, Smith responded to the demands of wartime production. The British and French governments were in need of army blankets and other war textiles. His colleagues 'shook reluctant or indifferent heads', but Smith rose to the challenge by accepting astronomical numbers of orders for blankets. He had acquired Long Meadow Mills in Dixon Street just before the war, when he took over the firm of Charles Harrison & Sons, and he transformed the premises into a felt factory. He alone seemed prepared to make a major investment in these unfamiliar products. His efforts further boosted the employment of women in Kidderminster, giving employment to 550 of them but to only 25 men.[22]

Prices rose quickly at the start of the war. In April 1915 the weavers' union put in a claim for an increase of 10 per cent in pay. This was turned down. However, Herbert Smith was to rise to the fore, leading to a new era of better relations between workers and employers. Some members of the union thought they had been too patriotic in delaying their pay demands, but there was progress in May 1916 when Smith led the way in agreeing a claim which included a 10 per cent increase. Two months later the other manufacturers agreed. Yet industrial relations were still poor, because by September the *Shuttle* was reporting that some employers were refusing to pay the 10 per cent. There was even a strike in October of that year by women in the Chenille Axminster section of the trade who were organised by the Workers' Union. By March 1917 Smith was chairman not only of the Kidderminster manufacturers, but also of the UK manufacturers as a whole. A further 10 per cent pay increase was agreed, followed by another four months later, making a total of 30 per cent over pre-war rates. In May 1918 the war bonus was raised to 60 per cent, and then to 75 per cent the following October through an intervention by Smith. Such evidence of Smith's commitment to partnership with the workers sits oddly with his reputation for ruthlessness, which was probably created by some of his fellow employers who did not appreciate his extraordinary rise to the top. The War Office clearly recognised his leadership qualities and he became chairman of the Carpet Trade Rationing Committee, which was responsible for allocating available supplies of wool and jute to companies.[23]

70. Horsefair 1915, showing the clock, yet another town landmark to disappear.

The war years saw a historic step taken by the carpet weavers' union. By 1916 their membership was reduced to 820 from a peak of 1,410 in 1890. The male weavers of Brussels and Wilton carpets, which formed the backbone of the membership, were an increasingly select group. Furthermore, the officers were regretting the indifference of members to the affairs of the union. A decision was taken to open membership to all workers in the carpet industry. On 17 July 1917 women attended a meeting of the Carpet Weavers' Association for the first time. Over 800 women had already become members of the union and total membership rose to over 2,000 by January 1918.

The Great War was coming to an end. It is perhaps a remarkable fact that the slaughter did not produce open opposition to the war, but only what other authors have referred to as 'intense disillusionment'.[24] The government did their best to maintain morale by such means as films like 'The Advance of the Tanks', the official War Office picture. In January 1917 this was showing at both the Grand, 'where everybody goes', and the Picture House, 'the cosiest hall in the district'. Nevertheless, advertisements during the same month by the Stourbridge Recruiting Officer showed that the authorities needed to control war weariness and ensure a continuing supply of soldiers. One called for information in strict confidence on named men, including 16 from Kidderminster, who had evidently slipped the net. Another gave notice to employers that they must prepare statements about all their workers of military age, that is between 18 and 41 years old.[25]

# X

# *Homes for Heroes*

The history of Kidderminster after the war was dominated by the story of housing, as the nation's rulers felt a sense of duty to provide decent homes for those who had fought and suffered during the war. Local councils acted as agents of government policy. It was the time of the rise of the Labour Party, but in Kidderminster the Tory party was dominant. The town's housing policy inevitably reflected a Tory preference for encouraging private home owners. Progress was restricted by only modest growth in the carpet industry, which the town depended on for its prosperity. Stability prevailed in the 1920s, and at least fears of serious unemployment proved unfounded. However, it is probable that output in the industry did not recover to pre-war levels. Exports certainly did not achieve their former volume and by 1930 Britain had become a net importer of carpets.[1] Yet production was in part sustained by demand arising from house-building programmes. Further stability during the inter-war period was due to the absence of major technological changes. Production techniques remained broadly the same and firms survived by renewal and sometimes by reorganising.

It was a quiet time in Kidderminster's history, and even Herbert Smith dropped from view only a few brief years after the war. In 1920 he was rewarded for his wartime work with a baronetcy, and in August he celebrated by taking his 1,300 employees on a pleasure steamer trip down the River Severn to Tewksbury. In the same year he added another company to his group, that of Edward Hughes & Sons. This firm had been run by the oldest of Edward's sons, Frederic of The Mount in Trimpley, until his death in 1919 at the age of eighty-four. Sir Herbert now brought all his acquisitions under the name of a new company, Carpet Trades Ltd. That he was still ambitious at this time is further suggested by his becoming chairman of the Joint Industrial Council for the Carpet Trade which met for the first time in July 1919. This body was formed as a result of recommendations by the Whitley Committee, which was set up by the government to improve relations between employers and workers. The JIC was a national body of representatives from both sides, designed to

71. Sir Herbert Smith with
Lawrence of Arabia. Smith
considered Lawrence to be
an intimate friend and often
entertained him at Witley Court.

settle disputes by negotiation. Sir Herbert was an obvious chairman, having
formed the view that workers should take places in management and on the
board as co-partners in the industry. However, the JIC never really got off the
ground, perhaps contributing to a disillusionment which provoked Sir Herbert
into a sudden early retirement at the age of 49 in March 1922. Ill-health was
the official reason given. He later sold his shares and there was no question of
his son taking over the firm. By this time his extraordinary wealth had enabled
him to purchase Witley Court and to put Blakebrook House up for sale.[2]

The fate of Blakebrook House showed that the conditions were not yet
ripe for the conversion of grand estates into much-needed housing. It was
purchased in 1922 by Charles Lovegrove, who ran it as a boarding school until
it went bankrupt in 1926.[3] Then the house which had been home to some of
Kidderminster's foremost citizens steadily declined into dereliction. The fate
of Franche Hall, after the death of Michael Tomkinson in 1921, was more
dramatic and fully exposed the sluggish state of the town economy. In 1924,
after failing to be sold, the historic mansion was pulled down. The land was to
be developed for housing, but half a century was to elapse before this happened.
In the 1920s growth in the housing stock was unspectacular and the promise
of homes for heroes was largely unfulfilled in Kidderminster.

By the mid-1920s the firm with the famous name, Doolittle and Dalley,
was well established as an estate agency. The company had been founded by the
Eymore farmer, Edward Doolittle, in 1893. He died in 1918, and it was probably in the two years preceding his death that Reginald Dalley joined him.

## A TORY TOWN

The vigorous class conflict of the 19th century was well in the past. Kidderminster
was now content to be employed and governed by the same people. It was to
be a Tory town for much of the next fifty years, despite a fundamental political

change with the Representation of the People Act of 1918. This gave the vote to all adult males and to women over thirty. In addition there was a reorganisation of constituency boundaries. Since 1832 Kidderminster had elected its own MPs, but this ceased with the expansion of the constituency to include surrounding urban and rural areas. The total electorate was nearly 40,000 people. This was to make it very difficult for the rising Labour Party to win the seat. Indeed, the sitting Conservative MP for Kidderminster, Eric Knight, won the new seat in the 1918 election as a supporter of the Lloyd George Coalition, and Labour had to wait until 1945 for a victory here. Irrespective of the rural areas, it remained a matter of doubt as to whether the

72. Louis Tolley
(1889-1959).

working class of Kidderminster were natural Labour supporters. Although the Carpet Weavers' Association was affiliated to the party, there was opposition to this from many members. The problems for the Labour party in the town were illustrated by the reaction to the election in 1919 of their first borough councillor, Louis Tolley. He was refused time off for his duties by his employer, Messrs Greatwich, and was eventually dismissed.[4] Nevertheless, the hesitant rise of the Labour party in the town was marked by the founding of a Labour Club in Park Street in 1921.[5]

In 1922 John Wardlaw-Milne, a partner in a firm of ship and mill owners, was returned as Conservative MP and his tenure was to last until 1945. By 1925 he had already been re-elected in two further elections by clear majorities. In that year the Labour MP for Bilston, John Baker, spoke at a meeting in Kidderminster Town Hall. He had been the defeated Labour candidate in the town in 1918, and in his speech he referred to what he saw as the conservatism of the local electorate: 'The mass of people in Kidderminster had faith in the present system, but none in themselves. Their attitude was "as it was in the beginning, world without end". That was not a proper attitude. The times were marching on, but evidently Kidderminster intended to stay behind the times.'[6]

The programme of house building introduced by the Lloyd George coalition government was based upon large subsidies given for council houses. Later, in the mid-1920s, tension developed between Tories, who favoured subsidising private building, and Labour, who tried to maintain the grants for council building. This produced only modest building in the 1920s in Kidderminster, which was run by a Tory council. Furthermore, many of the houses built by the council were intended for sale, though this was always a controversial matter. The first council housing projects were in Hurcott Road in 1920, followed by plans for an Aggborough site which were to be beset by difficulties. Despite the rhetoric of homes for heroes, costs were being kept down. The Hurcott Road development, which was built for rent, included houses with one living room only, or the 'non-parlour' type, described as 'mean houses for those who could afford nothing better' by at least one historian.[7] Such were the delays in construction that in January 1921 only one tenant was installed after 12 months of building. By April 1921, when it was agreed to name the site road 'Gheluvelt Avenue', 15 of the 40 houses were tenanted. All was not well, and tenants asked for a reduction in the rents because of lack of services. A certain cynicism concerning the quality of these houses was evident at one council meeting where Cllr Tandy asked if any of them were falling down yet. The houses had been built without cupboards and there was no gas main to supply the stoves and boilers. There were difficulties with the water supply, not helped by the refusal of the government's Unemployment Grants Committee to help lay a water main in Hurcott Road. The council agreed a reduction of rent all round of 2s. 6d. per week, which meant that tenants of non-parlour houses were paying 7s. 6d. rent plus rates.[8]

At first the council had high hopes for building on land they had purchased at Aggborough between Hoo Road and Worcester Road. By June 1920 the Borough Surveyor had produced a layout for 230 houses. The need to cut costs kept scaling down the proposals. By December the council had persuaded the contractors, the Kidderminster Federation of Builders, to reduce the price for what had become 160 houses. Cllrs Tandy and Wright, who seem to have been to the fore in all efforts to keep the lid on spending, then led a move to reject this proposal and seek tenders for the construction of 48 houses only on the Worcester Road frontage. By February 1921 the roads and sewers were being laid out by George Law Limited with government grant aid for the unemployed. Construction of the houses had started by the end of April. These were completed, but the government's financial crisis meant they were turning down further plans. Cllr Tolley regretted that they had delayed their proposals for 'the top of Aggborough'. He urged that the council try to push on with the scheme. He was supported by Cllr Dick Woodward, who commented that 'it would be years before they could hope to build houses by private enterprise, based on an economic rent'. Efforts were made to revive hopes of further building on the site, but it was too late and in February 1922 the council was told by the government that no more council houses could be approved.[9]

In 1923 legislation was passed to pay subsidies to the builders of private houses. Initially this was set at £75 for each house, and for the next few years houses were built all over Kidderminster with the aid of this money. By

October 1925, 192 applications had been approved. The vast majority were for individual houses, the main beneficiaries being the lower middle classes who could find the other several hundred pounds needed to build their house. It was still possible for the council to build, but they seem to have lost interest in doing so. An exception was in 1925 when they accepted a tender for the erection of four houses in Aggborough Crescent at a cost of £1,275. A proposal by Labour councillor Louis Tolley, that the houses should not be sold when built, but should be let to suitable tenants, was narrowly rejected, with all the senior members of the council against the proposal.[10] After the horrors of war the working classes were still heavily dependent upon private landlords, with no more than 100 or so council houses built for rent by the mid-1920s. Sanitary conditions, too, left much to be desired. In 1924 it was noted that Comberton residents of Somerleyton Avenue, who had become residents of the borough in 1912, were still awaiting the provision of sewers and drains.[11]

Other changes in the town included the opening in July 1922 of the Empire cinema in the Horsefair. In 1926 another historic landmark was lost with the demolition of the Elizabethan pub, the *Three Tuns*, in Vicar Street so that a new Woolworths store could be built. A step towards broadening Kidderminster's industrial base was taken with the opening of the sugar factory on Stourport Road in December 1925. The West Midland Sugar Company dealt daily with 500 tons of sugar beet which had been grown by local farmers. This was the culmination of at least twenty years of efforts to create such an industry, led by those such as Clement Dalley.[12] At the same time many centuries of flour milling at the town mills were drawing to a close. The importation of cheap Canadian wheat forced the Goodwin family to dispose of their business in March 1926. The *Shuttle* noted that there was only one working flour mill left in Worcestershire.[13] The name of Goodwin was purchased by another company, but it is not known if work was resumed at the mill.

## ROYAL VISIT

The steady, but not exactly booming, state of the local carpet industry was boosted in July 1926 by a visit to the town by the Duke of York, who inspected the works of Tomkinson and Adam. The firm still maintained a shed with handlooms operated by women, or 'old retainers', whose weaving of rugs was based on the same principles as when business was commenced in 1869. The Duke accepted as a present one of these hand-woven rugs. He was shown the Persian and Smyrna power looms, which reproduced almost exactly the hand knots of Oriental weavers. His Royal Highness was able to see an example of such a carpet being woven for his own use. Following his visit the finished carpet was displayed in the Town Hall, where a charge of threepence was made

73. **Fire at E.A. Broome & Co. 1927. The Castle Mill spinning complex in New Road was destroyed by this fire, but was rebuilt in fine style and now forms a small business park.**

for admission. No fewer than 3,800 people paid to see it, and they raised £50 for the hospital.[14] The firm of Tomkinson and Adam had been one of the leading carpet manufacturers in the country for nearly half a century. Michael Tomkinson had died in 1921, and when Peter Adam, the surviving son of Tomkinson's original partner, died in 1925 the ties of partnership were much loosened. In 1927 the two families went their separate ways, and two companies were created out of the one.

This was a period when relations between employers and their workforce were generally free from conflict. Stability enabled companies to consolidate their premises and equipment. Naylors had purchased Lowland Meadows at the bottom end of Green Street in 1916, and they gradually developed the site during the 1920s. By this time the street was filled by carpet factories from top to bottom, though four of them have now been demolished. In 1927 the Carpet Manufacturing Company doubled the size of the Rock Works, a building which now lies derelict in Park Lane. The character of industrial relations was encapsulated later in the decade by the creation of social clubs for their workforce by two of the town's major companies. Both used early 19th-century mansions built by carpet barons, which was further evidence that such properties were no longer attractive to the local gentry. In 1928 Tomkinsons opened their club at Oaklands in Chester Road, built by Henry Talbot. They were followed in 1929 by Brintons, who chose the fine Spennells House with its large grounds, once the home of John Broom II.[15]

A second public park was presented to the town in 1927 by three directors of Brintons. This was St George's Park, given by Reginald Brinton, Cecil Brinton and Dick Woodward. It was then a genuine town centre park, which stretched down to Waterloo Street. Today it lies ignored by most townspeople, having been halved in size and isolated by the ring road. In 1929 a new fire station was built in Castle Road. In the same year the tramway was closed, three years after the founding of Whittle's bus and coach company.

In the latter years of the decade there was more building by the council, who in 1927 purchased land between Franche Road and Marlpool Lane from William Cooke of The Lakes. By the end of September 50 non-parlour three-bed houses were ready for occupation and the site was called Marlpool Place. Unusually for the time the houses, which cost £708 5s. a pair to build, were built for rent. Other council projects showed the general preference of the majority of the council to build for sale. In 1926 they built houses in Adam Street and Marlpool Lane for sale, although Cllr Tolley had as usual proposed that they be let. In 1928 they decided that seven pairs of houses to be built in Greatfield Road would be sold at £385 for each house. In addition throughout these years a subsidy, which by September 1927 was reduced to £50 for each house, continued to be paid to private builders. By July 1929 the number of applications for these grants, since their introduction in 1923, had reached 488.[16] These had been almost entirely for single houses, typically in roads where vacant plots were gradually being developed in an haphazard fashion. Such roads included Hurcott Road, Turton Street, Connaught Avenue, Marlpool Lane and Franche Road, but many other streets in the town now have several houses built in the 1920s with such aid.

## SUTTON FARM ESTATE

In January 1929 the council embarked upon one of its largest building projects to date. Twenty acres of land forming part of the Sutton Park or Farm Estate were purchased from Mr William Johnstone. Eighty houses were to be built, half of which were of the non-parlour type with two or three bedrooms. They were all to be sold, despite the usual attempt to adopt a policy of letting, this time led by a new Labour councillor, James Ferguson, which was easily defeated by Tory leaders Cllr Grosvenor and Ald. Griffin.[17] By October 1929 plans were laid for a further 118 houses on additional land purchased adjoining this estate. The third stage of this development was approved in February 1931 with the acceptance of a tender for a further 56 houses at a total cost of £19,747.

The familiar inability to see the old house as the centrepiece for a new estate was evident here. A short note from the chairman of the Parks and Buildings Committee, Mr G.S. Tomkinson, simply read: 'Your committee recommends that Sutton Farmhouse be demolished'.[18] At this time the council returned to the Aggborough site off Worcester Road, which had been abandoned half-completed eight years previously. In July 1931 they approved the building of 58 houses, which would eventually comprise Cobham Road. Half were to be parlour-type houses. In this respect this estate and that of Sutton Farm were superior to the later ones at Broadwaters and Foley Park, which concentrated upon the 'mean' non-parlour type.

The council believed they needed far more land if further building was to take place. In 1931 discussions took place with the County Council regarding an extension of the borough boundary. Kidderminster was offered over 2,000 acres, but this was considered to be insufficient. A public enquiry was held at the end of the year. The Deputy Mayor Geoffrey Tomkinson said that the council planned to build 200 houses a year. He spoke of a 'serious shortage of labour already which was likely to become more acute unless more houses were built.' The 1931 census showed 3,100 females and 2,300 males who worked in the carpet industry and also lived in the borough. This compared with totals in the trade of 4,200 and 2,900 respectively. These figures showed a continuing preponderance of women, and Tomkinson spoke of 'girls being brought in from surrounding areas to Kidderminster factories to work'.[19] This was exactly what previous generations of carpet manufacturers used to deny when faced with the fears of the men from the carpet weavers' union. In any event the inquiry did not accept the Kidderminster case, and so Tomkinson and his colleagues had to be content with the addition of 2,136 acres, which took effect in April 1933. The new land included parts of Franche, Puxton, Habberley, Sion Hill, Hurcott, Offmore, Stone, Hoobrook and Rifle Range.

The early 1930s saw other development, in Kidderminster. In 1931 the gasholder was erected in Pitts Lane and this was to be a major landmark for many decades. The steady improvement of the streets continued and by March 1931 even the long-suffering residents of Somerleyton Avenue had obtained their sewer. Their road was among many to be adopted by the council now that they were sewered, levelled, paved, metalled, flagged and channelled. The expansion of the cinema industry continued and on 5 October 1931 the Central Picture Theatre opened in Oxford Street. It could accommodate 1,500 people and a fine organ was installed, fitted with the 'Western Electric Sound System'.

A very significant project was the widening of Blackwell Street, which was being planned in 1931. The narrow street contained many buildings of interest, including Rowland Hill's birthplace, but for many decades it had been home to

74. Rowland Hill's birthplace. Situated on the east side of Blackwell Street, it was demolished in 1930 and a telephone exchange built in its place.

some of the poorest residents in the town. Behind some of the frontages lurked courts which were to be identified as part of the slum clearance programme in 1933. The will was not there to preserve any of it. The council proposed to apply to the Ministry of Health for a loan of £1,530 to acquire numbers 95 and 96, and 105-115 for demolition. These properties constituted the line of buildings on the east side between the new *Red Man Inn* and the junction with Coventry Street. The building line was then to be pushed back to allow for the construction of a higher level carriageway 20 feet wide to take southbound traffic. The existing narrow street was to take the northbound traffic. The demolition was complete by May 1932. The council accepted a tender from contractors Messrs Towers, Wilson & Co. who were prepared to build first-class shops fronting Blackwell Street and Coventry Street for £3,500, which were duly completed in 1934. James Towers was evidently under the impression that the council were going to move quickly with comprehensive redevelopment of the street. In 1937 his solicitor wrote to the council to draw attention 'to the promise that was given to him by the late Mayor of Kidderminster, that immediately he proceeded to build these shops the property on the other side would be remodelled and the road made up to the level of the roadway in front of the shops'.[20] The promise to make a level road was eventually kept, but not until 1968.

## DEPRESSION

These were not easy years for the town. It was a time of national crisis with a Labour Government, elected in 1929, weakened by heavy unemployment and the collapse of the pound. These events were the background to a controversial debate in the town about whether new swimming baths should be built. In

75. Blackwell
Street demolition:
a picture taken in
the early 1930s
as redevelopment
was delayed.

September 1931 a well-attended meeting of the Ratepayers and Traders Association voiced their opposition to the obtaining of a loan of £20,000 for the project. The council was deeply divided, and only after several changes of mind was approval given by 12 to 11 votes. A handful of Labour councillors backed the scheme, but the Tories were split. The Mayor, W.H. Stewart Smith, criticised those who wanted to wait until Kidderminster was prosperous again, with the risk that they would lose a grant of £9,414 from the Unemployment Grants Committee. His fellow Tory, Cllr J.E. Grosvenor, admitted that the existing Mill Street baths were 'not a credit to the town', but to replace them was an 'unnecessary luxury'. He referred to the 'pernicious doctrine' of those who believed that 'the best way of meeting the present difficulties was by increased expenditure'.[21] Nevertheless, the baths were built in 1932 in Castle Road.

In the autumn of 1931 Labour was replaced by a National Government dominated by Conservatives. The election was fought on the issue of protectionism, which Labour opposed. In Kidderminster Wardlaw-Milne, the Conservative who canvassed in support of the National Government, had a majority of over 22,000 votes. In January 1932, when most of the town's factories were on a three-day week, the new government placed 50 per cent duty on carpets imported into Britain. Unemployment continued to be very high in Kidderminster, but by the end of the year the *Shuttle* was able to report that the industry had 'held its own'. Demand for Brussels was slack, but it was brisk for Axminster. Twelve months later trade was good for most fabrics. The output of the industry grew until 1937, stimulated by a massive boom in house building in the years between 1934 and 1938.[22] This growth was in part promoted by the Labour Government's Housing Act of 1930, which provided for slum clearance by the local council and house building to rehouse the displaced occupants. This legislation had considerable effect in Kidderminster.

During the depression the carpet weavers' union continued to defend the working conditions of its members by restricting overtime and night work. In November 1931 the union turned down the proposal of a temporary night shift at Carpet Trades Ltd and Naylors, but overtime was allowed. There was deeper conflict with the firm of Dutfield and Quayle. This company had been set up by two very young men, Harry Dutfield and Stephen (Ken) Quayle, both barely 21, in a 20ft by 60ft factory in Franchise Street in 1928. By 1931 they were struggling to make a profit and had decided to concentrate on some Gripper Axminster looms which they had acquired. Union rules were that weavers could only go on a loom if they had five years' experience by the age of 21, but Dutfield and Quayle were using ex-creelers from other firms who had not served the necessary time. Furthermore, they started to work two shifts, one of which finished at midnight. The union recruited all the firm's workers and the dispute was not properly resolved until December 1933. Dutfield was disillusioned by the episode. Further discouraged by Quayle's decision to get married, Dutfield quit Kidderminster in 1937 to restart the carpet industry successfully in Axminster, which had been abandoned in 1835.[23] His old firm continued in business with a unionised workforce, becoming Quayle and Tranter in 1945.

The depression provoked a historic reduction in the range of the town's production. The old spinning firm of Watson Brothers ceased trading. They owned the huge Pike Mills, a site now occupied by the Aldi supermarket and its car park. Their tenants were Naylors, their former partners, who used the premises to produce the reversible Kidderminster or Scotch type of carpet. Pike Mills was sold to Brintons, and in consequence Naylors left the site in 1932. No more of the carpets to which the town had given its name were to be woven in Kidderminster. This further highlighted the rise of Axminster carpets and the decline of the more traditional weaves. Naylors, however, were far from finished and in 1933 they built a spinning mill at Foley Park on Stourport Road just past Beauchamp Avenue.

The depression did not ease the financial problems of the hospital. Workplace collections, which had begun even before the building of the Mill Street infirmary, continued to be a major source of funding. They were overseen by the Saturday Fund Committee, who met in October 1932 to consider raising workers' contributions from twopence to threepence per week. It was approved, despite reluctance to ask more of people who had already been 'hard hit' and frustration that 'there were hundreds of homes in the town not contributing anything to the hospital'. A notice outside the Town Hall revealed the latest news on the debt, and at his inauguration in November 1933 Mayor Dick Woodward bemoaned the slow rate at which it was being reduced. Recent expense incurred by the hospital authorities included cooking accommodation, laundry facilities and a nurses' home.[24]

Woodward also noted that he 'had a task which none of his hundred predecessors had; to preside over a woman councillor.' This was Miss E.C. Addenbrooke, daughter of a local doctor. Another matter before the council was the need for more spending on sewage disposal, referred to by Woodward. The population of Kidderminster was now over 30,000 and for some considerable time it had been known that the system was no longer adequate. The sewage pumps and engines had been in use for over fifty years and were scarcely capable of dealing with the volume. The waste could be pumped only to fifty feet short of the highest point. Nevertheless the council resolved to continue with the 'open irrigation method', whereby the waste was spread over the land of the sewage farm on the site just south-west of today's Birchen Coppice estate.[25]

Their plan went to a public enquiry in 1933 where it encountered opposition from Stourport and Bewdley. The evidence given for Kidderminster by Cllr

Cecil Brinton revealed the characteristic slow pace and concern for economy of the town council. They preferred to continue with land treatment in part because it was cheaper than building a bacterial treatment works. The need to renew or replace the pumping engine, rising main and other works had been identified in 1911. 'The time had now arrived when action must be taken', Brinton commented, apparently without irony. Their plan was vigorously opposed by the clerk of Stourport Urban District Council, Mr Capel Loft. He claimed that 'for the last 25 years on a clear night the smell has been abominable, and still is abominable'. Others spoke of the sewage farm effectively preventing any building development of Stourport in that direction. It was gradually emerging also that much of the sewage escaped directly into the Stour. Mr Wyndham Parker, the county Medical Officer of Health, said that he did not want a scheme whereby all of the sewage went into the river the first time they got a heavy drop of rain. There was concern, too, from Bewdley, which under recent boundary changes had taken in Wribbenhall. It was pointed out that proposed new sedimentation tanks were to be placed on top of the ridge adjoining their water gathering area and there was the risk of contamination. Inevitably suggestions were made that the way forward was for the three towns to enter a joint scheme, and this was to be the outcome of the enquiry.[26]

## SLUM CLEARANCE

Meanwhile, under the Housing Act of 1930, the government asked the Borough Council to produce a programme of slum clearance by the end of September 1933. They duly identified 121 back-to-back houses in the Borough, of which 65 were capable of being reconditioned and made into through houses. They further identified 171 'single back' houses, of which 87 were recommended for demolition. This made a total of 143 houses which were to be pulled down and their occupants relocated.[27] For this purpose it was proposed to build 50 houses at Broadwaters and 50 houses at Foley Park. The Sion Hill area of Broadwaters was to be subjected to extensive development. The first scheme, approved in February 1933, was for 100 houses, followed by a further 50 houses approved towards the end of the year. All of these houses were of the three-bed non-parlour type and were intended for rent. Three more schemes were in hand by February 1934 to provide another 80 houses, half of which were built for sale.

Despite this apparently substantial commitment to new housing, there was considerable political argument on the subject. The National Government in fact suspended Labour's 1930 Housing Act for a while. At a council meeting in January 1933 James Ferguson condemned the government's proposed suspension of the housing legislation and he 'felt strongly that the Council should have an opinion on such a matter'. He was interrupted by John Wright, who warned him 'Try us, lad, try us!' The *Shuttle* also reported Wright's view that the working classes should have cheap houses at a rent of 5s. 3d., as they had before the war. 'These houses were good enough for everybody, although he knew that they were not equipped with an elaborate bath.' Alderman W.A. Edwards put the point more clearly: 'Some did not want houses with "posh" baths in them which were not used for that purpose ... they had to get back to provision of the necessity of life and houses which would not entail high rents'. Yet some Conservative opinion was sympathetic to Ferguson and assured him that provision of new housing would continue even without government help. However, their continued preference for building for sale was clear. Ald. Griffin, the carpet manufacturer, told the meeting that 'he could claim to have built more houses than anybody in Kidderminster by private enterprise, and today his family owned 80 houses ... they should bear in mind some of the things which caused property to decay and become slums if allowed to go unchecked. Nothing did more harm than a dirty tenant.' Cllr Tomkinson said they should adopt the slogan, 'Working men of Kidderminster, build your own houses.' He understood that Cllr Ferguson was one who had already done so.[28] A few months later, at the opening ceremony for the first 100 completed Broadwaters houses, which were for rent, Cllr Tomkinson again tactlessly made this preference clear. He urged that the adjacent plots available for sale be taken by working men, who 'for 10s. or 11s. a week, would be able to build a house which would be their own in a few years time.' Their houses might cost a little extra, but 'they had the satisfaction of getting the type of house they wanted and knowing they were not living at the expense of their neighbours.'[29]

## CORRUPTION

The political argument on housing culminated in a bitter election campaign for St Mary's ward in the autumn of 1933, the outcome of which was that James Ferguson lost his seat to Fred Pugh of the *Royal George Inn*, Hall Street. It was a late example of the survival of bribery in Kidderminster's political life. Ferguson fought the campaign on the basis that many landlords of overcrowded properties with high rents were Tories. He attacked 'the vested interests of slumdom from the Town Council'. A letter from G.S. Chadwick, the Church Street yarn agent and later a Borough Councillor, accused Labour of bribing the electors with houses to be let at uneconomic rents. This provoked Ferguson into fierce retaliation, in which he suggested that Mr Chadwick's party should give up the 'pernicious practice of shillings and beer at election times.'[30]

Despite the controversy, building did continue. By June 1934 the council had approved the building of 60 houses at Foley Park. Although these were all of the non-parlour type, there was greater variety in the type of accommodation than in earlier schemes, with the inclusion of six four-bed houses and 12 single-bed bungalows. Immediately the council were looking to a second scheme at Foley Park of 20 houses to be erected for sale. This was approved by the Ministry of Health, who made it clear that they did so as an 'exceptional measure'. The government now saw the council's role as building for rent only, but accepted that in Kidderminster the private sector was not 'within measurable distance' of providing smaller and cheaper houses. They also recognised there was 'an immediate demand from persons of the working class to purchase houses of this type'.[31]

Private building of middle-class homes proceeded swiftly as the decade progressed and many of Kidderminster's outer streets are characterised by 1930s houses. Both sides of Hurcott Road saw activity at this time. James Road was named in 1932. Highfield Road was built by October 1933, when the frontagers of the extension of Turton Street were objecting to the cost apportioned to them of the channelling, sewering and metalling of the road by the council, who wished to link Highfield Road with Hurcott Road. The same report revealed that other roads which had recently been made up were Russell Road, Oldnall Road and St John's Avenue. A 20-acre site belonging to Greenhill Farm, between Hurcott Road and Birmingham Road, was acquired in 1933 for development. At the same time houses of a 'superior type' were being erected at Comberton on a 100-acre site at the bottom of Somerleyton Avenue. Three months later Phipps and Pritchard were advertising a detached three-bed house for £750 on the 'charming Comberton estate', which it was claimed was 'the best in the district'. Other adverts included two detached three-bed houses in Batham Street at £595 and similar houses fronting Birmingham Road 'ready for occupation in a few weeks' at £750.[32]

The breaking up of some of the grand estates of the carpet manufacturers further encouraged the rapid extension of the town's streets in the middle 1930s. The Adam family homes of Cairndhu and Lyndholm were pulled down, leaving only the Music Room belonging to the latter. This opened up the land south of Linden Avenue for construction and Lyndholm Road was built by the side of the railway. The very fine Greatfield Hall on Bewdley Hill, the last great house of the Humphries family, was probably demolished in 1935 soon after Jimmy Humphries sold up and left the area. This enabled Oakfield Road and Birchfield Road to be built at the back, and both were complete and adopted by 1939. In July 1937 the 24 acres of Summerhill on the opposite side of Bewdley Hill were offered for sale after the death of W.H. Stewart Smith, the chairman of the Carpet Manufacturing Company. This 18th-century mansion did not survive the subsequent development of the site. Summerhill Avenue and Westville Avenue were named in 1939.

Progress was being made with plans for the long-delayed new sewage works. Bewdley, Stourport and Kidderminster had agreed to a joint scheme submitted by Messrs D. Balfour & Sons in March 1934. This was approved by the Ministry of Health after a public enquiry in May 1937, despite the inevitable opposition from the Kidderminster Traders and Ratepayers Association, who believed there was a 'better and cheaper' alternative. The scheme comprised a new pumping station between Hoobrook and Falling Sands and new sewage disposal works at Oldington. It also involved the exchange of 70 acres of Brinton's land, on the Stour side of the Stourport Road, for 70 acres of Corporation land on the other side of the road. More evidence was revealed at the enquiry about the discharge of sewage into the Stour. One witness claimed that even in dry weather most of it was pumped directly into the river, though this was disputed by Alderman A.E. Meredith. Dr Wyndham Parker described the pollution of the Stour as 'a matter of urgency', as sewage was going in 'at present in large quantities'.[33]

## BENIGN PATERNALISM

For many years a number of men had taken a leading role in both industrial and political life. Prominent among them had been Dick Woodward and Reginald Brinton, and the relative degree of harmony in town life was in part due to their approach. The type of management they brought to Brinton's has been described by Marsh as 'benign paternalism'. Woodward was well known for his good relations with workers and apparently adopted the principle that 'if you have a union the management can hit the men and the men can hit the management and neither side gets hurt.' He had shown political independence in earlier years by occasionally supporting Labour's Louis Tolley in trying to get the council to push on with housing schemes for rent. Brinton, as well as giving strong support to the suffragette movement, had once shown great magnanimity by offering Louis Tolley a job, after being defeated by him in the 1919 local election, when the latter was being prevented from having time off for council duties by his employer.[34] However, an era was coming to an end with the death of Woodward in 1934 whilst in office as Mayor, and with the retirement of Brinton in 1936 due to ill-health.

There had already been signs that a period of industrial peace was closing in two disputes involving women. In 1933, 45 Axminster weavers at the Carpet Manufacturing Company Ltd protested for eight months that the 'Dial' system which measured their production was faulty before the company finally accepted they were right. At the end of that year Gripper Axminster pickers at Naylors were given notice, with no prior discussion, that their pay rates were to be cut by nearly half. Brintons and the Victoria Carpet Co. soon followed suit, despite the prosperous state of the Axminster trade. Union resistance led to the companies backing down. The following four years were a period of growth for the industry, but as war began to look imminent trade faltered and companies strove to become more competitive. In January 1938 the weavers' union opened new offices built in Callows Lane, and soon they had to contend with a rash of disputes, starting with a three-week strike at Brintons which broke out in October.

One of the key reasons for the leadership of Brintons in the carpet trade has been their preparedness to break with accepted practice and be ahead of the game. In 1936 they withdrew from the Kidderminster District Council, which discussed problems in the industry, in order to pursue their own policies. One such policy was the appointment of an efficiency expert, the splendidly named Mr Odd, to study the time taken by workers. This resulted in gripper Axminster weavers being offered reduced rates of pay. It resulted also in another chapter in the saga of the introduction of youths, still called 'creelers', into the trade. This had been a vexed question since the formation of the union seventy-five years or so previously. Brintons reduced the number of creelers and also refused to honour an agreement about rates of pay to weavers for working without their assistance. The anxiety of the Weavers' Association was increased further by the company opening a factory in Bridgwater, to which the union was denied access. They feared Brinton's might transfer work there from Kidderminster. The resultant strike was only settled by the intervention the Mayor, Sir George Eddy.

In 1939, 'the worst year for trade in the previous four decades' according to weavers' leader Arthur Smith, a far worse conflict arose involving Carpet Trades Ltd and the Victoria Carpet Company, who unilaterally gave notice of reduced pay for gripper Axminster weavers. It was all reminiscent of 1828. The union insisted on negotiations, but none was offered and a 14-week strike of 500 workers ending in late May was the consequence. It narrowly missed involving Woodward Grosvenor. Later in the year Naylors got in on the act by refusing to pay recently agreed rates of pay to gripper Axminster weavers. Another strike was declared and averted only by the declaration of war on 3 September. The union backed down at the request of the government.[35] There is no doubt that industrial relations were very poor at the opening of the war. The breakdown of the paternalistic approach was illustrated by the termination of Brintons experiment with their social club at Spennells House. According to Melvyn Thompson the project was 'never really successful', and during the war it was to be taken over by a munitions company.[36]

# XI

# *War and Recovery*

During the Second World War Kidderminster lost 146 men and women, all killed on active service. In that respect the trauma was less than for the 1914-18 conflict, yet the effect upon the carpet industry was to be far greater. The collapse of the export market and difficulty in getting supplies caused the industry to go into steep decline. Many companies were already involved in munitions production when the government shut down the industry completely in early 1943. After the war Brintons led the recovery, but it was a slow process which was not completed until the 1950s.

By the end of 1939 the effects of the war on the town were already significant. These included rationing, the blackout, evacuees, identity cards and registration for military service. In October 317 young men between the ages of 18 and 21 registered under the National Service Act, which provided for the call-up of all fit men up to the age of 41. Employers were no longer free to recruit workers by their own efforts, but had to use an Employment Exchange or an approved trade union. Arrangements were made for the evacuation of children from urban areas thought to be at risk from air-raids. Kidderminster was twinned with Smethwick for this purpose and several hundred arrived by train in September to be billeted with local families. The feared air-raids did not happen and most had returned to Smethwick by February 1940.[1] Some of the old unoccupied mansions were taken over for the military effort. These included The Newlands in Franche Road, which had been the home of Alexander Hamilton until his death. Underground bunkers were installed at The Elms in Blakebrook and the house became known locally as 'Hush Hush House'. The bunkers were part of a network of such facilities designed to broadcast the spirit of resistance in the event of the Germans occupying the main broadcasting station in London.[2]

## WORKING WOMEN

In March 1941 the government sent Margaret Bondfield to Kidderminster to urge women to assist their country by working. Bondfield, who in 1929 had become the first woman cabinet member when appointed Minister of Labour by MacDonald, asked her audience of women in the Town Hall to 'place their services at the disposal of the Labour Exchange and to be ready to respond to anything'. She appealed to those living in 'nice little suburbs' like Hillgrove Crescent, Chester Road and Blakebrook to forget about paid work being undignified. She concluded by praising the efforts already made by local women: 'Last year Kidderminster showed the finest piece of organisation in her experience, when within 24 hours they got a thousand women transported from the carpet factories to a munitions factory to finish an urgent contract.'[3] A year later the local MP, Sir John Wardlaw-Milne, at a Town Hall meeting organised by the Ministry of Information, called for 500 women to take on factory work. The Ministry of Health asked the Borough Council to aid the effort by building at least two nurseries, each to accommodate 60 children. After making 'exhaustive enquiries' the council declined to do so. They could find few women who would use the facility. Married women had made their own arrangements for many years and the large expenditure would be unjustified. In any case it was unlikely that 'adequate staff' could be recruited. At least one mother of two disputed all this in a letter to the *Shuttle*. She had not been asked for her views and had not heard of anyone who had.[4]

One curiosity of life in the town during the war was the existence of a branch of the Russia Today Society. In December 1941 the secretary, Mrs Noel Gray, sought and obtained permission from the council to hold a picture and poster exhibition of life in Russia in the Museum and Art Gallery. The council's attention was already ominously directed towards traffic congestion in the Bull Ring. The Chief Constable attributed this in part to the presence of the Richard Baxter statue. For the time being the members were clear that the statue should not be removed. Council elections during wartime were suspended and the same meeting saw the council voting for a new member. Arthur Smith was duly elected, defeating Ernest Pearsall by ten votes to three.[5]

The war did not prevent the completion of plans made for two new secondary schools. On 1 October 1940 the Harry Cheshire and Sladen Church of England 'Modern Schools' opened in Habberley Road and Hurcott Road respectively. In its early days part of the former school was occupied by children from Clacton-on-Sea.[6] Nor did it prevent the already long-delayed measures to improve the sewage disposal system. The new works at Hoobrook and Oldington were complete by September 1942 and officially opened in July 1943. They served Kidderminster, Stourport and Bewdley. The winding up of the sewage disposal functions of the corporation lands based upon Birchen Coppice and Oldington farms was eventually to have tragic consequences. The long-serving manager, Mr G.F. Stones, committed suicide in December 1945, when he was found by his wife hanging in the foal yard at Manor Farm. He

76. Coventry Street School, the first School Board school. It was used for other purposes after the war, before being pulled down to allow the building of the Edward Parry Centre.

had been manager of the Corporation Farms since 1916 and prior to that he had assisted his father in the management since 1898. It was thought that he had become depressed by the difficult task of bringing back to its proper state land which was so surcharged with sewage that it had lost a great deal of its agricultural value.[7]

## FROM CARPETS TO MUNITIONS

At the outset of the war there was some hope that the carpet industry could be sustained at some level. Yet it was obvious that a luxury trade would struggle to survive in time of war, particularly as export markets were cut off. By June 1940 at least one local manufacturer, Roland Worth, was calling for the government to take over the carpet factories. A year later moves were made in that direction with a policy of 'concentration'. This involved confining production to certain selected firms and six Kidderminster companies were licensed for carpet production. The effect of the policy was not great because shortage of materials, particularly jute for backing, had already considerably reduced output. In early 1943, when the licences were withdrawn and the industry closed down, only 290 persons were still employed making carpets as against 10,760 in 1938.[8]

Kidderminster was now a military engineering town. Concern was such that unions and employers came together to form a Carpet Trade Reconstruction Committee which met for the first time in May 1943. The fortunes of local firms had varied. Brintons had been producing a range of products for four years, including gun mountings, bomb components and petrol containers. Tomkinsons contribution ranged from blankets and tarpaulins to aircraft fuel tanks and mortar bombs. Woodward Grosvenor, Jellymans and Victoria were other companies to be involved in this transformation of an industry. On the other hand Naylors had been closed down since October 1941.

Kidderminster was almost totally unaffected by air-raids, but there were several incidents. In November 1940 two bombs fell on Hoo Road one Sunday afternoon when a lone German plane flew over the town. One of the bombs dropped on The Copse, the 19th-century mansion built by the carpet manufacturer, Joseph Bowyer. Like many of the town's grand houses, it had in any case been derelict for some years and was falling into ruins. The other bomb dropped on tennis courts on the other side of the road, causing minor injuries to the occupants of the nearby converted vicarage. One night in December 1940 many incendiary bombs were dropped in the neighbourhood of Marlpool Lane. In May 1941 a more serious raid occurred on the western side of town, during which Harry Cheshire School was hit by high explosive bombs and Habberley Valley was set alight by incendiary bombs. In St John's Avenue 'Crantock', the home of leading Labour stalwart A.E. Meredith, was destroyed.[9]

## RECONSTRUCTION

Immediately after the war Kidderminster was, briefly, no longer a Tory town. The general election was held in July 1945 and the veteran socialist, Louis Tolley, defeated Sir John Wardlaw-Milne, who had held the seat since 1922. This was followed by victory for Labour in the November council elections. In the new council Labour had 17 votes to only seven for the Tories. The change was accompanied by some acrimony. In the campaign James Ferguson repeated his attack upon the Conservative housing record which he had made in the early years of the previous decade. He alleged that there was much dilapidated property that had not seen paint or repairs since the last war. A great deal of it was owned by Tory landlords, and some were on the council, though he did not name them.[10] The Tory campaign was unusual. A list was issued by Alderman F.D.H. Burcher containing 13 candidates named as Independent, Unionist or Anti-socialist. The group did not believe party politics should enter municipal affairs. In the end most stood as 'anti-socialist'.

The representation of carpet manufacturers on the council was beginning to wear thin. In the remaining years of the borough they were never to regain the dominant civic role of pre-war years. Instead, they had the major task in front of them of reconstructing their industry. Brintons recovered quickly and by

November 1946 they were exceeding pre-war production. The key to a speedy recovery may have been a question of whether premises had been requisitioned outright by the government. Jellymans, for example, took an advertisement in the *Shuttle* at the end of 1945 to reassure the public that their factory was 'NOT REQUISITIONED'. It was true that they had been entrusted with contracts for 9,400 gun mountings, but now a reasonable proportion of their textile machinery had been reinstated and a number of looms were in production. On the other hand Naylors had the Admiralty occupying their premises and they were slow to move out. Tomkinsons found it impossible to end their wartime activities and concentrate on making carpets until the end of 1946.[11]

Concern about the prospects for the carpet trade were so great that in January 1946 the President of the Board of Trade, Sir Stafford Cripps, met with the nation's carpet manufacturers and trade unions. The conference was held in Kidderminster, reflecting the town's standing as the leading centre for production. A working party was to be formed to lead the recovery. It was said that only 3,000 Kidderminster workers were employed in the industry as against 12,000 or 13,000 before the war. Sir Stafford and Lady Cripps visited the Mill Street factory of Carpet Trades Ltd. A hint of the way ahead for the industry was given by the report that Lady Cripps was interested in the new technology of 'moth-proof carpets of spun rayon', which it was claimed would 'have a life three times longer than the ordinary woollen carpet'.[12]

Requisitioned property was not simply handed back to the owners. In December 1945 the Ministry of Health placed a number of properties at the disposal of the council for housing purposes. These included The Newlands in Franche Road, The Hawthorns in Comberton Road, Yew Tree House (presumably that in Habberley Valley), Springfield House in Stourbridge Road and The Croft in Sutton Park Road. The owners wished to deal with the properties themselves, chiefly by converting them into flats. However, the council decided they would take them all over for conversion, with the exception of Springfield House which had already been divided into flats. In the event The Newlands was derequisitioned, and the owner, Mr A.H. Hipkiss, himself converted the mansion into five flats. On the other hand the council did proceed with the purchase of The Croft, which had been the home of Reginald Brinton until his death in 1942, and it was converted into a maternity home.[13]

## BIRCHEN COPPICE

The council had already embarked upon the building of the Birchen Coppice estate prior to Labour's victory in the local election. This was a project which would run for years and building was still continuing in 1953, by which time 590 houses had been completed. Partly due to shortage of manpower and materials, the slow pace of both council house construction and slum clearance was to be a feature of post-war Kidderminster. In 1948 the council found time to consider clearing rubble and debris from Queen Street and complete the clearance which had been interrupted in 1939 by the outbreak of war, but it was to be another five years before work started.

A development of some significance was the revival in 1946 of the Opera House on Comberton Hill as a place of live theatre. It had been closed since 1938 and had been used as a food store during the war. The purchaser was a group of amateur players called the Nonentities, which had been formed in 1937 by a talented Heightington farmer, Kenneth Rose. The price was £6,000, but refurbishment was to cost £18,816. The Arts Council gave a grant of £3,500 and the borough council loaned £1,500, but the Nonentities were in debt to the tune of £11,000. The Playhouse was in the news again in November 1951, when it was announced that the Nonentities were free from debt. This was no more than a book-keeping exercise undertaken because a council loan of £1,000 could be turned into a gift provided all liabilities were cleared. This rather lukewarm support from the council has always been a feature of the history of the Nonentities. By 1952 the debt was back in place. During these years the Playhouse combined both amateur and professional repertory. In 1952 the professional company included a young actor, John Osborne, who sat typing his play 'Look Back in Anger' when he was not on stage. Yet audiences were dwindling and in 1955 the theatre was forced to close down its regular professional work. The council responded by withdrawing its annual £500 grant.[14]

Kidderminster's experience of Labour rule was brief. In the 1947 local election the Conservatives took four seats from Labour, including the return of Tatton Brinton. That was the last November poll and the next election was in May 1949. By 1952 the Tories were back in control and four years later their majority was 18 to 10 seats. Labour never held power again on the borough council. Meanwhile at the general election of 1950 Gerald Nabarro regained the seat for the Tories, defeating Louis Tolley by 22,950 to 19,145 votes. He increased his majority in a further election called in October 1951. It was clear that Kidderminster remained a Tory town.

## SLUM CLEARANCE

Housing conditions continued to be very poor in Kidderminster's older streets. Bromsgrove Street contained well-built properties, but they were completely neglected by small-time landlords such as Bert Coates, who owned many of the houses in the area. The Coates family had been hairdressers in the town for many years. Coates waged a constant struggle to persuade tenants to open

77. No. 1 Arch Hill Square. This unusual house with its ogee window and gable was mentioned by Pevsner, who thought a date of *c*.1770 was likely. It became derelict in the post-war period.

78. Arch Hill Square: another view of the square and its listed buildings, taken in 1966.

their door to pay the rent. Repairs and improvements were rarely carried out. If tenants whitewashed their own walls, then some of the rent was waived. Three houses shared an outside toilet and everybody had a pot under their bed. Most houses relied upon gas lighting downstairs and candles upstairs. There was a slaughterhouse near to the Coventry Street junction, and houses there were plagued by bugs, flies, rats and mice. There were modest signs of progress in the 1950s. Some tenants started papering their walls, and by the time they were moved out in 1961 one or two people had inside toilets. The area was a distinct community with shops and public houses. Most of this was lost in the clearance, with the exception of the *Freemasons' Arms*, already known as the *Barrel* in the 1950s. This pub was once the meeting place for striking weavers in 1828, and Chartists in later years, but today it stands empty. The shops included a pawn shop, where children raised a few shillings on a Monday morning on the strength of their fathers' suits and shoes. Horse transport was still evident around this town centre area until the early 1950s. The Co-op had a small stable at the top of the steps leading from Worcester Street and their horse-drawn carts delivered bread and milk. Since the late 19th century Bantocks had been major carriers, based at the Marlborough Street and Oxford Street junction, and throughout that period their horse-drawn vehicles had transported goods to and from the carpet factories.

The post-war conditions of Bromsgrove Street showed the continuing struggle for many working-class people, despite the success of the carpet industry. This may be the key to understanding why there has been little evidence of pride in the old landscape and buildings of the town. The 1950s was a time when housing and amenities finally began to improve again. One remarkable man can recall this emergence from poverty, when it became possible to win the battle against filth, cold and degradation. Brian Smith, brought up in a Bromsgrove Street weaving family, learned that concern for health and fitness was not a waste of time. He took up weightlifting and succeeded to such an extent that he was mid-heavyweight British Strength Champion in 1963.

The long-established poverty of the north-east side of town became the focus of some attention in the 1950s. In 1953 work finally started on completing the clearing of Queen Street that was begun before the war in readiness for building council houses. It appears that the street had lain empty and rubble-strewn for 14 years. The *Shuttle* displayed a picture of the last house to be pulled down 'opposite the *New Inn*, against the wall of which it had been propped for years'. The houses to be built were 16 two-bedroom flats and eight three-bedroom houses using the 'Reema' method of construction. This involved the use of concrete panels transported to the site from the Reema factory on Hoo Road, and no bricks were needed at all. The concrete was required not just for the outside walls, but also the downstairs partitions, first-floor joists and ground floors. Already 100 such dwellings had been built on the new Franche estate.[15]

The appalling conditions in Chadwick Square, Clensmore, had been the subject of council scrutiny in 1950. The square comprised 22 houses at the north end of the warren of streets immediately to the west of Tomkinson's factory. They were home to more than a hundred people who shared five wash houses and ten primitive toilets. There were no baths or sinks in the properties. The landlord refused to carry out an order for repairs, and his lack of co-operation resulted in demolition in 1953. The residents were rehoused in the new Queen Street development. There were to be unfortunate consequences in the following year. Chadwick Square had been built 20 feet below the six late 18th-century almshouses funded by Sir Edward Blount's bequest, which stood across the top of Rackfields. In September 1954 a retaining wall left over from the clearing of the square collapsed. The soil slipped away leaving the almshouses perched two feet away from a precarious drop. The council were also giving attention to the early 19th-century houses of Broad Street. In

79. Pleasant Street 1959. By 1835 some of these houses had been built as an offshoot of Broad Street. Both streets were part of the slum clearance programme.

July 1954 they pondered a scheme for pulling down 89 houses and the *Albion* public house. This also envisaged the redevelopment of Pleasant Street and the allotments at the north-east end of Broad Street. The councillors wished to retain the *Woolpack Inn* and six almshouses, but they were not to survive. This was an early example of the council being unable to maintain a commitment to conservation in a redevelopment scheme.[16]

At this time the Baxter statue remained in the Bull Ring, even though in 1948 it was proposed to move it to the island at the junction of Worcester Road and Stourport Road. However, the council were gradually resorting to extreme measures to accommodate the demands of motor traffic. In the

80. **Blakebrook Drinking Fountain** *c*.1908, given to the town by Daniel Wagstaff Goodwin in 1884 and demolished by the town council in 1954.

autumn of 1954 the Blakebrook drinking fountain, presented to the town in 1884 by Daniel Wagstaff Goodwin, was pulled down in an extraordinarily crude attempt to deal with the dangerous junction between Blakebrook and Mason Road. Within weeks some councillors were arguing that nothing had been achieved. They had wanted a 'nice wide open road', but the road was as narrow as ever because of 'bulges' designed to slow traffic down.[17] Another dramatic change to this area at about the same time was the building of a new police station with 26 police houses on land on the north side of the junction. This was opened in May 1955 by the Home Secretary, Major Gwilym Lloyd George, on land cleared by the demolition of Blakebrook House.

## GREAT FLOOD

The continuing ability of the Stour to flood the town centre was dramatically revealed on Sunday 27 March 1955. There was no warning and no awareness of the calamity to come. Many tradesmen were away from their premises and had to be contacted by personal visits from the police. It was the worst flood since 1924 and certainly the worst recorded by the Callows Lane gauge in 25 years. On that Sunday morning the water rose to 60 inches above the gauge, more than double the previous record. The extraordinary lack of preparation was indicated by the *Shuttle*'s report that 'the causes are not at present clear'. A flood of some sort had been expected, and 'normal flood preparations had been taken on Saturday night, including extensive sandbagging'. It was assumed the flood would take its normal course by rising by 1½ to 2 inches per hour. However, between 3.45 a.m. and 4.30 a.m. it rose by a staggering 18 inches in Mill Street, which eventually had five feet of water covering it. The town bridge had nine inches of water on it and many of the leading carpet manufacturers were affected. Considerable damage to carpets was suffered by Carpet Trades Ltd at Mill Street and water came pouring out of Brintons 'like a river'. The torrent extended across to the Green Street factory of Chlidema Carpet Co. where 'water to a depth of two to three feet rushed through the works and did considerable damage'. Two cinemas were badly affected. In Mill Street the Grand had 10 feet of water in the front stalls and amongst its losses was a new Cinemascope screen. In Vicar Street the Futurist took in eight feet of water and was contemplating the replacement of 500 seats. Insurance could not compensate for some of the destruction sustained by the library. 'The newly made archive, in which all the old records of Kidderminster were stored, was completely flooded and many old historical documents have been reduced to a pulpy mess.'[18]

## GOOD TIMES

It has been said that 'in the mid-1950s Kidderminster was a good place to live and work. The town was rich and prosperous, and in the carpet industry things had never been better.'[19] This has to be seen in perspective. Certainly membership of the weavers' union reached a peak in 1954 at 5,243, but this was only just over the number they recorded in the pre-war years. Whilst the prosperity of the carpet trade would have stimulated the general economy of the town, it may well have been that there was a substantial part of the working class which was not directly benefiting. If we look at housing as an indicator of quality of life, for another twenty years at least public enquiries would reveal very poor conditions in the town. There was also an ever-present fear that any boom would be followed by a downturn, and the weavers' union was definitely cautious. The increased demand caused a backlog of outstanding orders for Wilton in the early 1950s due to a shortage of qualified weavers, but the union refused to relax the rule concerning the minimum age of 21 for the occupation of a Jacquard loom.[20]

The carpet industry was being boosted by the house-building programme which had gathered pace from 1948 onwards.[21] This was reflected in Kidderminster, particularly in the council house programme of the mid-1950s. During these years the long period of construction of Birchen Coppice estate reached its conclusion, and the school for 340 children was opened in October 1952. By June 1952 the Franche estate was underway and 50 houses were completed. This figure had risen to 240 by April 1955. The development included the Franche County Primary School, which was officially opened in May 1955 for the education of 320 children. The massive Comberton estate grew more quickly. In April 1953 16 houses had been started and two years later 573 were finished. Nevertheless, the council house programme was not without its problems. There was uproar and accusations of 'betrayal' in 1954 when the plans for the Habberley estate were severely reduced from 600 to 200 homes, and all were to be of the non-traditional type. The penny-pinching caused havoc in 1957 when in the middle of a winter's night many families had to be evacuated from homes on the Birchen Coppice estate after snow entered roof spaces and brought bedroom ceilings down. The whole of one side of Kinver Avenue was affected. It was revealed that when the houses were built just after the war the torching of roofs was omitted to bring the cost down to Ministry requirements.[22]

## TUFTED CARPETS

By the mid-1950s Axminster and Wilton carpets were the dominant British products. The output of Chenille and Tapestry carpets was under 20 per cent of pre-war levels in 1957. Wool remained the standard material used for yarn. However, the use of man-made fibres and a new tufting process was gaining ground in America. Inevitably manufacturers in Kidderminster began to respond. Eventually the industry would be transformed and the traditional weaving techniques for producing a carpet would give way, more or less completely, to that of tufting. In weaving a carpet, the backing is woven on the loom and the pile is secured in it at the same time. In tufting, a ready-made backing is used and the pile is inserted at a rapid rate by a large number of needles. The first Kidderminster company to commit to tufting was Empire Carpets Ltd at its Foley Park factory in May 1956. The new process strengthened the demand for female labour in the industry. The new loom was designed for operation by two

81. Royal Visit 1957: the royal car taking the Queen and Duke of Edinburgh away from the reception in the Music Room to the railway station.

82. The Music Room looking immaculate after redecoration for the royal visit.

girl weavers, a tufting machine mechanic and one girl mender. In the same year Brintons and Bond Worth joined a tufting consortium called Kosset carpets. Very soon advertisements were claiming 'everybody loves a Kosset carpet'. The new man-made fibres were extra tough and moth-proof, cleaning them was very simple and the carpets were a 'new low-cost luxury'.[23]

It is likely that the necessary transition led to an uneasy period for the town. Membership of the carpet weavers' union went down from 5,243 in 1954 to 4,695 in 1957. Then the figure rose gradually, but it was not until 1963 that the 1954 total was surpassed. Certainly the end of year messages for 1956 in the *Shuttle* were sombre and the Mayor, Louis Tolley, hoped for better times. Early the following year local MP, Gerald Nabarro, complained about the dumping of cheap Belgian carpets, but by the end of 1957 the *Shuttle* was able to report on a 'better year for the carpet industry'. These were the years of Harold Macmillan's premiership, and he visited Kidderminster in the autumn of 1958, when he impressed the farmers and toured Brintons.[24] He once famously asserted that 'most of our people have never had it so good', but Kidderminster's best years probably lay ahead.

Traditionally leading carpet manufacturers had been very influential on the town council since its creation in 1834. This had continued up to the Second World War. It is noticeable after the war that their representation dwindled considerably. By 1958 only two members of the 28-strong council, Tatton Brinton and George Rainsford, were carpet manufacturers. Tory interests were also represented by industrialists such as Sir George Eddy and F.D.H. Burcher, a chemical manufacturer and director of an engineering firm respectively. There were three solicitors: Frederick Adams, John Ellis Talbot and William Percy Hill. Two other notable Tories, Arthur Dudley and Alfred Humphries, were builders. The broader interests involved led to a concern that the borough should be less dependent upon the carpet industry, and accordingly, in February 1959, it was agreed to create the Stourport Road trading estate for this purpose. The first factory to be opened there was that of Henry Beakbane in January 1961.


## BROAD STREET PROBLEMS

The periods of prosperity in the carpet industry in the 1950s through into the next decade could not conceal that there were still social problems in Kidderminster. This was graphically illustrated by the controversy which erupted in 1957 prior to the redevelopment of the lower end of Broad Street. Labour councillors were furious when they heard that the proposed houses would cost £2,100 each as against £1,400 for houses being erected at Habberley. Alderman Burcher explained that the Broad Street houses were 'designed to meet the needs of problem families and were to be provided with concrete floors and stairs and tiled skirtings … This form of construction would prove economical in the long run as otherwise the houses would be liable to suffer considerable damage'. Cllr Ricketts was incredulous at the idea 'that these families will tear up wooded floors and burn them!' The first five-storey block was eventually opened in November 1959.[25]

Other development during the decade included the new College of Further Education at Aggborough under the county education authority. Building commenced in September 1952, but classes did not move there until 1955. This represented a reorganisation of the work which had previously taken place at the School of Science and Art in Market Street. However, the transfer of classes was a gradual process and some continued to be held at the old school for 10 years.[26] The crisis about what to do with the historic buildings was thus postponed. Market Street was undergoing major change and very soon the cattle market was to leave for a new site off Comberton Hill close to the station. The project was subject to the delay which inevitably seemed to afflict Kidderminster schemes. The new site had already been cleared when work was shelved in early 1956 because a loan was unavailable. A resumption was made in 1957 and the new market opened in September 1959. The old site was used for a car park thereafter, although the highly unusual manager's house survived and has been occupied for many years by the Royal Air Force Association. Another development was the completion of the King Charles I room in the Town Hall, which was opened by the Duke and Duchess of Gloucester on 27 October 1959.

In 1958 the Kidderminster motor racing driver Peter Collins was killed in the German Grand Prix. He had been lying third in the world championship at the time. Also at the beginning of that year the world's only recorded centenarian sisters, Carrie and Jane Badland, died within 11 days of each other. They had lived together at Short Heath, 29 Comberton Road, for over 90 years and had been presented to the Queen and the Duke of Edinburgh on their visit to the town in 1957. They had been committed members of the congregation of New Meeting church and their deaths were a sign of the closing of an era. Many of the town's churches were struggling to maintain attendances and were a declining part of local social life. Another sign of change in the pattern of social life was the closing of the Grand cinema in Mill Street in February 1959.

TRIUMPH OF FLOOD PRECAUTIONS

After two days of torrential rain serious flooding again hit Kidderminster on Monday 25 January 1960. This time the damage was far less than in 1955, even though the water rose to within a few inches of the level which had caused so much havoc. This was hailed as a 'triumph' for the modest precautions taken.

Readings of the Callows Lane gauge were taken during the course of the weekend and information was sought from upstream at Stourbridge, Stourton, Kinver and Cookley. The authorities were then able to warn property owners of the impending flood, and they had time to do what they could to safeguard their goods. The Carpet Trades works in Mill Street was again badly affected. At one point they had two feet of water in certain parts of the factory. Brintons was also flooded again, but this time Green Street escaped lightly, probably due to changes to the weir at Greatwich Ltd since 1955.[27]

The changes faced by Kidderminster in the post-war period were nothing compared with what was to come. The traffic congestion in the town centre had not been dealt with, but by 1956 the council was planning a ring road. A period of relentless redevelopment spread over more than four decades was in store, by the end of which Kidderminster would be virtually unrecognisable and many of its finest buildings would be pulled down. Protest would be muted and would be brushed aside by the power of the developers, who would not meet with such resistance as they encountered in an extraordinary incident in March 1958 at Blakebrook. Messrs Bridges and Grove purchased The Cedars in 1956 and intended to build 20 houses on the land around and behind the house. They engaged a firm to cut down trees that were in the way and attempts were made to start felling. However, they had reckoned without a redoubtable resident of Blakebrook who climbed over a fence to resist the efforts to cut down the trees. This culminated in Messrs Bridges and Grove calling their solicitor, John Ellis Talbot, to the scene. He was met by Mrs Margaret Jordan 'dressed for battle' wearing trousers and carrying a first-aid kit. She forced her way past the solicitor, clambered up the tree and challenged the men to cut it down. The publicity quickly persuaded the council to obtain a Tree Preservation Order and only two trees were lost, one being rotten and the other 'felled as a genuine mistake'. Nevertheless the developers and their solicitor did not admit defeat with dignity. In January 1958 Mrs Jordan found herself in the County Court facing claims for damages for trespass and assault and battery. She denied 'shoulder-charging' Talbot, but the judge was displeased that she was not sorry and 'was more proud of what she had done'. Even though there had been no physical injury to Talbot and only a slight delay was caused for the developers, the judge felt that the matter was not trivial because Mrs Jordan's actions had been 'deliberate' and 'insulting'. He awarded Talbot 100 guineas and costs, while Bridges and Grove received £50.[28] The episode was a warning that the forces of the law would be intolerant of any who tried to interfere with the requirements of development.

# XII

# *Permanent Redevelopment*

In matters of planning it is often true that the authorities get away with murder because most of us do not care enough at the time. We look around us some years later and find that our town has lost its character. A few see what is coming and fight an unequal battle against what they are always told is 'progress'. Thus it was that Mrs Elizabeth Chambers and Dr James Craig found themselves struggling to save their property at a public enquiry in April 1959 into the council's plan to pull down the historic buildings of Hall Street, and some of those in Church Street, in preparation for the first stage of the Ring Road. There was only one other objector to the scheme, Mr Frank Coates, owner of nos. 11 to 18 Hall Street, and he objected not to the principle of demolition of his properties, but to their compulsory purchase. He wished to redevelop the land himself. The council had once spoken of the need for conser-

83. No. 2 Hall Street, once the home of the Rev. Price's mother and later the Kidderminster Savings Bank.

vation of the almshouses and houses adjoining in Church Street, but such promises were now abandoned. They were proposing to build a car park on the site cleared by pulling down the north side of Hall Street and three courts which lay behind. One of these courts had been identified for demolition in 1933 as part of the slum clearance programme. The Borough Surveyor said that the area had a 'very limited claim to be of architectural interest', which sidestepped the historical significance of Hall Street,

181

the one completed part of the 1753 plan. His assessment did no justice to the almshouses and the dignified masters' houses forming 17-21 Church Street, where Dr Craig lived, nor to the fine home of Mrs Chambers at 2 Hall Street. The council embroidered the decision to destroy these houses with an elevated purpose. The deputy Town Clerk solemnly told the enquiry that the council felt 'that this was an opportunity, which will only come once, and ought to be taken, to open up the view of the Parish Church'.[1]

## NEW VISTA OF PARISH CHURCH

Dr Craig lived at 17 Church Street, which he described as 'one of the few remaining town houses in Church Street, the only street of "town houses" in Kidderminster'. Mrs Chambers was 87 years old and she said the house had served the needs of her family for over 100 years. She thought a better way of dealing with the traffic problem would be to have a bypass further out. The dismissal of their claims was a prelude to decades of destruction of Kidderminster's historic central streets. The first stage of the destruction was the demolition of nos. 5 to 18 on the north side of Hall Street in February 1961.[2] This terraced range of houses, carefully built up the sharp slope in pairs, with their attics and railed pavement, were described in the *Shuttle* as 'slum property'. The benefit of the 'new vista of the ancient parish church' was still

84. Church Street 1959: the almshouses and grammar school houses which had to make way for the ring road.

being claimed, apparently without irony, even though it was planned to place a ring road between the town and the church in due course.

The home of the Chambers family survived until 1965, by which time Mrs Chambers had probably died. The adjacent Church Street almshouses were undoubtedly lost at the same time, as was Dr Craig's property at nos. 17 and 18. These would have been sad days for Dr Craig, who had been Kidderminster's part-time Medical Officer of Health from 1922 until 1947, when it became a full-time position. His point about the lack of town houses was emphasised by the electoral register of 1968 which listed no one at all in Church Street. He was a pillar of the Church Street community, having organised the 'peace and good neighbourhood' midsummer suppers for over twenty years before his death in January 1969 at the age of 82.[3] During that time he had been secretary of the Brecknell's Charity under which the suppers were held and are still held today. Construction of the first stage of the Inner Ring Road began with clearance work in Dudley Street in August 1965. The south side of Hall Street, containing a row similar to that removed on the other side, was taken down leaving only the *Royal George* public house. It stood in isolation until 1973, when it yielded to the inevitable closure. The first stage of the ring road was opened in May 1967. This extended from Mill Street round to the Birmingham Road. The route cut off St Mary's church from the town and put paid to those newly created vistas. This was noted by Pevsner, who described it as a 'crying-out crime against the town'.[4]

## MODERNITY

During the 1960s, of course, Kidderminster was in part doing no more than following the fashion for bright new structures. It was also doing no more than responding to the pressures experienced by many towns of dealing with motor traffic. This latter problem was arguably particularly acute in Kidderminster because so many main roads meet there. In 1961, in order to meet the crisis, the council decided to delegate the planning of the work needed to a specially created redevelopment committee. This consisted of three senior members from each the two main political parties. The committee was not simply concerned with seeing through the ring road: three other projects were specified as requiring attention. The first was the widening of the Bull Ring and the provision of rear access to the properties on the west side of Vicar Street. The second was to provide a modern shopping area north of the High Street. The third was redevelopment of the cattle market site.

The pages of the *Shuttle* during the following years often carried impressive pictures of planned buildings, whose crisp outlines must have presented a pleasing contrast to some of the town's neglected old buildings. One particular example was a proposal to replace the Dr Barnardo's home at Spennells House, former home of John Broom II. The modern structure was complete by December 1965, and a *Shuttle* reporter commented that the many concrete pillars reminded him of 'Cape Kennedy on a busy day'.[5] The hopes for the future were short-lived and the space-age Dr Barnardo's has itself been replaced by a housing development. These were not good years for the heritage of the Broom family. The magnificent Broomfield Hall, built around 1809 on the lower Franche Road by John Broom III, was pulled down in late 1962 to be replaced by The Patios. Yet it was a listed building. Other visions of the future included planned new offices at Tomkinsons, who had acquired land opposite their main entrance at Duke Place. By February 1964 site preparation had been proceeding for a year and the company were able to conclude a deal with the council for the sale of their existing offices, which formed most of the west side of Church Street. In September of that year the *Shuttle* featured an artist's impression of the Hoobrook high-rise blocks, to be built by Tarmac Buildings Ltd for £40,000, looking clean and neat. Work was to start later that month and take 19 months to complete. A further example was a picture in March 1965 of the three-storey Tesco store to be built in Worcester Street. It was shown forming a sharp and strong contrast with the older buildings, from which it was set back, creating a wider street.[6]

Yet there were some who questioned the changes. Prominent among them was Mr E.A. Cookson, one of the leaders of the Kidderminster Retail Traders' Association. In 1964, at their annual dinner, he warned that modernisation was robbing Kidderminster of its character, and that it was becoming a town of 'glass and steel boxes' like every other town. The following year he added to his criticisms by remarking that outsiders regarded Kidderminster as a 'dirty little town' which had never been in such a 'filthy and disreputable condition'. This was a recurring theme of those years. It was not so much a criticism of the changes themselves, but of their consequences. Paradoxically it was frequently suggested that the scale of the redevelopment was such that small developments could not take place. Individual property owners or builders would often have planning permission refused because the council always had other plans for the area. In this way many buildings fell into decay and disrepair. For example, in 1964 the Witnell's Alms and Clare's Charities were unable to proceed with new almshouses near to Dudley Street, because of plans not just for the ring road, but for a new Town Hall and swimming baths in Hall Street and the Horsefair. There was some surprise at the plans for these facilities and they were described by the estate agent Stanley Cattell as 'just an artist's dream'. In 1965 similar complaints were made at the annual dinner of the Kidderminster branch of the Retail Newsagents Federation. Their president, Charles Fryar, also complained that the council would too often give only a nominal sum for property purchased compulsorily. The only way back into business was to pay a high rent. His remarks matched those of Cookson who regretted that there was only one retail trader on the council. He was concerned that Tesco had obtained planning permission for their Worcester Street store 'without any difficulty' and expressed the hope that small businesses would be catered for adequately and be able to take their places alongside the big stores.[7]

## RING ROAD

In general, however, there was no substantial opposition to the transformation of the town. A typical view was that of the Mayor in 1964, Cllr Robert Oakley, who stated that 'Kidderminster was an old town and everyone agreed that it needed a drastic face lift'. There was very little pride in the older buildings of the town and very little concern about the ring road, although in early 1966 the *Kidderminster Times* did issue a warning:

> The inner ring road may yet strangle Kidderminster … It could become the means of motorists by-passing the town to get to neighbouring places where there is better entertainment and comfortable licensed hotels … There surely cannot be as many places as large as Kidderminster so lacking in hotel accommodation … We can only wonder at man's monster and pet – the motor car – running our lives to the extent that everybody apparently must be subordinated to its demands.[8]

The council themselves seem to have experienced few doubts about the ring road or any of the other major developments of this period. Their confidence in the steps they were taking to resolve the traffic problems was no doubt eased by the fact that they had to pay only ten per cent of the cost of the ring road. The rest was met by the county council and the government. In January 1966 the route for the remainder of the ring road was agreed. Obvious casualties were to be the *Black Horse Hotel* in Mill Street and The Playhouse theatre. The long section from Worcester Road island to Bewdley Road, which was destined never to be built, would have destroyed the fine terraced houses of Park Street and also taken a slice out of the cemetery. It was expected that the disturbance of a number of graves would rouse some opposition in the town, but this never materialised. Nothing was sacred, except perhaps the carpet industry. The original thinking was to take the ring road through the Green Street area, causing disruption to firms such as Woodward Grosvenor. However, the final plan took the road over the hill at the back of Green Street, leaving the carpet factories unscathed, but requiring considerable construction work.[9]

## LISTED BUILDINGS

The council's lack of pride in the old buildings of the town had been clearly shown in 1952 by their opposition to the proposed listing of many buildings.[10] Even at that early stage they wanted to ensure that no listed building would

85. *Bell Hotel*, Coventry Street. Built in the late 18th century, this inn was listed in 1953 as a building of outstanding historical or architectural interest. It was nevertheless carefully dismantled in the late 1960s, leaving adjoining buildings intact.

inhibit development. Subsequent events showed that they need not have worried. Redevelopment severely reduced the ranks of listed buildings in Kidderminster. Broomfield Hall was Grade II, as was Mrs Chambers' home in Hall Street. Time was running out for the three surviving inns of special historic interest out of the four listed in 1953.[11] The *Lion Hotel* was waiting for demolition in February 1965 to be replaced by a new Woolworths, which was not complete until nearly four years later. Part of the hotel was occupied by the National Provincial Bank and, in order to accommodate the bank, the High Street entrance to the Retail Market, itself Grade III, was demolished in 1965. The *Fox Inn* in Swan Street had a long wait for demolition. It had closed in March 1960 and lay empty for years before demolition work started in 1968 in preparation for building the Swan Centre. Finally, the *Bell Hotel* in Coventry Street was acquired for redevelopment in 1968.[12]

Many of the town's listed buildings were of the now obsolete category Grade III. They were buildings of 'some importance' and, had they survived, many would have been reclassified as Grade II. The impunity with which the council treated this category was shown in a curious episode involving Ald. David Samuel in February 1968. He had been a leading member of the Redevelopment Committee from the beginning and had never previously shown any hesitation in supporting the widespread demolition programme. However, on this occasion the *Shuttle* reported him as making a 'moving plea' to save the picturesque Arch Hill Square. This was not unreasonable given that nos. 1 to 7 were Grade III listed buildings. Unfortunately, their condition was poor. Much of the internal woodwork of no. 1 had been removed and cut up by Mabel Payne, who had lived there in poverty after her father died. Samuel's proposal was greeted with cries of derision from other members of the council. Ald. W. S. Carter described his suggestion as 'ridiculous' and went on to say 'the place was a slum'. Cllr J.S. Perrin said the square was not the 'jewel' it was thought to be. The plea was decisively rejected.[13]

## TOWN CENTRE 1965-69

The town centre changed beyond all recognition in the latter part of the 1960s. The unstoppable momentum of change was such that it was as if nothing at all amidst the network of Kidderminster's historic streets was worth saving. A bustling and varied urban landscape was to be transformed into an environment dominated by the activity of shopping. Much of the planning was directed at opening out the narrow thoroughfares with tall Georgian or Victorian frontages. In 1965, before work started on the first stage of the ring road, the Bull Ring began to be altered in this way with the demolition of the old premises of Attwoods clothing store, which had stood there for at least a century. Its frontage had been in line with that of the High Street shops, but the new building, which is now occupied by T.J. Hughes, was set back. A public house called the *Golden Lion* had once stood there and from at least 1810 had been incorporated in a drapery store. It had been an inn of some distinction because many meetings are recorded there, including the Annual Friendly Meeting

86. Attwood's *c*.1910. Situated at the junction of the Bull Ring and Vicar Street, it was another casualty of 1960s redevelopment.

87. New Meeting School: a 19th-century picture of the school pulled down for the Swan Centre.

88. Harvey & Co., Swan Street. Pictured c.1905, these premises and their large cellars were lost to the Swan Centre development.

of the Gentlemen of the County in 1754. As demolition began, the *Shuttle* recorded that the old beer ramps where the beer was stored still remained in the cellars.[14] The transformation continued when the Richard Baxter statue was finally removed in March 1967, after decades of pressure from those who argued that it contributed to traffic congestion. Ironically, only five years later pedestrianisation put an end to through-traffic in any case. The developments of the Swan Centre and Crown House took down three Grade III listed buildings and completed the virtual destruction of the historic Bull Ring.

The massive construction project of the Swan Centre required the loss of much more. Work began in 1968, and in that year the raising of the western carriageway in Blackwell Street was finally completed, over thirty years since the promise given to James Towers. As part of this project the Kidderminster Brewery buildings and the *Black Star* pub were pulled down to be replaced by the town's first multi-storey car park, which was opened in October 1969. From there round to the Bull Ring everything was flattened. The losses included a row in Coventry Street with very fine frontages, all of Swan Street, which ceased to exist, and the tall buildings on the east side of the Bull Ring. Behind the latter, and also doomed, was the historic New Meeting School, the closure of which had been confirmed in 1965. The entire block lying between Swan Street and High Street also had to go, and this included Richard Baxter's house.

Among the history lost forever were the vaults at Harvey's at the top of Swan Street. A final opportunity to examine them was given prior to the demolition in 1968. Legends used to abound concerning these vaults, including the existence of a supposed Saxon chapel or a secret passage running between them and the parish church. No such passage was found, although the leader of the emergency excavations, Ian Walker, did consider that in view of the shape of some of the window openings it was 'more likely that the building was at some time used for religious purposes than it was not'. No graves were found under the floor. A spiral staircase, probably of Tudor date, was discovered, as was another floor 15 inches below the existing one.[15]

At this time Pevsner wrote of Vicar Street that it was 'where properties have a more cityish scale than elsewhere'. Yet although the work here was directed at pulling down the muddle of buildings between the rear of premises and the Stour, the frontages were being affected. In particular the complex known as Kingsley Buildings was removed in work which was underway in November 1968. This included the former Futurist Cinema which had closed in June 1962. Also removed was the fine house which had once formed part of the Barton factory complex.

In the background to this activity was the continuing devastation wrought by the ring road. The perverse planning, which had enabled stage I to cut off St Mary's from the town centre, had also destroyed half of St George's Park,

89. Vicar Street 1933. The majestic three-storey house shown here had formed part of Barton's carpet factory in the second half of the 18th century.

leaving the remainder similarly cut off from the town. It was an example of gratitude for a gift to the town to equal that shown by the destruction of Daniel Goodwin's drinking fountain. There was now no genuine town centre park. The council, presumably inadvertently, was creating a situation where there was little reason for people to linger or walk in the town centre once they had completed their shopping. In 1969 demolition was well in hand for stage II of the ring road. This included large parts of Anchorfields and George Street, and the mission church of St Andrew in South Street. The area around the junction of Hoo Road with Comberton Hill was seriously affected, and the *Worcester Cross Hotel* and the *Leopard Inn* were among the losses here. Gradually the town was having its life drained away. A shopping centre was replacing a town where people lived, stayed, drank or were entertained. Houses, hotels and public houses were being lost and the ABC was the only cinema left in town. This transformation was symbolised by the lingering decline and eventual sacrifice to the ring road of the Playhouse theatre, whose story says so much about Kidderminster.

## THE LAST YEARS OF THE PLAYHOUSE

The final years in the life of Kidderminster's only theatre saw heroic efforts by the Nonentities and their chairman, Kenneth Rose, to sustain live theatre in the town. Even though they had reduced their repertory to three months in the year audiences were poor. In January 1964 Rose adopted shock tactics by taking out whole-page advertisements in the local press carrying a 'warning' that the theatre would close in the following May unless more support was forthcoming. The wording was deliberately provocative and included a criticism of the local council for inadequate grant aid. Although the theatre was able to struggle on, less than three years later Rose was referring to the determination shown by Kidderminster 'to stay at home twiddling television knobs when it cannot claim kinship with anyone across the footlights'. The *Shuttle* made a similar point in 1967: 'The only times in the year the Playhouse seems really full is when as many children as possible crowd the stage, and their mothers, sisters and their cousins and their aunts pack the house.'[16]

The final years were also a story of continuous sparring between Rose and a council which could never quite bring itself to support the theatre effectively. It was a conflict that was to be replayed at the end of the century. The Nonentities have been reluctant proprietors of a theatre, seeing themselves first and foremost as a performing theatre company. It was Kenneth Rose's plan that the theatre should belong to the people of Kidderminster, but councillors were weak in their commitment and sometimes hostile to any plan to preserve or develop the Playhouse. Rose's controversial tactics occasionally gave them a perfect excuse for negativity. Nevertheless, the initial response to Rose's 1964 warning was encouraging. The secretary of Kidderminster Trades Council, Cyril Yarsley, said that it would be a sad day 'if we lose these vestiges of culture'. He was also secretary of the Carpet Weavers' Association, which voted to donate £100. It was true, on the other hand, that politicians were not so supportive. The Conservative MP, Gerald Nabarro, thought it was 'very dubious' that the town could support a theatre. The sensitivities of Labour councillor Bill Micklewright had been strained and he complained that the Playhouse had 'insulted' people. However, by March the doubts seemed to have been set aside and the theatre saved. The council voted to buy the theatre for £25,000. There would be an initial grant of £3,500 for the year 1964/5, which would be followed by four instalments until the completion of purchase in 1969. It was a narrow vote of 14 to 11, and it succeeded despite the opposition of most of the largest party, the Conservatives, because two of their number were in favour. Ald. Burcher warned against taking over a 'derelict and bankrupt enterprise'. Cllr K. Tomkinson said that Kidderminster had failed to support the theatre in the past and it would be unwise 'to buy an old building which was ready for demolition'. He reminded the council that their finance committee advised against the purchase. As a victory, therefore, it was less than convincing and time was to tell that it was a hollow one.

A draft contract for the purchase of the theatre was drawn up and then apparently consigned to the drawer of the Town Clerk, John Evans, for some considerable time. Matters came to a head in January 1966 when the agreed route for the ring road was announced. It was evident that in the intervening period the council had had second thoughts about the line to be taken by the road. Instead of going through the Worcester Cross factory of Woodward Grosvenor, the road now went through the Playhouse. As the council put it at the subsequent public enquiry: 'This was the dilemma, the town's staple industry or the Playhouse'.[17] Rose responded with programme notes headed 'Honour in Danger', in which he demanded that the council honoured its agreement to buy the theatre and then either save it or build a new one. This did not please councillors, who threatened to withdraw grant money unless they received an apology. The Town Clerk rejected the 'wild ranting' of Rose. Cllr George Dance remarked that 'all we get is this stream of insolence'. Cllr B. W. Smith was just as upset, saying 'he has continually insulted us'. Under pressure from the executive committee of the Nonentities, Rose was persuaded to issue the required apology.

The extraordinary drama being played out by the council and the Playhouse continued with the death of Ald. Sir George Eddy immediately following his collapse on stage in April 1967. He had just finished a speech after the final performance of 'The King and I'. He was seen to be ill and asked for a chair. A member of the cast supported him as the curtain came down. He was rushed to hospital, but was found to be dead on arrival. The four-times former Mayor of Kidderminster was 88 years old. He had joined the firm of Hepworth Ltd as a clerk and had eventually become its owner. According to the *Shuttle*, he expanded the company into 'one of the most successful chemical manufacturing concerns in the Midlands.' Among his gifts to the town were a nurses home at Stanmore House on Chester Road, the old pals' shelter in Brinton Park and electric bell-ringing apparatus at St Mary's church. He was renowned for small acts of generosity. For years he visited the hospital every morning and there he distributed sweets, newspapers and silver coins. In his will he left sums of money to be shared by journalists who had reported his speeches. His final speech contained a mystery, for he gave an 'assurance that the Playhouse would continue.'[18]

In fact a new Playhouse to replace the doomed theatre looked no more than a far-off possibility. Negotiations for its purchase by the council were broken off by July 1967, because the District Valuer was prepared to offer only £30,000, which was totally inadequate for the building of a new theatre. The Playhouse was to be the subject instead of a Compulsory Purchase Order and only a site value would be paid to the Nonentities. This forced them to go to a Land Tribunal in order to seek compensation which would enable them to build a new theatre. An award was by no means a foregone conclusion, as the accepted procedure at the time was to pay only site value. However, the council showed goodwill in July 1967, voting by a substantial majority to put £50,000 towards a new theatre, subject to reconsideration in the light of the Land Tribunal award. Cllr John Cotterell felt that the town's cultural heritage was in question and the theatre was more important than the ring road. Cllr R.A. Ricketts asked if they were 'going to have a town of supermarkets with no culture at all'.

The soap opera starring the council and the Playhouse continued to run until the final curtain. The last play to be performed was 'Gloriana', which had been written by Rose himself 25 years previously. So many people wanted to attend the last performance that the seats were allocated by ballot. The council were not invited. Rose commented: 'What have we to thank the Borough Council for? For knocking us down? For cutting off our grants when we needed them most?' For good measure Rose told the Mayor, Cllr Harry Purcell, who was a member of the Nonentities, that he would have to remove his chain of office if he wanted to come on stage at the end with everybody else. The Town Clerk, John Evans, described this as an 'insult' to the Mayor, and the result was a boycott of the final showing by the council and its officers. In their absence, an epilogue on the theatre's work was spoken by Ruth Dalley, who had spoken the original prologue when the theatre had opened in 1946. In January 1969 the Playhouse was reduced to rubble, and the *Shuttle* commented that 'many will be pleased'.[19] One commentator suggested it had been 'loved by few and ridiculed by many'. A letter from D.M.L. Smith of Far Forest challenged this view. The theatre had been 'an Edwardian gem and beautifully preserved' and 'known to be coveted by the citizens of some of Kidderminster's more enlightened neighbours'. Another commentator said: 'Only a local authority with little feeling for its past and even less for the social life of a theatre would decide to drive a road over the site of Kidderminster Playhouse.'

## A NEW IMAGE

The image of Kidderminster as an old manufacturing town was being shed and other familiar landmarks were being lost. In early 1968 the huge Pike Mills factory was pulled down. At the same time the town's Victorian railway station building was also demolished. British Rail officials declared that the building was unsafe and should be taken down. They wasted no time and work started a month later. Although the *Shuttle* was moved to describe the black and white structure as 'famous', nobody protested.[20] The town centre also continued to lose its resident population. Traditional family shops with living accommodation above were being replaced by chain stores, whose managers and employees went away to their own homes after work. This trend was evident in Worcester Street, where Woolworths and Tesco were built on either side of a three-storey building containing ground-floor shops and *The Grapes* public house. By November 1971 a vacant site was created where Littlewoods was to be built. All three modern stores were set several feet back from the old building line, thus widening the road. Above them the residential area centred around Bromsgrove Street had been cleared and was awaiting redevelopment. The town centre was now primarily designed for shopping, as exemplified by the Swan

90. *Lion Hotel* 1967: awaiting demolition after being closed for four years. The lion on top of the porch had already disappeared.

Centre, which was opened on 31 October 1970.

Development of estates on the outskirts of town was essential if enough homes were to be provided. In March 1964 a public enquiry found in favour of Whitbread build-ers who wished to develop allotment land east of Marl-pool Lane. They had claimed that there was an astonishing and unprecedented shortage of building land in the town. By 1966 Willowfield Drive was built, and the estate grew

91. Rack Hill, Orchard Street 1970: another drawing by Miss M. Robinson, who documented the rapidly disappearing townscape.

during the next two years. Much development at this time centred around the Franche side of town. In 1965 houses were for sale on the Franche Park estate in Wolverley Road. In the same year the Habberley View estate was com-menced on the corner of Habberley Lane and Habberley Road. This consisted of 98 houses with oil-fired Swedish-style warm air heating. The Mayor, Ruth Chamberlain, commented that 'central heating is no longer regarded as a luxury, it is within everyone's range'. In 1965 the Ferndale estate in Franche was taking shape with the construction of Ferndale Crescent. Within the next two years Coningsby Drive and then Audley Drive were built. In the latter part of the decade Puxton House and Puxton Farm were sold and demolished, opening up the area for the extension of Willowfield Drive and the building of Puxton Drive. These years saw the complete transformation of the historic community of Puxton. Many centuries of farming drew to a close and the farm buildings, instead of forming a feature of the new community, were obliterated as if they had never existed.

One of the further effects of a declining population in the town centre was an even greater struggle for a church to retain its congregation. The Baptist Church in Church Street closed in March 1970 and was pulled down three months later. By this time the remaining housing in the neighbourhood was being destroyed. The demolition of Arch Hill and its listed buildings began in February 1970. The Baptists relocated to the Franche Road, where the new church opened in May 1971. Also relocated to Franche were the Witnell and Clare Almshouses, which found a site in Wilton Avenue. As the *Shuttle* put it in 1970, 'a town centre designed for the horse and cart era is being converted into a spacious traffic-free precinct … The slums of the 19th century are being swept away to make way for modern homes in keeping with more hygienic factories.'[21]

## CARPET METROPOLIS OF THE WORLD

In 1970 Kidderminster was confident enough to be steadily taking down the unique townscape which was part of its identity. The carpet industry appeared to be in good shape, despite the challenge set by massive production of the cheap tufted variety in America. Membership of the carpet weavers' union was nearly 6,000, which was 20 per cent up on the 1960 figure. The *Shuttle* went so far as to describe the town as the 'carpet metropolis of the world'. The industry employed over 10,000 people in Kidderminster. Nothing better represented the new forward-looking town than the startling Mill Street office building with the legend 'Gilt Edge Carpets' above the lines of glass windows to grab the attention of those who arrived at the junction with Park Butts. It was built in 1962, replacing the classic line of old buildings occupied for half a century by Carpet Trades, who in 1953 had gone into partnership with Crossleys of Halifax. They began to trade as Gilt Edge in 1967 and in 1969 they merged with the Carpet Manufacturing Company to become Carpets International Ltd. According to the *Shuttle*, this was probably the 'biggest carpet combine in the world (outside the USA)'. Production in Kidderminster was now concentrated among only about twenty manufacturers and the trend was towards 'bigger and more financially powerful' companies.[22] Unhappily, the strength of this particular combine was to prove to be an illusion two decades later.

The positive state of the carpet trade was reflected in the peaceful industrial relations which had existed since the war. Arthur Marsh summed up this period as 'an age in which easy and tolerant relationships still prevailed'. Matters such as low pay and dismissals met with a 'conciliatory' response from the union. 'On three matters only did it invariably insist on the union's rights: to issue qualifications to occupy jacquard looms, to regulate excessive overtime and to require agreement on shift working.'[23] There was to be increasing competition within the industry during the 1970s, which would strain the happy relationship between the union and the employers, but for the time being the partnership was sustained. This was due to the durability of the traditional woven carpet trade, where production was at a record level in 1968. This could not conceal the ominous advance of the tufteds, whose products in that year exceeded the sales of woven carpets for the first time in the home market.[24] Many of these came from America, where nine out of ten carpets sold were tufted.

## DREAM AND REALITY

Sadly, Kidderminster was planning for a future that was not there. It had a reputation for being one of the wealthiest towns in the West Midlands and confidence was high. In 1970 it was preparing for a population within its borough boundaries of 70,000 by 1981.[25] This was a wildly over-optimistic assessment of the capacity of the carpet industry to attract future employment and of the ability of the town to draw in overspill population from the West Midlands. The population eventually reached in 1981 was to be only a little over 51,000. The threat posed by tufted carpets was ultimately to prove very damaging. It was just as well that, in terms of employment numbers, the advance of the carpet industry in the post-war period had been only steady at best and Kidderminster was not as dependent upon carpets as it might have been. The 10,000 workers employed in 1970 was two or three thousand less than one estimate of those in the trade before the war.[26] Also, there was always a preponderance of female labour in the industry with all its problems of low pay. The prosperity of many families in the town may have been based upon wages of one or more women which were viewed as supplementary to the main income. Hopes for the future already partly depended on the prospects for other industry, and in 1970 it was estimated that the town provided jobs for over 11,000 workers outside the carpet industry.[27]

The gap between dream and reality was illustrated by the consideration of grandiose construction projects. The council was having some difficulty bringing its plans to fruition. One of its critics was the estate agent, Stanley Cattell, who in 1969 repeated his charge made in 1964 that much of their thinking was based on 'artist's dreams'.[28] On this latter occasion he was referring to the ideas for developing the Bromsgrove Street area. He had a personal interest as his premises were to be pulled down. The proposal was to put a temporary car park on the site, before erecting a civic centre, a youth centre, a theatre and swimming baths. At the public enquiry Cattell noted that a civic centre seemed to pop up in plans for various parts of the town and he dismissed it all as fanciful.

Two projects which did come to pass were outside the remit of the council. Trimpley reservoir was constructed to enhance the supply of water to Birmingham by taking water out of the Severn. Work began in 1964 and the reservoir was officially opened in May 1968. The road and the landscape in that remote corner of Kidderminster Foreign was transformed. Unfortunately the historic Eymore Farmhouse was pulled down because restoration was uneconomic. On Bewdley Road Blakebrook hospital was being transformed into the District General Hospital. In 1970 Phase I had been completed, including operating theatres and administration offices. The old workhouse buildings had been modernised, with sun lounges built on to them. The Mill Street hospital was to be used solely for elderly people who were chronically sick. A further three phases of the development were being planned.

The new Kidderminster was typified by the completion in 1971 of Crown House, built on a massive concrete slab spanning the river Stour. This was the new post office and government headquarters. Work began in September 1969 and more damage was done to the old character of the Bull Ring with the loss of two more Grade III listed buildings. Crown House presented an ugly visual clash with the nearby churches and industrial buildings, but it was completely in keeping with the new Attwoods and the Swan Centre. The artist's impression in the *Shuttle* gave the usual gleaming futuristic impression. The extraordinary claim was made that the reinforced concrete structure, with its plastic sheathed metal windows and white ceramic fibre glass moulded panels, was entirely 'self-cleansing'.[30] It is true that Crown House was imposed upon the town by the government, but it was clearly in line with the council's scheme for modernising the town. It also enabled the level of much of the lower end of the Bull Ring to be raised by five feet to alleviate the risk of flooding.[31] There is no evidence of any objections to the scheme, even though thirty years later the building is now widely reviled. By August 1971, when Crown House was opened, there was no going back. Too much of the unique landscape of the country's leading centre for carpet manufacture was already gone. It was beginning to look like any other town and its identity was in jeopardy. As long as the industry itself appeared to have a certain future, this thought may not have troubled many. Unfortunately, difficulties and decline lay only a few years ahead. Symbolically, these were to be accompanied by Kidderminster's loss of its borough status, which it had enjoyed for nearly a hundred and fifty years, and its absorption into the new Wyre Forest District Council.

92. Crown House. This artist's impression appeared in the *Shuttle* in February 1970 and, typically, showed a bright gleaming future. Completed in 1971, it has recently been voted by viewers of the BBC's Midlands Today as the Midlands' ugliest building.

# XIII

# *Wyre Forest*

A lthough so many of the Georgian and Victorian buildings had gone by the beginning of the 1970s, there was still much work to be done to complete the transformation into the modern townscape. The remarkable political unanimity as to the destruction of the old continued for the most part into the 1980s, with just occasional public concern revealed by features in the *Shuttle* suggesting, for example, that there was too much concentration on shops at the expense of places of entertainment and that Kidderminster was becoming a 'ghost town'.[1] There was also further uncoordinated opposition by individuals at the various public enquiries into the latest demolition plans. Such was the confidence of councillors that they were happy to consider the inclusion of all of the names of the Redevelopment Committee on the foundation stone for the Swan Centre. Four years later, when the plans for redeveloping the area between Vicar Street and Worcester Street were approved, Ald. David Samuel expressed the hope that the council would go out in a 'blaze of glory'.[2] The demise of the Borough Council in 1974, to which he was referring, was to be one factor which hindered the smooth rebuilding of Kidderminster. Funding was a continual problem, exacerbated by the repeated redundancies and closures in the carpet industry during the late 1970s and early 1980s. The assumption that Kidderminster would have a modern carpet industry to match the modern town began to look shaky. Development slowed down and there were complaints about planning blight and dereliction.

Nevertheless, a start was made reasonably quickly with building on the cleared space at Bromsgrove Street. Ever since the end of the Second World War there had been criticisms of the lack of social facilities to occupy young people. In 1965 the youngest ever Mayor of the town, Cllr Charles Talbot, had used his Mayoralty to launch Kidderminster's Youth Trust. In April 1970, with the aid of a government grant of £55,000, work was started to build a youth centre, which opened in September 1971.[3] Unfortunately it was to be many years before Bromsgrove Street was fully developed. Plans for the leisure centre were to recede into the middle of the following decade, whilst those for the theatre and the civic centre never materialised.

## SITE VALUE ONLY

In April 1970 the council's offer of only £16,000 to the Nonentities for the purchase of their theatre was considered at the Lands Tribunal. Kenneth Rose and the society were claiming the full rebuilding costs of a new theatre, as opposed to the simple site value which was being offered. The result was an unqualified victory for Kenneth Rose and the Nonentities, who were awarded £167,500. The council again had to consider their position regarding a new theatre. The Tories were still in control, and most of them were against council funding for the theatre, but they were undermined by one or two of their number. In November it was agreed to create a Theatre Trust, on which the council would have four representatives. The Bromsgrove Street site and a grant of £13,750 were to be provided for a new theatre. This infuriated the solicitor, Ald. F.C. Adams, chairman of the Finance Committee. He maintained that 'a town poll would show a 20 to one majority against the grant.' The Mayor, Cllr George Dance, presented a petition with 684 signatures against the council's decision.[4] In the same month Kenneth Rose died suddenly, at the age of 74, so he did not endure the further dashing of his hopes for a theatre which genuinely belonged to the town. Inflation was to erode the value of the award and by 1974 the estimated cost for a 370-seat theatre had escalated to £350,000. The plans had to be scrapped. Although the trust continued to exist until 1981, the reality was that the Nonentities were on their own and would eventually again have to build their own theatre.

Site value only was also an issue at a public enquiry into the council's wish to demolish 167 houses in the Wood Street area adjoining Bewdley Road. The other streets affected were Hill Street, Park Street, Chapel Street, Rock Terrace, Park Terrace and Edward Street. The council needed to pull down the properties to make way for a further phase of the ring road. Residents were forced to argue that their homes were not 'slums', as the council contended, conveniently, that 165 out of the 167 houses were 'unfit for human habitation'. At the enquiry it was objected that the houses were needed for road building and it was 'wrong that they should be purchased as unfit houses which would mean the owners would receive only site value instead of current market value.' It was denied in any case that the houses were unfit, and Rock Terrace properties in particular were said to be 'well maintained and repaired'. The council argued that 37 houses had no internal water supply, 80 shared sanitary accommodation, only seven had internal sanitary accommodation, and baths were installed in only four of the houses.[5]

## RING ROAD STAGE 3

The inhabitants of Comberton Terrace were not inclined to trouble the authorities to the same extent. In 1972 work was proceeding to take the ring road from Worcester Cross through the hillside to avoid the factories, and down to the junction of Worcester Road and Stourport Road. The Hoo Road had formerly run straight to Worcester Cross, next to Green Street, but now it had to be made to turn at two right angles to emerge into Comberton Hill well above the ring road roundabout. This required taking a chunk out of the hillside right underneath Comberton Terrace. This group of mid-19th-century houses had once seen better days, set on an open space looking over the slopes down to Comberton Hill and Hoo Road. Now a vertical drop was being created a few yards from their front doors, with the aid of 40-foot steel piles 'being hammered relentlessly into the ground'. They were needed to support the foundations of the houses as well as to protect the new section of road underneath. The pile driving was going to last a month, but the residents were not complaining. One had got used to the noise and another was reassured by a workman who 'made daily checks to see there were no cracks in the buildings'.[6] This was a major engineering project, which disturbed the natural landscape and effectively destroyed much of the Worcester Cross part of town. This third section of the ring road was opened in August 1973 by Keith Speed MP, Under-Secretary at the Department of the Environment. He praised the foresight of the council and said the road had 'actually improved the environment of the area through which it passed'. Alongside the road ran a huge retaining wall holding up the Hoo Road which was 320 metres long and up to eleven metres high. Underneath the road the branch of the Stour had been diverted through a culvert. Ald. Samuel, the chairman of the Redevelopment Committee, said that the borough was being 'taken by the scruff of the neck out of the horse and buggy age into the motor car age and beyond.'

## HOSPITAL EXPANSION

The general hospital was gradually expanding. In June 1971 the postgraduate Medical Centre had been opened, funded by public subscription. It was designed as a centre for lectures and courses to enable staff to keep abreast of the continuous developments in medicine. The key to further growth was the programme of taking down houses in neighbouring streets. Fifty houses in Crescent Road, Hume Street, Franchise Street and Sutton Road were the subject of compulsory purchase orders, and demolition had begun by 1973. Much further along the Bewdley Road changes of a different kind were in hand. The Safari Park opened in 1973 on the 300-acre Spring Grove estate.

Kidderminster was not quite ready to look at a post-industrial age, but there were other signs of the growing importance of the leisure sector. The Severn Valley Railway Company was steadily acquiring the line which had been abandoned by British Rail in 1970. In 1974 they added the two-mile stretch from Bewdley to Foley Park. For a decade this was to be used only on special occasions until further purchases enabled the line to be extended into Kidderminster Town.

## DOING VERY WELL

In 1972 there was great optimism concerning Kidderminster's industry and employment prospects. The district could be described as 'the world's largest centre of manufacture' of carpets and the mood was 'buoyant'. It was noted that the total workforce in the Kidderminster area, including Stourport and Bewdley, numbered 37,670, of which over a third was engaged in the carpet industry. Commuting was minimal, because no fewer than 34,730 were employed locally. Unemployment had been below national levels for years.[7] One expanding company was Tomkinsons. The growth of their Clensmore site necessitated the demolition of yet another historic building. St Mary's Church of England School in Churchfields was pulled down in October 1972 for what were described as 'amenity improvements' (presumably a car park). Opened in 1818, it had been empty since 1967 when pupils moved to Stoney Lane School. Further growth of the Clensmore complex was announced in November 1972. In 1973 record profits were announced by Bond Worth, the Stourport firm who in 1963 had acquired Jellyman & Sons Ltd based in Puxton Lane. In the same year Brockway announced plans to increase the capacity of their Axminster and Wilton plant at Hoobrook by 25 per cent.[8]

By 1975 national economic problems were beginning to have an effect in Kidderminster. In January Bond Worth announced they had enjoyed another record year, but a week later Brockway announced 12 redundancies 'of a minor nature' out of their 112 workforce. The mood was growing cautious. An article on prospects for the CMC branch of Carpets International Ltd referred to the decline in demand for narrow width Jacquard Wilton production. Throughout the century the market had been sustained despite the advent of the broadloom, but now there were signs that it was waning. It was thought that the adverse economic climate might ultimately result in a reduction of 100 jobs in the workforce of 3,000. In April 1975 Bond Worth revealed falling profits, explained partly by a downturn in exports. In the same month Carpets International also announced reduced profits, partly because of the poor performance of their Australian interests.[9]

# WYRE FOREST DISTRICT COUNCIL

If there were signs that the carpet industry was losing its way, there had long been indications of a lack of direction on the council. This occurred before the demise of the borough council, which gave way to Wyre Forest District Council in April 1974. For the most part, with the exception of the period following the Second World War, Kidderminster had been governed by Tories since the First World War. Usually the Tory group had included several names which had been familiar to generations of the townspeople and several names associated with the carpet industry. By 1971 the Tories were of a different character and they were about to lose control. After the May election they were reduced to exactly half of the council seats. Solicitor Charles Talbot was the one remaining representative of the old governing families of the town and there were no carpet manufacturers at all. A brief period of ascendancy for the Labour Party as the largest party followed. For a time they formed the initial administration of Wyre Forest District Council, before being ousted by a Tory/Liberal alliance in March 1975. The Liberal Party gained in strength, but for most of the period up to 1991 Wyre Forest had a hung council.

Under the new arrangements the three principal towns making up Wyre Forest retained their own Mayor. In Kidderminster's case the Mayor was to be elected annually by a body known as the Charter Trustees, who were simply the Wyre Forest district councillors from the wards within the old borough boundary. In fact, this was the sole function of the Trustees. The new structure provided no forum for discussing purely Kidderminster affairs. Stourport and Bewdley retained parish councils, but Kidderminster was considered to be too large. This anomaly has continued to be a source of frustration and to this day efforts are being made to gain a town council. Another feature of the new council was that all seats on the council were occupied by members directly elected by the public. The seven aldermen elected by councillors themselves were abolished.

One of the first tasks for the new council was to deal with the extraordinary story of the long evacuation of Hoobrook Flats. The inhabitants had been woken up at 7 a.m. on the morning of 15 January 1970 to be told they were being moved because the blocks might be unsafe in high winds. After years of secrecy it was announced in January 1975 that an out-of-court settlement had been reached with the two companies involved in the construction. The unapologetic chairman of the housing committee, Cllr Wilf Keeley, was satisfied that the council had a 'good bargain'. He explained that they had 'had to exclude the press and public from meetings, but that is entirely different from saying we have been secretive'. In July the council proudly announced that the whole episode had cost them only £23. Work of reinforcement was well under way with a deadline for completion in May 1976. It involved the insertion of steel stanchions into the walls.[10]

## HOWLS OF OUTRAGE

The Labour administration which had concluded the Hoobrook flats agreement was driven from office by the traditional thriftiness of the Kidderminster ratepayers. Against a national background of high rate increases, partly due to inflation, the Labour council wished to introduce some growth into the council's budget. This new type of leadership proved too much for some and a campaign to restore the town to normality was launched. Prominent among them was Sir Tatton Brinton, who had stepped down as MP in 1974. The chairman of Brintons re-entered political life in a less conventional guise. At the end of January 1975 he announced that the company were refusing to pay £90,000 in rates as a protest against 'county and district extravagance'. However, he added that he was 'not going to tell them what to cut out. That was up to them.' In the same week 450 people crammed into the civic centre at Stourport to hear councillors try to explain the need for growth. Labour councillors were jeered, but the Liberals and Conservatives won support by opposing these plans. The *Shuttle* reported that the audience showed that 'it was not interested in what environmental benefits the growth programme held. All that mattered was keeping the increases as small as possible'. When figures were given for the rate increase there were 'howls of outrage'.[11]

In March what the *Shuttle* described as the 'quiet revolution' occurred. The Labour Party had only 20 seats on the council to the combined Tory and Liberal total of 25 seats. Labour's proposals for growth, including improvement schemes at council depots of Hoobrook and Green Street, were doomed. There was some bitterness at this. Cllr Paul Thomas noted that they had '150 refuse workers sharing two showers, doing a job which probably carries the highest risk of disease'. Cllr Michael Williams said that he had visited the incinerator where low-paid men were 'working like pigs'. It was 'disgraceful' that improvements were unlikely to be achieved in his time on the council. Also lost was a flood alleviation scheme to be funded jointly with the new Severn Trent Water Authority.[12]

## NO ARTS CENTRE

The *Shuttle* interviewed members of the public informally in the town centre on the morning of the council meeting which saw Labour's programme defeated. They discovered a majority in favour of paying more for improved services. 'They have spoilt the town. Where can a bachelor boy go on a Saturday night in today's Kidderminster?' said Mr Wilfred Hardiman of St George's Terrace.[13] Among the cuts was a scheme to create an arts centre in the School of Science building in Market Street. In 1974 the library, museum and art gallery occupied two-thirds of the building, but the rest was vacant following the creation of the College of Further Education at Aggborough. The abandoned plans had incorporated a theatre to be accessed from Exchange Street, a cellar bar, rooms for lectures and film shows on the first floor, and conference facilities on the second floor.

The history of Kidder-minster is littered with reports

93. Methodist Church, Mill Street.

of widespread derelict property, but it does appear to have been an acute problem during the economic crisis of the mid-1970s. This was not helped by lengthening delays in extending the ring road. In 1973 work on the remaining two sections had been scheduled to start in 1975. However, the Park Butts section was not to be opened until early 1984 and in December 1978 it was announced that the Park Lane/Park Street section was not to be built for 10 years. Old shops in Park Butts had been boarded up by June 1975 and already there were complaints that mice and rats were attracted to rubbish being left there. The fine old buildings at the lower end of Mill Street were blighted for years before they were finally pulled down. These included the 1803 Methodist Chapel, a Grade II listed building, and the *Black Horse Hotel*. The latter was probably Kidderminster's last surviving coaching inn. Its undignified demise is another indictment of planners with no feel for the history of the town. It functioned as a hotel until October 1973 and was fully booked to the end, even though by then the *Shuttle* could describe it as a 'dirty old building' and its fate had been known for many years. Also, in the latter years it had been 'almost the sole regular venue for live entertainment'. Its weekend pop dances had given it a reputation for brawling, but it was the one place youths could go to let off steam. 'Now they have nowhere.'[14]

The instinct of the planners remained unchanged. Having done their best to ruin the one reasonably well preserved street in the town by driving the ring road through it, they decided in 1975 to complete the process by pulling down nos. 2 to 13 on the west side of Church Street, all of them listed buildings, including the former Tomkinson and Adam offices. The council had the usual reports that the buildings were 'structurally unsound'. There were many protests, including one from Church Street solicitor and former Mayor, Charles Talbot, who described the proposal as 'a gross piece of municipal vandalism'. Fortunately this was one plan which did not come to fruition. In another compromise, the planners' determination to remove most of the old buildings encircling the retail market was softened by a petition to save *The Swan* public house opposite the Town Hall.[15]

## THE END OF AN ERA

The achievement of Kidderminster had been extraordinary. Though only a small town, it had succeeded in maintaining its place as one of the world's greatest centres for carpet production for over a century. The severity of its decline from the mid-1970s can be gauged by figures for membership of the carpet weavers' union. In 1974 a peak of 6,683 was reached, but by 1983 it was down to 3,200. The first major shock was the demise of Naylors, founded in 1853. Although the firm became a public company in 1953, the family involvement continued with David Naylor becoming chairman in 1965. They made a modest profit of £117,192 in 1973, but profits were down in 1974. In January 1975 dwindling sales led to 450 employees being told not to come to work for a fortnight. The company was heading for a loss of £569,898 in 1975. After a further drop in sales, the directors invited their bankers 'to appoint a receiver and had requested the Stock Exchange to suspend dealings in the company shares'. Closure meant the loss of 600 jobs.[16] David Naylor had made a firm statement in support of family firms in 1970, when he had said that the industry was 'still very much a family oriented one'.[17] After the demise of his firm, the industry was never to be the same again.

In 1976 the Bowater Corporation had taken over the spinning firm of Greatwich with their tufted manufacturing subsidiary, Georgian Carpets. In March 1978 a reorganisation led to a reduction of 100 jobs. Further unemployment was stemmed by government grant aid to two family firms, Quayle Carpets and Chlidema Carpets. They were paying £20 a week for each employee. The *Shuttle* claimed that most of Kidderminster's carpet factories had been taking advantage of the scheme. However, the Hoobrook firm of Morris Carpets were also in trouble. They had become a public company in 1965 and had been taken over by an Irish concern, Youghal Carpets (Holdings) in 1968. They closed down Morris Carpets in 1979 with the loss of 250 jobs. The closures were not creating much unrest in Kidderminster. A local Trades Council member, Ken Orme, called upon workers to fight for their jobs. 'When the proposed closure of Morris's was first announced, I don't recall one letter of protest in the local press,' he said. He added that workers in the town were 'concerned only for their own problems' and were too ready to believe that another company's plight would mean 'more work for us'.[18]

During this period a three-week strike at Brintons in October 1977 was the only significant example of resistance of the workforce to the efforts of the employers to reduce costs. It was a time when companies sought to be more efficient by having a reduced number of looms operating for longer hours. Night shifts had been introduced some years before. Brintons, unlike other manufacturers, also broke with custom and practice by reducing loomage from 51 to 42 in the Axminster Department rather than resort to expensive short-time working. They then sought to introduce even greater flexibility with weavers moving between looms to avoid the necessity of setting up looms on a short-time basis. The resulting strike produced no agreement, but it served to warn both employers and union officials that complacency might have 'overtaken them after a long period of overtly peaceful relations'.[19]

Nevertheless the relentless tide of redundancies produced little reaction from either the workers or the town. In September 1979 the efforts to prop up the private limited company of Quayle Carpets seemed to have failed when the receivers were called in. Their factory in Franchise Street was closed, but their Wilden Lane site formed the base for a new company using the old name which commenced trading three months later. Jobs were found for 46 of the original 170 employees. The subsequent history of the firm illustrates the merry-go-round of proprietors to which the modern carpet industry was vulnerable. In 1985 Quayle Carpets collapsed again and 65 people were 'dismissed at a minute's notice without pay'. The general secretary of the Carpet Weavers' Union, Brian Moule, angrily said: 'This workforce has gone out of its way to co-operate with the management and all they get is a kick up the backside.' There had been rumours that Quayles were to be taken over by Georgian Goodacre Ltd, a company within the Milton Medes Group who had recently taken over Bowater Carpets, who it will be remembered had previously taken over Greatwich and Georgian Carpets of Clensmore. In the event Quayles were purchased by Lionel Rowe's company, Carpets of Kidderminster.[20]

Other losses included 230 redundancies at the Carpet Manufacturing Company in December 1979, where 800 employees were on short-time work. Another 300 lost their jobs there in August 1980. The receivers were called in at Chlidema, which finally closed in February 1980 with the loss of 114 jobs. In the same month Carpets of Worth announced 100 redundancies, including many on the Jellyman's site in Puxton Lane. That unemployment was now a very serious matter in Kidderminster was shown by a report in January 1981 that 300 people queued outside a new DIY store in Spennells Valley Road for 12 jobs. Still the losses continued with Brintons announcing in February 1982 that 100 jobs were to go in a rationalisation. Only in 1983 were there signs that the worst was over. In March of that year Brintons announced their biggest profits for seven years at £3.9m. In September Carpets International, still operating in Kidderminster as the more familiar Carpet Manufacturing Company, declared half-year profits of just under £1m. In December Tomkinsons too announced a profit.[21]

Another sign of the times was the demise in February 1979 of the firm of Bradley and Turton, which had been formed many years before out of two of Kidderminster's 19th-century iron founders. It had continued to operate from Turtons original Park Lane base, and lately it had specialised in 'custom-made presses'. It was taken over by the Manchester company Francis Shaw & Co., who were part of the BTR group. Unceremoniously it was announced that the business would be moved to Manchester. Only key workers from Bradley and Turton were to be offered jobs and there were to be 90 redundancies. The *Shuttle* noted that there had been difficulty in demolishing Margate pier recently, so strong were its 34 iron legs provided by Turton over a century ago. The new generation of companies in Kidderminster was represented by Kidderminster Steel, who arrived in the town in 1960 by taking over Tansley Brothers in Mill Lane. They claimed to have been 'the first steel stockholders and constructional engineers' in the town. They expanded and moved to Worcester Road trading estate in 1972. Ironically, they specialised in industrial demolition.[22]

## COMPREHENSIVE EDUCATION

Comprehensive education in Kidderminster began in September 1977, when the three selective schools were closed. These were King Charles I Grammar School in Bewdley Road, the girls' High School in Chester Road and Hartlebury Grammar School for boys. The change had been met with some resistance. The basic scheme had been known since 1970, when the private Sebright School in Wolverley closed for financial reasons and was acquired by the County Council. The plan was to use it as one of the three comprehensives, along with Harry Cheshire and a new school on the site of the girls' High School. However, campaigners to save the selective tradition were encouraged by the election of a Conservative government with Margaret Thatcher as Minister for Education. A petition was organised by the Old Carolians Association, who collected 5,000 signatures. In January 1972 came the reprieve for the three threatened schools. Nevertheless, the principle of comprehensive education was established at the Harry Cheshire and Wolverley schools, and with the election of a Labour Government in 1974 the pressure for further reform mounted. In March 1975 the education committee of the new county of Hereford and Worcester approved a plan for a 1,000-pupil comprehensive school on the Chester Road site. This time there was little resistance. The governors of the Grammar School agreed to the absorption of the King Charles Foundation Trust in the new school, which it was agreed in February 1976 should be called King Charles I School. The scheme for complete comprehensive education in Kidderminster was implemented in September 1977. The Hartlebury school was closed, whilst part of the Bewdley Road site was to be adapted for a new middle school, which opened in August 1978. The girls' high school had grown from a roll of 85 in 1912 to 601 in 1973. The new comprehensive school incorporated its fine buildings, erected in 1912, and also the lovely Hillgrove House and its grounds which had been acquired in the late 1940s.[23]

## CONTINUING REDEVELOPMENT

The industrial decline was accompanied by the continued destruction of many of the town's old buildings. One further casualty of the absolute priority given to modern traffic needs was the demolition in 1977 of the 200-year-old *Three Crowns and Sugar Loaf* in Franche, despite the protests of local folk singer, Dave Cartwright, who then lived in Lowe Lane. It was regarded as a necessary measure to improve the traffic island, which 25 years later remains an awkward junction for drivers to negotiate. A number of important schools were also pulled down. These included two school board buildings: one in Coventry Street in 1977, and one in Bennett Street in 1978. The Edward Parry Centre was built on the site of the former school and opened in January 1980. The latter school was a victim of the ring road extension up to Proud Cross. Also to go in 1978 was St George's School in Offmore Road, built over 150 years previously. Another notable loss, in July 1980, was the old post office on the corner of Market Street and Exchange Street. This was followed by one of the occasional eccentric gestures towards conservation which have been made in the planning of Kidderminster. As part of the development of a Sainsbury's store, which was opened in 1982, a new building was erected on that corner in the same style as the post office.

Demolition began in June 1978 for the proposed rebuilding of the area between Vicar Street and Worcester Street. Work was in hand at once to remove a line of commercial buildings on the east side of Vicar Street, including the 19th-century Barclays Bank. By August one of the town's great landmarks, the Victorian retail market, was being destroyed. Kidderminster was becoming less and less like a market town. Again traffic considerations were paramount. The

94. Retail Market 1978, pictured shortly before demolition.

removal of the market was essential to allow access for delivery vehicles into an area behind the shops of Vicar Street, High Street and Worcester Street, which for years had been due for pedestrianisation. The impressive entrance to the retail market next to the *Swan* was replaced by a cavernous entrance for goods vans. Nothing could be left alone. The statue of Sir Rowland Hill, around which traffic had moved for 100 years, was moved closer to the Town Hall, thus giving the delivery vans a wider approach and also paving the way for a pedestrianised area extending into Vicar Street. The statue's time capsule was opened to reveal a mass of mouldy pulp and a new one was installed.[24] Along the west side of Worcester Street other old buildings were pulled down, including the fine premises of Bywaters.

During these years the destruction of Mill Street as a street of any consequence was completed. It was one of the town's earliest streets and for centuries was the principal means of entry from the north-west. In the late 18th century it started to present to visitors a formidable sight of industrial buildings and tall town houses on either side. Now it is a backstreet and a shortcut to the Crossley Park retail estate. The architect Alan Brooks has commented that Mill Street is a 'disgraceful example of a town itself destroying an area that once possessed considerable historic interest'.[25] Between 1979 and 1984 the line of old town houses below Park Butts, in which families such as the Brooms and the Leas may have lived, was pulled down. These included no. 28, a Grade III listed building.

In January 1983 the ravine-like Park Butts was closed for three months to allow for work on stage IV of the ring road. A historic street in itself, its derelict buildings were finally removed and so was its character as a street. It had always stood out as a reminder to townspeople of the triumph of previous generations over the natural landscape. Many years ago they had cut a way through the towering sandstone cliffs to Bewdley. Now the street was gone and had become a raised ringway, concealing the cliffs, rising to a gigantic roundabout where once had been many terraced houses, a few pubs and some shops. The roundabout was built in March 1983 and the new stretch of the ring road was opened in February 1984 by local MP, Esmond Bulmer. The development included a new stretch of road leading to Proud Cross, where another new roundabout took traffic on to the Franche Road. A notable loss was the *Barley Mow* public house on the corner of Bewdley Street. Some people affected by the ring road received no compensation at all from the council. Willie and Nellie Edwards, newsagents on Park Butts, were ruined by the raised ringway, which passed within a few yards of their shop. Customers had to climb down a flight of 25 steps to gain access and trade dropped by 80 per cent.[26]

The economic imperative which has demanded the demolition of many old buildings, some of them of great character, has to be contrasted with another economic imperative which demands the retention of the tower blocks of Hoobrook and Hurcott Road, despite concern about their condition and the quality of life enjoyed by residents over many years. In 1976 the *Shuttle* revealed that the Hurcott Road blocks could collapse under certain conditions. The saga was to run for over two years before a repairs programme was agreed.

95. Mill Street dereliction 1970s. 19th-century industrial buildings which, like so many others, once offered potential for conversion.

96. The Library and old Schools of Art and Science. By the late 1980s plans were well in hand to demolish these buildings. This picture from 1955 shows some of the fine detail.

Tenants had difficulties with heating and water penetration. In addition to strengthening work, it was necessary to replace the external cladding with traditional brick-facing. The projected cost was £1.25m, but the council ruled out the more expensive option of demolition and rehousing the tenants.[27]

## SPENNELLS

In order to provide much needed housing Kidderminster expanded considerably to the south-east in the late 1970s. Spennells Pool was drained and the building of Spennells Valley Road was underway in April 1976. By 1977 the Mallard Avenue area was being constructed and in 1979 the new Aggborough and Spennells ward was created. In 1980 many of the roads around the eastern part of Captains Pool Road were adopted. The potential for further development of the area was enhanced by the closure in February 1982 of Dr Barnardo's, which was to be pulled down. The futuristic building, which had required the demolition of Spennells House, had survived for less than twenty years.

Another important indication that Kidderminster town centre was not the focus of progressive planning at this time was the erection of the Rose Theatre in outlying Broadwaters. After the Playhouse had closed in 1968 the Nonentities had occupied St Oswald's Hall, which they soon purchased. Their hopes to create a town theatre had been extinguished in the early 1970s as inflation pushed up the cost beyond their reach. Yet their capital, sustained by high interest rates, was eventually to prove enough to expand their premises beyond all recognition to create a new theatre named after their deceased leader, who had battled heroically, and with little civic recognition, for nearly thirty years to preserve live theatre in the town. The Theatre Trust, drawn from every section of the community, was wound up in 1981, and the Nonentities' own theatre began to take shape at a cost of £300,000. It opened on 21 November 1981. The souvenir programme of that night stated that the Rose Theatre would 'remain the home of the Nonentities, but it is also hoped that it will become the Theatre of Wyre Forest'. Meanwhile, the range of entertainment on offer in the town centre continued to decline. By January 1985 the last cinema in town, the ABC in Oxford Street, formerly the Central, had not only closed but had been demolished.[28]

## FOREST GLADES LEISURE CENTRE

A very positive development was the opening of the leisure centre in March 1986. After more than fifteen years the vacant space in Bromsgrove Street was finally covered. The project had been subject to much delay and controversy. In the end it had been financed by the council selling the freehold of the Swan Centre shopping complex for £3,457,000. There was opposition from various parish councils and the town councils of Bewdley and Stourport. This resulted in divisions within Wyre Forest District Council itself. There were regular reports of soaring costs. In February 1984 opposing councillors, led by Stourport's Pat Duffy, were infuriated by the belated discovery of seven freshwater wells which were going to hamper construction. The unusual roof design, with eight octagonal domes, gave rise to the nickname of 'Nipple City'. There were predictions that the centre would turn out to be a 'white elephant'. Nevertheless, the administration was not diverted, and the chairman of Wyre Forest's Policy and Resources Committee, Cllr Mike Oborski, said: 'We reckon the new centre will be the finest of its kind within a 100 mile radius.' The opening of Forest Glades Leisure Centre by Diana, Princess of Wales, was a memorable day for the town and the chairman of the council, John Wardle.[29]

Another project, to be planned in the early 1970s and to come to fruition in the mid-'80s, was pedestrianisation. A limited start had been made in January 1972 with two small areas in Coventry Street and the Bull Ring, which prevented traffic getting through to the town centre. This had effectively isolated Vicar Street, High Street and Worcester Street, which were made one-way. However, it was always intended to proceed to comprehensive pedestrianisation of the area. This finally came to pass in late 1985 with the prohibition of traffic into Vicar Street, High Street and part of Worcester Street on weekdays between

10.30 a.m. and 4.30 p.m. The plans had been controversial. Local bankers, for example, had feared that their customers would be put at risk walking the Kidderminster streets with large sums of money.[30] There was even a dispute about whether to allow exemptions for disabled people, although this was eventually resolved in their favour.

## TROUBLE SPOT

As the 1980s progressed it was clear that the closures and redundancies had been indicative of a fundamental change in Kidderminster's standing in the carpet industry. It was not being claimed any more that the town was the carpet capital of the world, and the town no longer enjoyed any sort of favoured status among manufacturers as a carpet town. On the contrary, they were successfully operating in other places. When the multi-national company Carpets International announced profits of £1.42m in April 1985, they referred to their UK operations in Kidderminster and Yorkshire as a 'trouble spot'. Later in the year, when Tomkinsons revealed their own profits of £1.1m, a good performance was noted at Steeles and Mid-Wales Yarns. The former was a Wilton plant based in Banbury, which had become part of the company in 1960. The latter had been set up in Llandrindod Wells in 1969 to spin their yarn requirements.[31]

The growing detachment of Brintons from the town was illustrated in January 1986. They had been making yarn at Telford since 1968, but had continued production at the Slingfield Mill. Now they wanted to concentrate on the Telford factory and sell Slingfield Mill. However, they were so concerned about the 'desperate unemployment' in Kidderminster that they wanted it to be used for small industrial units. They were angered when the council decided that the building should be preserved and was worthy of listing. They were probably surprised as well, because this was a rare occasion when the council acted decisively in favour of conservation. Brintons were worried that listing would leave them with a 'white elephant', which 'cannot be sold in the market and will cost large amounts to maintain'. In any case they also considered the building to have 'very little historical interest'.[32] In the event Slingfield Mill was listed and Brintons vacated it in 1988. Eventually Brintons were to vacate the entire site, which was to be redeveloped as Weavers Wharf. The building which they underrated is one of the most beautiful sights in a town which has too few visual attractions. Brintons are now based out of town on the Stourport Road, but in recent years they have established factories in Portugal, India and the United States.

## COLOROLL

The bringing of the town's historic carpet firms under the control of larger and more remote corporations approached a disastrous conclusion. In 1985 Carpets International was purchased by the John Crowther Group. Three years later it was sold on to Coloroll, 'a home furnishings group floated by John Ashworth, once described by Margaret Thatcher as her favourite industrialist'. Coloroll borrowed heavily to finance the purchase at a time of high interest rates. Their position was unsustainable and in May 1990 the banks called in the receivers, Birmingham accountants Ernst and Young. The group had estimated debts of £400m.[33] The premises included the massive factory complex at the bottom of Mill Street, which extended across the meadows beyond the Stour, and also the fine 19th-century buildings in New Road erected by Mortons. Around 1,100 jobs were at stake.

At first there were hopes of a management buyout, but the sackings started very quickly. In June the union was advised of 243 redundancies, and within 24 hours workers were receiving their cards. There was much bitterness at the 'barbaric' way that it was handled. From then on the redundancies at the doomed enterprise proceeded gradually and by November 600 workers had gone. In December it was reported that a property company had purchased the site and that the majority of the remaining workers would be dismissed in early January. The local firms which over the many decades had been incorporated into this giant company included James Humphries, Edward Hughes, Charles Harrison, James Morton and Richard Smith. An era was drawing to a close.

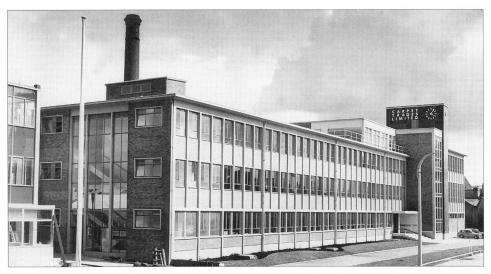

97. Carpet Trades Ltd Offices, a striking example of 1960s architecture. Unfortunately the demise of Coloroll doomed these offices, which fronted Mill Street near the Park Butts junction.

The initial angry reaction of workers seemed to die away, and the predominant feelings were of sadness and resignation.

In the midst of the crisis Brintons were running a four-day week, and Woodward Grosvenor announced 30 redundancies, which they blamed on stock from Coloroll flooding the market. Considering these additional difficulties for the town, it is perhaps surprising that there was not more anger, particularly in view of the way the Coloroll workers were treated. Legislation required a 90-day consultation period prior to redundancies, but this was completely ignored by the receiver. The weavers' union was then obliged to bring a succession of cases to an industrial tribunal for compensation for each worker. Their victory was inevitable and the receiver did not even bother to attend the tribunal, whose chairman spoke of a 'brutal lack of consultation', and 'contempt for the spirit behind the legislation'. The compensation awarded was paid out of public funds.[34] By 1991 total membership of the union was down to 2,167, less than a third of that in 1974. These figures betray the possibility that the subdued reaction to the job losses was due to the unpalatable fact that the carpet industry was no longer the major aspect of town life. The *Shuttle's* review of the year 1991 referred to Croucher the alligator arriving at the Safari Park in August and to the closure of the infamous Cobra roller coaster ride there in September. It referred also to the June tiddlywinks championship at the Forest Glades. There were no references at all to the carpet industry.

XIV

# *Rebellion*

The history of Kidderminster has been one of struggle, sometimes of an heroic nature, to push a small town to the forefront of the industrial world. The subplot has been one of sacrifice, with the town's environment failing to reflect the wealth being created. Yet recently, just when the carpet industry was playing a reduced role in town life, local people have been moved to make some vigorous protests concerning the environment and services. It is as though, after decades of behaving themselves, the inhabitants of Kidderminster decided enough was enough and it was time to fulfil their earlier reputation for nonconformity and awkwardness.

The headline story of this period was to be that of the hospital and the election to Parliament of Dr Richard Taylor, and we shall cover this in some detail. Yet throughout these years runs the equally important theme of the ineffectual role of the council in planning. It contrasts with the leading role taken by the Borough Council and later the District Council in planning the redevelopment of the town in the decades following the Second World War. On reflection, however, we must not exaggerate the former power of the council. Their strategy was based on demolition and clearing the ground for commercial interests to develop. When provision of amenities by the council was an issue, we have seen the difficulties it caused. These included the long-running arguments concerning the funding of the theatre and the many years of delay in building Forest Glades. Even when, as in 1975, the council was prepared to raise a little extra money through a rate increase, organised ratepayers created such a furore that the proposals were abandoned. Given that councils were deliberately further weakened by Thatcher governments, and then by Labour under Blair, it should not be surprising that in the period 1992-2004 we find little evidence of strong planning.

## THE OLD SCHOOLS OF ART AND SCIENCE

The first such protest involved the old library buildings along Market Street, which represented a brief flowering of civic spirit in the town in the late 19th century. They had been created by the bequests of Daniel Wagstaff Goodwin and by the energy and enthusiasm of Michael Tomkinson. It might have been thought that the town would have seen some value in retaining them. As Alan Brooks has said, concerning the destruction of earlier decades, 'most towns seem to have since learned the lesson however and have attempted to save and incorporate what remains'.[1] Unfortunately, the authorities in Kidderminster had evidently learned nothing by the early 1990s. Unmoved by opposition, both district and county councils over a period of many years drove through the policy of demolition, which finally began on 21 December 1992. Ultimately the authorities were able to complete this work only by the cynical exploitation of a bureaucratic technicality. For some years there had been a desire to create a new library. The path for planners to rebuild on the Market Street site had been made easy for them by the Tory government's device of a Certificate of Immunity (COI), which prevented a building from being listed for five years. Such a procedure was bound to exploit public apathy, but there were objections to the proposed COI. There was no Kidderminster Civic Society at the time, but John Cotterell objected as an individual and it is known that the Victorian Society also objected. Nevertheless, after English Heritage refused to recommend listing, a COI was granted and was valid until September 1993.

Opposition to demolition came from a group of individuals led by John Cotterell and Liz le Grove, who enjoyed little open political support. The letter columns of the *Shuttle* probably revealed apathy to experienced politicians. Contributions were divided and one described the old buildings as an 'eyesore'. The Labour candidate in the forthcoming general election, in a letter of reply to the campaigners, prudently declined to give a view on the matter until after the election. The only politician to offer consistent open support was, ironically, the Conservative MP, Anthony Coombs. Yet the few campaigners fought very hard and appeared to have secured a surprising victory, when Liz le Grove was notified on 22 January 1992 that her application for listing had been successful. English Heritage had this time decided that the building was of 'significant local importance historically and architecturally'. Clearly something had gone wrong with their filing system and they had failed to realise the existence of a valid COI. The celebrations were cruelly curtailed less than a week later when Liz le Grove was advised there had been a 'clerical error'.[2]

## PHILISTINES

The issue was becoming a national scandal and was covered in the columns of *Private Eye* and the *Daily Telegraph*. The press coverage provoked the 'appalled' great-granddaughters of Daniel W. Goodwin to write to a national newspaper of their horror that his gift was being abused. The Ancient Monuments

Society wrote to County Hall to express its objection to demolition 'in the strongest possible terms'. Far from being ashamed of themselves, the officers and members of the council proceeded towards the demolition of a building which everybody now knew was considered by English Heritage to be worthy of listing. Much to the disgust of the Senior Architectural Adviser of the Victorian Society, Richard Holder, 'philistine' county councillors dismissed the 'bleatings' of campaigners and were quoted as saying that the building was 'a Victorian slum which no one in his right mind would want to retain … let's get it knocked down as quickly as possible'. The district council proved themselves to be just as impervious to inconvenient views, when they were asked by campaigners to consider protecting the buildings by declaring a Conservation Area. On 8 October they replied to say that the area was 'too small and its shape too irregular' to be so designated, although this has not prevented them from doing so in 2003.

No serious attention was given to another possible site for the new library. Indeed the campaigning group was depicted as 'busybodies' preventing the town from having the new facility.[3] No serious consideration was given to refurbishing the existing buildings, and the county council argued, despite some scepticism, that refurbishment would cost £4m, whereas demolition and reconstruction would cost only £2.25m.[4] The completion of the plan ultimately required the cooperation of the Kidderminster Educational Foundation. This trust had been created in 1973 by bringing together various trusts and gifts to the town, including two-thirds of the Market Street complex, the old School of Art on the Exchange Street corner and the old School of Science which formed the middle section. The remaining third was the library itself, which historically had belonged to the Borough before being transferred to the County Council after the Second World War. The plan was for the new library to be erected on the site held by the K.E.F. This depended on a deal, whereby the K.E.F. swapped their two-thirds for the other one third plus £250,000. However, given that the K.E.F. was simply Wyre Forest District Council with another hat on, there was every reason to expect the deal to go through. At the decisive meeting in the autumn of 1992 a named vote was taken and, although there was some opposition, the deal was agreed.[5] So the last hurdle was cleared for demolition to begin, and by January 1993 the historic buildings had gone. There was no concession to conservation, with even the bricks dumped in a landfill site.[6] For their stubborn work the district and county councils were jointly rewarded by *Private Eye* with the Macmillan Award for the most philistine local authority.[7]

The new library opened on 15 July 1997 and it is a fine building to visit and to work in. That is some consolation, but there was no room for the museum and art gallery contained in the old building. The pictures and artefacts belonging to the old town of Kidderminster have been stored on a trading estate ever since demolition. The property deals entered into by the Kidderminster Educational Foundation should have left it with a substantial fund to fulfil one of its objects, which is the 'provision and maintenance of a museum and art gallery'. However, it sold its third of the site to Kidderminster College for £75,000, and there has been little indication since of any political will to undertake such a project.

Perhaps the bitterest disappointment belonged to John Cotterell, who had once worked in the buildings as Principal of Kidderminster College. Out of the ashes of the campaign came the formation of Kidderminster Civic Society in April 1993 with Cotterell as chairman and Charles Talbot as secretary. Ten years later insult was to be added to injury for Cotterell as the Civic Society fought to save the Piano Building. A number of hostile letters to the *Shuttle* appeared from people who were angry that the Civic Society was fighting to preserve an 'eyesore', but had not been around 'when the bulldozers removed Kidderminster's beautiful Victorian library and school of arts'. Stung into a reply, Cotterell commented on the 'apathy of the majority' and said that he and a small group of campaigners had 'worked their guts out fighting both the district and county councils'. Of one of the correspondents Cotterell simply asked: 'What did he do towards preserving that historic building?'[8]

## KIDDERMINSTER HARRIERS

An unexpected success story in recent years has been the rise of Kidderminster Harriers Football Club. Its history has been one of an unpretentious non-league club but, under the guidance of managers Graham Alner and Jan Molby, Harriers has developed into one capable of competing in the Football League. After winning the FA Trophy in 1987, Alner's team made two visits to Wembley Stadium as finalists: in 1991 and 1995. In 1994 the Conference Championship was secured, which should have given Harriers a place in the Football League, but entry was harshly refused because the ground had insufficient seats. This ruling was doubly harsh because a planned new stand was to be ready by the autumn of that year. Nevertheless, Harriers were to be taken seriously and their next manager, Jan Molby, had been a supremely talented footballer at Liverpool and a Danish international. It was Molby who took Harriers into their rightful place in the league in 2000 when the team again won the Conference Championship.

## POST-INDUSTRIAL LANDSCAPE

Although by the 1990s much of Kidderminster's town centre had long been redeveloped, there remained considerable potential for further change as the process of withdrawal of the carpet industry accelerated. Coloroll were not going to be replaced by another carpet company, so their massive site was free to be developed for other uses. Brintons were ready to cease production completely in the town centre and concentrate production at Stourport Road. By 1996 plans for the transformation of the old site were being discussed. Furthermore a developer, Morbaine Ltd, had acquired a large site at the bottom of Green Street, having found that Victoria and Rowe Carpets were prepared to vacate the site. The opportunity was there to salvage something of Kidderminster's character from its unique industrial landscape.

The early indications were that Kidderminster was to get the kind of new buildings appearing in every other town and city. The Coloroll site was sold by the receivers Ernst and Young in 1991, and the developers Inoco Ltd were ready with a proposal for a Sainsbury's superstore in November 1992. The historic site had been developed by Kidderminster manufacturers such as Broom and Humphries, but the brochure was already calling it the 'Crossley Site' after the Halifax firm, which only became part of the conglomeration from 1969 onwards. Surely any town proud of its history would have demanded a more appropriate name. The planned store was given the go-ahead in May 1993. At the Local Plan Enquiry in 1994 the inspector recommended retail warehouse development for the rest of Crossley Park. Application was made in 1995/6 but the council doggedly refused permission, apparently because they were worried about the effect on the plans for the Brintons site, known as KTC1. After appeals to the Secretary of State, planning permission was finally given in late 1998.

## UNIQUENESS OF PLACE

The council's protectiveness towards KTC1 may be explained by their ownership of about 17 per cent of it, but its potential was completely different from that of Crossley Park. The Coloroll premises had consisted of a massive expanse of buildings of no great merit, so there was no heritage issue concerning demolition, except perhaps the passing of the startling 1960s office block fronting Mill Street. The former Brintons factory, on the other hand, contained many buildings of historic interest. This was reflected in the council's planning brief issued in January 1996, which spoke of the town's 'unique manufacturing heritage'. The 'majestic mill buildings and spaces between them' offered exciting possibilities. Apart from the listed buildings, including Slingfield Mill, the council considered that the Piano Building and the third mill, known as the Wool Hall, were both worthy of retention. In addition they wished to preserve the chimney adjacent to the Sling. In June a Summary of Proposals was issued by Lyons, Sleeman and Hoare, the architects appointed by developers, Centros/

Wimpey. This exactly reflected the enthusiastic planning brief. The intention was to take 'full advantage of the site's existing under-utilised attributes and historic background'. A mix of uses was to be established, with the 'correct balance between the commercial demands of the retailers and the needs of the local community'. Slingfield Mill was to be refurbished to provide five floors of 'high quality residential accommodation'. The 'unusual' Piano Building was earmarked for an arts and heritage centre. The Stour was to be diverted to follow a course closer to the new library under construction on the east side of the site, and it was to be landscaped to create a new leisure attraction. The vision was apparently completely different from that for Crossley Park and its retail warehouses.

However, by 1996 commercial reality meant the need to compete with Merry Hill, the huge shopping mall at nearby Brierley Hill in the Black Country. This was made explicit in the proposals produced in March of that year by the developers of Crossley Park. It may be that there were already doubts about whether the vision for KTC1 could be seen through. The council's recent record on heritage was poor. In 1994 they had delivered the *coup de grace* to Mill Street. In June of that year English Heritage refused to list the one remaining building which had anything to do with the carpet industry. This was the imposing four-storey office block built in 1884 by Richard Smith & Sons, which stood between the Town Mill and the Infirmary. The council at once conceded demolition for the provision of a site for a car sales company. Cllr Rachel Gittins regretted 'the loss of this building, but I can't see on planning grounds what argument we have got'.[9] This certainly raised questions about the future of the mills and other historic buildings on the Brintons site. In due course the KTC1 plans were to be turned on their head.

During this time another plan, which had been blighting part of Kidderminster for as long as anybody could remember, was finally about to be scrapped. Responsibility for Stage V of the ring road, which would destroy Park Street, had passed to the County Council. The project had last been approved in 1980 and had continued to be listed among other schemes to be implemented if funds permitted. Finally, in January 1996, a county committee decided they were minded to scrap the plans. Wyre Forest District Council, who had been able to contemplate the disaster of the ring road for many years, could not bring themselves to agree, but their flawed vision was doomed and was eventually to be abandoned.

## KIDDERMINSTER HOSPITAL

Although the redevelopment of large swathes of the town was going to affect the quality of life of residents for decades, the issue of most concern to Kidderminster people was the future of the town's hospital. This helped David Lock to defeat the sitting Conservative MP, Anthony Coombs, in the general election of 1997. It was an event of some significance, which has since been eclipsed by Lock's extraordinary defeat four years later. Lock was only the second Labour MP in Kidderminster's history. In 1992 Coombs' majority had been over 10,000, but in 1997 Lock defeated him by nearly 7,000 votes. It was an historic moment for the local Labour Party. Yet by their handling of the hospital crisis they were to toss away their political advantage almost immediately.

It was Lock's misfortune that he had barely settled down when dark pronouncements concerning the hospital started to emerge. In the October after his election the health authority proposed to axe Kidderminster's Accident and Emergency Department and also 82 inpatient beds in order to deal with a £20m deficit. Furious opposition grew very quickly. There was a feeling of injustice that Kidderminster was being sacrificed so that Worcester might benefit from a pre-election commitment to a new hospital by Tony Blair. There was anger because so much money had been raised from local people by the League of Friends to assist the funding of developments at the hospital. Only two years previously a new block had been opened with operating theatres, a maternity ward and medical beds. An action group was formed under the chairmanship of a retired consultant, Dr Richard Taylor, with David Lock as one of the vice-chairmen. On 1 November a rally attracted 4,000 people, who were told by Lock that 'the hospital facilities are simply too good to close'. The anxiety extended well beyond Kidderminster, because the hospital was used by residents of Bridgnorth and other parts of south-east Shropshire. Within four weeks a petition of protest had gathered 66,351 signatures. Dr McCloskey, the Director of Public Health, fought back and attacked the 20-year-old 'myth' of the 'golden hour', which was widely regarded as the critical time for patients to get to hospital in an emergency. In February 1998, when the health authority opted for a draconian reduction of Kidderminster beds from 296 to little over a hundred, he referred to studies which showed that 42 per cent of patients did not need to be in hospital and could be nursed or cared for in other ways. The vision of the future saw Kidderminster Hospital converted into an 'ambulatory care centre', or in other words a bedless treatment centre.[10]

On 17 March the 1300-seat Forest Glades Arena was packed to hear the health authority Chief Executive, Pat Archer-Jones, attempt to convince doubters. She and Dr McCloskey were jeered and heckled. David Lock, sitting in the audience, said that 'people were well-informed and angry because they felt the pain was not being equally distributed around the county'. He was treading a tightrope, because he was on the brink of a promising ministerial career, having become parliamentary private secretary to the Lord Chancellor

98. Hospital Demonstration, March 1998. The hearse symbolised the death of excellence. Dr Richard Taylor is shown in the right foreground.

just before Christmas. His belief that local people were well informed was soon to change. The protests continued with a demonstration in March attended by an estimated 12,000 people. At its head was a horse-drawn hearse, which carried the message 'Death of Excellence'. Eight months later the dreaded verdict came from the Health Secretary, Frank Dobson. Kidderminster was to lose its A & E department and the capacity was to be reduced from 296 to 120 beds. It was no advance on the proposal of the previous February, and the optimistic response by David Lock sealed his fate as MP. 'This is good news for the people I represent,' he announced. The following day Dr Taylor said that it was 'laughable to say it's good news.'[11]

## HEALTH CONCERN

In April 1999 it was announced that campaigners would stand in elections for Wyre Forest District Council. In May Health Concern won seven seats, so that Labour lost its majority, having being reduced from 24 to 18 seats. Though Labour was still the largest party, the other parties combined to exclude them from office. Health Concern were to make progress every year and by May 2002 they held 21 seats, giving them control with the casting vote of the chairman. Labour's demise had an inevitability about it and they seemed to march headlong to defeat after defeat, convinced that they were right and everybody else was wrong.

The Labour Party had many experienced politicians, and throughout these events they clearly saw themselves as the professionals. Before the general election in 2001 Lock characterised Dr Taylor as 'naive'. Yet Labour treated the hospital not as a political issue, but as a matter for medical experts. Lock claimed to have the support of local doctors, and indeed GPs did declare their backing for the changes in November 2000. He also took seriously the Royal College of Physicians' belief that Kidderminster hospital was too small to offer adequate training opportunities to doctors. Lock told the local press that it was not the role of an MP to fight for what his constituents believed, but he had a 'responsibility to do what is right'. With the rest of his party offering largely silent support, Lock was in fact leaving the political field to Health Concern. They alone were able to give expression to the desire for essential health services close to the community. Health Concern were even able to make all the running on the finance issue. The new Worcester hospital was to be built and owned by a private company under the Private Finance Initiative. This was one of the Conservative policies which had been enthusiastically adopted by New Labour. Throughout the controversy, research was being produced by Professor Alison Pollock suggesting that in the long run this was a very expensive option, costing £30m more than a publicly funded hospital. It was left to Dr Taylor to oppose PFI and to ask if Kidderminster was to be sacrificed because of the cost.[12] The huge groundswell of support for retaining the hospital services had little impact upon the Labour Party. David Lock was not diverted from pursuing his ministerial career. In August 1999 he was promoted to parliamentary secretary in the Lord Chancellor's department, putting him on the government's payroll. In June 2000 a lobby of 500 Kidderminster people attended parliament, but the minister, Alan Milburn, refused to meet them. Lock came face to face with them and afterwards spoke of 'mob rule' and complained of being 'jostled' as he tried to leave. In November later that year Tony Blair visited the floods at Bewdley and was confronted by hospital campaigners. Lock complained that it was 'outrageous that protestors had hijacked the visit'. A senior Labour Party member, Barry McFarland, denounced the crowd as a 'thoughtless mob'.[13]

Health Concern was free to become the major local political force as Labour quit the field. Only two of the party's significant members ever voiced disquiet about their position. In a joint statement in December 2000 the veteran John Wardle and Kidderminster Mayor Nigel Knowles called for the reinstatement of the A & E unit and the lost beds.[14] Otherwise Labour headed for inevitable defeat in the general election, for which Dr Taylor announced his candidacy in February 2001. Towards the end of May, less than two weeks before the

99. Dr Taylor with Martin Bell and John Fortune. They shared a platform at a public meeting in May 2001 prior to the general election.

election, Dr Taylor addressed an audience of over 400 people at a public meeting in the Town Hall, where he stated that doctors had been prevented from revealing their true opinions because of the threat of disciplinary action. By contrast the Labour Party held no public meetings, even though Lock evidently believed that the majority of his constituency was ill-informed and misguided. Their remoteness was inexplicable for a party which had waited so long for the opportunity gained in 1997. On 7 June Dr Taylor romped home, securing 28,487 votes as against Lock's 10,857. Dr Taylor's personal vote and his majority were among the biggest in the country. Lock was far from chastened. Within a few weeks of this trouncing he commented that single issue campaigns 'use experts' reports like a drunk uses a lamp post – for support not illumination.'[15]

## PRIVATE FINANCE AND THE INCINERATOR

The impact on Kidderminster of New Labour's commitment to principles developed by Margaret Thatcher has been considerable. Public bodies have been unable to raise their own finance for new projects, and have found it necessary to involve private companies in funding arrangements which might prove very costly in the long term. The changing reality of financial power in the town was graphically illustrated by the final closure of the cattle market on Comberton Hill in 1998 after years of decline. In October 2001 a new magistrates court was opened on the site under the Private Finance Initiative. It was Britain's first privately funded magistrates court. Less than a year later questions were being asked as to whether it had been value for money.[16] Another PFI project was the incinerator planned for Stourport Road, and this potentially most damaging development was stopped only by the courageous hard work of SKI

(Stop Kidderminster Incinerator), a small group of campaigners boosted by the efforts of the Forest Gate Residents and Friends of the Earth.

The provision of incinerators was one of the government solutions to the problem of finding landfill sites for huge amounts of waste. Having seen a large part of their historic town dragged off to such sites, it was the final insult to Kidderminster to be selected as the host for the county's incinerator. Furthermore, the chosen location was very close to residential areas and the threat of pollution was obvious. On such a vital issue the County Council managed to tie itself closely to private interests, whilst failing to consult the public adequately. In July 1998, when consultation started, the council had already appointed FOCSA, a Spanish company, as their preferred contractor, and by December a 25-year contract had been signed. The attempts at consultation were widely seen as half-hearted and there were many claims that the real discussions were taking place in secret. Questions posed by the public and others went unanswered because of contract confidentiality and the PFI agreement. According to Friends of the Earth, the council's determination to 'railroad the scheme through in secret' cost ratepayers £950,000.[17]

The convoluted nature of the events saw FOCSA, through a company called Mercia Waste Management, identify part of the British Sugar site for their operations, which were to be carried out by yet another company, Severn Waste Services. The land consisted of a narrow strip adjoining the Stourport Road,

100. Celebrating victory in their campaign to stop the incinerator are, left to right, Kate Brookes, Ian Brookes, Hilary Mueller, Chris Connor, Melvyn Thompson and Martin Mueller.

but broadening out by the canal, the whole being north of the water treatment works. The persistent and skilled work of the campaigners resulted in a major triumph in April 2001, when the County Council's own planning committee threw out the application by eleven votes to two. The County Council, as the waste authority, was now in conflict with itself. The matter went to a public enquiry for resolution, which was held in the Town Hall between 19 February and 27 March 2002. The dedication of campaigners was rewarded in July, when the decision of the Planning Inspector, Ken Smith, was announced confirming the rejection of the scheme. In his decision he noted that a high degree of confidentiality surrounded the award of the contract and its content. He found that there had been no realistic Best Practicable Environmental Assessment. In its absence he concluded that there was no evidence that the proposed incinerator was needed at all, on the Stourport Road or on any other site. The town waited to see whether Severn Waste Services would appeal, especially as it had been revealed that the County Council would underwrite their costs under the terms of their agreement. Fortunately, it was announced in August that there would be no appeal.

By this time British Sugar had vacated their entire site. Production ceased after 76 years on 25 January 2002. At the end it was employing 52 staff, plus 60 casual staff for four months every winter. British Sugar was to concentrate processing at other sites and the Kidderminster sugar beet was to be taken to Telford. Two years later, in early 2004, the site remains vacant.

CONSERVATION

Whilst public attention was gripped by the controversy about the hospital and the incinerator, the efforts to conserve the town's heritage were boosted. In 1998 the council sold Caldwall Tower to Richard Davies, who in the space of four years has restored it magnificently. It is regularly open to the public and is now one of Kidderminster's finest assets. In February 1999 the work of the Civic Society was rewarded by the listing of three former carpet factory buildings. One of them was the Stour Vale works at the top of Green Street, which contains fine brickwork. Another was the former Mortons factory between Green Street and New Road, incorporating the magnificent Paddington House and its tower. The third site to be listed comprised the equally attractive buildings at the lower end of Green Street, which had been erected by William Green in 1869.[18] The latter were part of the property acquired for redevelopment by Morbaine Ltd from Victoria Carpets. They have been well restored by Morbaine, whose fine work was recognised by the Civic Society in April 2003 with its Jubilee Award.

## WEAVERS WHARF

The wisdom of the Civic Society in seeking listing for these buildings was highlighted by the drastic changes in the plans for the Brintons site, when proposals began to emerge in July 1999. The exciting ideas of three years ago had been dropped. There were no plans to use the Piano Building, which was clearly threatened with demolition. The building on Castle Road, with its striking Art Deco frontage, was to be pulled down. The entire concept of mixed use had been abandoned, with no provision for cultural facilities or housing. The development was to be dominated by retail use. With public attention focused firmly on the hospital, the planning application produced only four letters commenting on the proposals. At a public meeting in October organised by the Civic Society, with no councillors present, planning officers admitted that the plans were driven primarily by commercial interests. It was a theme to be repeated many times by leading councillors as work on the Brintons site took shape. Commercial reality seemed to mean that above all Weavers Wharf needed an 'anchor tenant' to be financially viable.[19] This was to be the Tesco

superstore, which opened well before the rest of the site was ready. Tesco had been in discussion with Morbaine, who wanted them on their Green Street development, but so vital were they to the success of Weavers Wharf that Brintons refused an offer of £8m from Morbaine to let Tesco go.[20] In the end the developers of Green Street had to be content with a B&Q superstore as their anchor tenant. Truly Kidderminster was taking on the appearance of Merry Hill.

Between early 1996 and July 1999 the lauding of Kidderminster's majestic mills had apparently become a luxury the town could ill afford. Only Slingfield Mill, because it was listed, was to

101. Wool Hall, one of the trio of mills originally intended to give Weavers Wharf unique character, but pulled down in 2002.

be restored, but even that was to be devoted to commercial use. Until 2000 there had been high hopes that it would be converted into an arts centre, but these were dashed under the new council led by Mike Oborski. There was little appetite for expenditure among the council. In June 1999 a proposal to turn the derelict Rock Works in Park Lane into a youth club was rejected by a council committee because the site would be 'unsafe' for youngsters and would lead to increased 'vandalism and anti-social behaviour', despite the fears of John Wardle and other councillors that youngsters were being branded as 'hooligans'. This lack of vision began to lead to the dismantling of the historic buildings at Weavers Wharf. In February 2001 a chimney was demolished, followed several months later by the very fine mill, known as the Wool Hall. Both structures had been identified in the original planning brief as buildings worthy of retention. The Wool Hall was destroyed within days of the rejection of an application for listing by the Civic Society. However, there was to be some success for the Society in that the Art Deco frontage on Castle Road was preserved and incorporated in a new building as part of the Tesco development. Yet the relentless push by the developers for clearing away the old buildings was continuing, and the Civic Society was to find itself under fire in a bitter struggle to save the Piano Building, which also had been designated by the council as worthy of preservation.

## A QUESTION OF LEADERSHIP

The transformation in the plans for Weavers Wharf coincided with the rise of Health Concern and the removal of Labour from power in May 1999. Leading Labour councillor, Nigel Knowles, warned that the town-centre development would require 'political steerage'. The chairman of the Nonentities, Colin Young, is in no doubt that this change in leadership led to the scrapping of plans to convert Slingfield Mill into an arts centre. The Nonentities had been prepared to contribute all their capital tied up in the Rose Theatre to the project in order finally to realise their hopes of creating a genuine town theatre. Cllr Mike Kelly was one of those on Labour's side who had led the discussions, and he confirms Young's account of the optimism that existed in early 1999. Under the alliance led by Cllr Mike Oborski, the mood and the plans changed, and it is said that Young and Kelly never had any reason for optimism. In 2000 a report on the feasibility of the conversion of Slingfield Mill revealed that the developers, Centros Miller, would charge a commercial rent for an arts centre. This effectively killed off the scheme, because to be financially viable an arts centre requires a peppercorn rent. The suspicion remained that the council could have extracted a deal for the town. In May 2002, when he resigned as leader, Cllr Oborski said that he and his colleagues had got the development 'moving'. His Labour counterpart, Jamie Shaw, saw it differently, referring to it as a 'fiasco' which had been 'ceded to the developers'.

After overseeing the loss of the chimney and the Wool Hall, Cllr Oborski announced in October 2001 the possibility that a cinema could be built at Weavers Wharf, but it would require the 'sacrifice' of the Piano Building. Built in 1868 over its own arm of the canal, the mill had a curved northern wall, which followed the historic track known as the Sling. It was a building of great character and it was entirely predictable that there would be opposition to its demise. Its demolition would have meant that the council had permitted the destruction of the greater part of the area which in 1996 they believed gave Kidderminster its unique character. Nevertheless for a while it seemed that the town might enjoy both a cinema and the Piano Building. In autumn of 2002 approval was given for a cinema to be built on Crossley Park, against the advice of planning officers. The Civic Society, which had strongly backed this site for the cinema, then applied for the listing of the Piano Building. In February 2003 the council, on the advice of planning officers, gave approval to the demolition of the Piano Building so that a cinema might be built. Events immediately unfolded to leave the town with no plans for a cinema and the Civic Society as scapegoats.

102. Weavers Wharf. The development takes shape with the new college in the background and the Piano Building awaits its fate.

The application for Crossley Park had included a store which sold small goods. Planning officers doggedly argued that this contravened the town plan which required only 'bulky' goods be sold. The application was called in by the Secretary of State, and in the face of such uncertainty the developers pulled out in February 2003. Shortly afterwards it was announced that the Civic Society had been successful in its request for the Piano Building to be listed. Cllr Mike Oborski, who had waged his own campaign for a cinema, denounced the Civic Society. They were 'half-baked' and had 'idiotically sabotaged the whole enterprise'. The Piano Building was now described as 'useless' and part of the 'debris and rubbish of the past'. For good measure he attacked the Society's work in the listing of

103. Worcester Cross Factory. Formerly the Magistrates Court and the last home for the indoor market, much of this building now lies empty and its future is under threat.

bombazine weavers' cottages in the Horsefair, which were 'useless and hideous'.[21] Oborski received a good deal of support in the letter columns of the *Shuttle*, where the mill was regularly dismissed as an 'eyesore' or a 'monstrosity'. The furore exposed the lack of political will concerning conservation, even though the 1996 planning brief for Weavers Wharf had been committed to it. In its campaign to save the Piano Building the Civic Society had the support of the government watchdog CABE, and of the national charity SAVE. English Heritage was in no doubt about the merit of the Piano Building. Their inspector's letter said, 'the listing of this distinguished and unusual Victorian warehouse is highly recommended'. Yet in Kidderminster there was evidently little pride in the building.

The unique character of the town is being progressively eroded. As well as being an industrial town, Kidderminster has been a market town for about 800 years. In 1996 planners envisaged three markets for Weavers Wharf, but now it is possible that Kidderminster has ceased to be a market town of any kind. In December 2003 the indoor market at Worcester Cross closed with no prospect of new premises. The Piano Building was available, but the council lacked the resources to pay a rent which would satisfy the developers. Like other towns, Kidderminster is dominated by big money and chain stores. Small businesses continue to struggle to survive. In 2002, for example, the Coventry Street electrical stores, J. and H. Russell, announced they could no longer compete and would be closing after eighty years or so trading in the town.[22] Another serious loss came with the decision of Fagins, the only specialist bookshop in the town, to close in March 2004. The council's capacity to influence events seems to be minimal, particularly as they have released so many freehold interests in the town. We may further illustrate the apparent powerlessness of the council. In September 2003 the new college opened next to the library, and the old Hoo Road site was being redeveloped. A condition was attached that the old hedge along the road be preserved. Yet in May 2003 trees and hedging were removed, despite council officers and councillors being informed that it was taking place.

On 18 March 2004 the *Shuttle* announced the 'dawn of a new era' and the 'complete shopping experience' at Weavers Wharf, which was to be opened seven days later by the Duke of Kent. The town would now be able to compete with Merry Hill and Worcester for shoppers. The ballyhoo surrounding this

104. Slingfield Mill 2004, the magnificent centrepiece of Weavers Wharf.

partial revitalisation of the town centre for the moment obscured the work still needed to restore residential, entertainment and cultural facilities, and also to enable local traders to survive or to start up new businesses.

## A PLACE WHERE CARPETS ARE MADE

This story must end somewhere, although the story of Kidderminster will go on. So far it has been a colourful story of the struggle of a small town to develop an industry which made it famous across the world. It has been a story of much sacrifice by its inhabitants along the way, as comfort and a decent environment have been postponed or compromised to ensure the health of the industry. We leave the town at a time when its identity is by no means clear. The carpet industry has declined so much, and the authorities have continued to permit the destruction of its industrial architecture. Kidderminster is a town where people live and shop, and whether it can be much more remains to be seen. The battles of the last decade, though they have sometimes been waged by small groups, show that many aspire to something better. There are some positive developments. Kidderminster is in the public eye a little because of the rise of the football club to League status, but their fine football has so far attracted disappointing crowds. The role of the College in promoting young rock groups and developing a record label is another promising contribution to the future growth and culture of the town.

At the end we must return to carpets, and sadly mark the continued decline. In 1999 the last spinning mill in Kidderminster closed, when Greatwich Ltd shut down its Clensmore site with the loss of 80 jobs. The historic firm of Tomkinsons has been taken over by a northern company, Gaskells, who abandoned production in Kidderminster. Only part of the Clensmore site is now in use, purely for storage and distribution. Another historic name was taken over when, in May 2003, Brintons acquired their rival Woodward Grosvenor.[23] Other companies remain, such as Adam Carpets, Brockway, Carpets of Kidderminster and Victoria. They have to carve a niche for themselves in a market dominated by cheap tufted carpets from countries such as Belgium. Brintons remain the most important, and in 2000 their profits exceeded £10m for the first time. They have specialised in high quality contract work. The future is uncertain, and in December 2003 Brintons were reported to be making a loss as a result of cutbacks in orders from hotels and cruise liners after the terrorist attack on New York.[24] Although the excellence of Kidderminster's Axminster product, led by Brintons, has long been recognised, demand has been undermined by the recent fashion for either a plainer carpet or a wooden floor. Kidderminster is no longer the centre of the carpet world, but at least for the time being it remains a place where carpets are made.

# Notes

**Abbreviations:**

BWJ      *Berrow's Worcester Journal*
HER      Historic Environment Record, University College, Worcester.
KS      *Kidderminster Shuttle*
KT      *Kidderminster Times*
PRO      Public Record Office
SRO      Stafford Record Office
TTM      *Ten Towns Messenger*
TWAS      *Transactions of Worcestershire Archaeological Society*
VCHW      *Victoria County History of Worcestershire*
WCHS      Wolverley and Cookley Historical Society
WRO      Worcester Record Office

## Chapter One: Before Kidderminster

1. Oliver Rackham, *Trees and Woodland in the British Landscape* (2002), p35.
2. HER, refs. 29913, 5128, 8167 and 2082.
3. WCHS, Journal Number Three (1992), pp7-17.
4. HER, ref. 1180.
5. HER, refs. 29913, 29914, 5446, 7584, 5734 and 31023.
6. Rev. H.R. Mayo, *The Annals of Arley* (1914), p7.
7. KS 10.8.1958.
8. Victoria Buteux, *Archaeological Assessment of Kidderminster* (Dec. 1996), pp1,4; KS 6.6.1980; Edward Broadfield, *A Guide to Kidderminster* (1889), p33.
9. Sir Frank Stenton, *Anglo-Saxon England* (1971), p40; Sarah Zaluckyj, *Mercia* (2001), pp14, 102.
10. Della Hooke, *The Landscape of Anglo-Saxon England* (1998), pp46, 62.
11. This translation is taken from an article by P.W. King, 'The Minster *Aet Sture* in Husmere and the Northern Boundary of the Hwicce', TWAS (1996).
12. Stenton, *op. cit.*, p279.
13. Margaret Gelling, WCHS, Journal Number Twelve (2002), p9.
14. Stenton, *op. cit.*, p160.
15. Gelling, *op. cit.*, pp7-9; Don Gilbert, WCHS, Journal Number Four, p72.
16. Dr McCave, *Kidderminster Sun*, 6.5.1876; J.R. Burton, *A History of Kidderminster* (1890), p9. Margaret Gelling favours Cydela's minster, even though the 'l' appears only briefly in the town's name in the 12th century.
17. *The Story of Kidderminster Parish Church* (10th edition), p2.
18. Lucy Torode, WCHS, Journal Number Three (1992), p20; Hooke, *op. cit.*, p13.
19. Hooke, *op. cit.*, p62.
20. Burton, *op. cit.*, p7.
21. Michael Aston, *Interpreting the Landscape* (1985), p124.
22. Rackham, *op. cit.*, p186.

## Chapter Two: The Middle Ages

1. This translation is taken from Domesday Book published by Phillimore (1982).
2. H.C. Darby and I.B. Terrett, *The Domesday Geography of Midland England*, p262.
3. J.R. Burton, *A History of Bewdley* (1883), p3.
4. Darby and Terrett, *op. cit.*, p242. The authors broadly agree with Burton by suggesting a multiplier of four or five, p430.
5. Domesday Book, note 1,1c.
6. Michael Aston, *Interpreting the Landscape* (1985), p111; Oliver Rackham, *Trees and Woodland in the British Landscape*, pp166 and 168.
7. J.R. Burton, *A History of Kidderminster* (1890), p14.
8. Articles by R.A. Lewis KT 19.10.1951 and KS 24.9.1954.
9. Burton, *op. cit.*, pp101-13.
10. For legend see R.A. Lewis article, KT 19.10.1951; for Crossfield reference see SRO D/1317/6/20/5.
11. Burton, *op. cit.*, p48; Ian Walker, *West Midlands Annual Archaeological News Sheet*, No.2 1959.
12. See p6 of article by Don Gilbert in *Kidderminster 350* (1986), a souvenir publication to celebrate 350 years of the town's charter.
13. A.J. Perrett, 'The Blounts of Kidderminster', TWAS (1942); E. Lipson, *The Economic History of England* (1962), Vol. I p223.
14. HER, ref. 30046; the second mill of Domesday is generally thought to have been at Mitton.
15. R.A. Lewis, *Kidderminster Stuffs* (1959), p4.
16. Burton, *op. cit.*, p25; Lay Subsidy Roll available at Worcestershire Library and History Centre in Worcester, ref. L336.22.
17. VCHW iii p170.
18. Burton, *op. cit.*, pp106-12. For comparison, in the 13th-century list printed by Burton, which excluded Hurcott, 13 tenants from Oldington were paying a total of 50s. rent. The house on the south side of the church may have developed into the manor house of the Blounts.
19. J.W. Willis-Bund, *Inquisitiones Post Mortem County of Worcestershire* (1242-1346), pt. II, pp15-20.
20. HER, ref. 23983.
21. VCHW iii p171.
22. Richard Lockett, *A Survey of Historic Parks and Gardens in Worcestershire* (1997), p102.
23. Burton, *op. cit.*, pp108 and 110.

24. Don Gilbert and Richard Warner, *Caldwall Hall* (1999), pp2 and 22; Ian Walker, 'Excavations at Caldwall Hall Kidderminster 1961-69', TWAS (1992).
25. E.D. Priestley Evans, *History of New Meeting House* (1900), p158, confirms these 18th-century boundaries of the Caldwall Estate.
26. The attempts to understand the history of Caldwall involve at least two current schools of thought. Ian Walker, as an archaeologist, is preoccupied with the possibility that the ground level of the Stour valley has been raised considerably around the castle over the centuries. He doubts whether there was ever a moated castle with a number of towers. Richard Davies, as a dedicated owner exploring every aspect of the property's history, is convinced there was such a castle. He doubts the theory of the raised ground level.
27. Lucy Torode, WCHS, Journal Number Four (1993), pp19-21.
28. Willis-Bund, *op. cit.*, pt. II, viii.
29. Don Gilbert, *Kidderminster 350*, p7.
30. This figure is arrived at by using tenant figures from inquisitions of 1294 and 1307 for the Burnell and Biset manors, adding in appropriate numbers for Oldington, Comberton and Hurcott, and assuming an average household of four. The Lay Subsidy Roll of 1275 suggests a lower figure of about 560, but it may have excluded very poor people.
31. Lay Subsidy Roll, 1327, introduction by the Rev. F.J. Eld.
32. VCHW iii pp160/161.
33. Don Gilbert and Richard Warner, *op. cit.*, p2. Richard Davies, on the other hand, prefers a mid-14th-century date.
34. Cal Pat Rolls Henry VI 1446-52 p224.
35. Cal Pat Rolls Henry VI 1422-29 p423.
36. Cal Pat Rolls Henry VI 1446-52 p386.
37. Lewis, *op. cit.*, p5.

### Chapter Three: The Making of a Cloth Town

1. J.R. Burton, *A History of Kidderminster* (1890), p173.
2. R.A. Lewis, *Kidderminster Stuffs* (1959), p7.
3. Alan Dyer, *The City of Worcester in the sixteenth century* (1973), pp93, 117-18.
4. Lewis, *op. cit.*, pp7-9; T.R. Nash, *Collections for the History of Worcestershire* (1782), ii p39. Nash thought that only 300 of them lived in the town of Kidderminster, which was only an 'inconsiderable village'. That estimate was probably too low according to A.J. Perrett in KS 30.1173.
5. *The Itinerary of John Leland* is available at Kidderminster Public Library.
6. A.J. Perrett, 'The Blounts of Kidderminster', TWAS (1942); the will of Sir Edward Blounte available at Public Record Office, prob 11/159; David Hazell, WCHS, Journal Number Nine, p12. It is thought that the mill may have forged blades for the Royalists in 1643.
7. Worcestershire Archaeology Newsletter no. 2 July 68.
8. Soley information from Add. MSS 31,003 available in British Library; Richard Crane will at WRO, probate 1609; Sebright purchase SRO, D593/B/15; Comberton Hall VCHW iii pp 167, 169.
9. Arthur Marsh, *The Carpet Weavers of Kidderminster* (1995), p2.
10. Lewis, *op. cit.*, p29.
11. Dyer, *op. cit.*, p119.
12. Christopher Hill, *Reformation to Industrial Revolution* (1969), pp69-70.
13. Lewis, *op. cit.*, p19.
14. Despite their confident presentation, the Ship Money assessment of 1635 was to reveal Kidderminster as a town of modest wealth below Worcester, Evesham, Droitwich, and Bewdley. The town paid £30 as against Bewdley's £70. Burton, *op. cit.*, p72.
15. Don Gilbert, *Kidderminster 350*, pp9-15.
16. G.F. Nuttall, *Richard Baxter* (1965), p25.
17. Burton, *op. cit.*, p48. This raises the possibility that ownership of the manor house should be traced back to the Maiden Bradley portion, not the Biset portion, as previously assumed by VCHW, p161. See also note 18 to Chapter Two.
18. Don Gilbert, 'Kidderminster at the Outbreak of the English Civil War', TWAS (1988), pp37, 46. The remains of the mutilated cross were moved in 1876 to a position south of the chancel.
19. Lewis, *op. cit.*, p7. Baxter himself estimated it to be between three and four thousand, Nuttall, *op. cit.*, p46.
20. Lewis, *op. cit.*, p22.
21. Malcolm Atkin, *The Civil War in Worcestershire* (1995), p123.
22. Don Gilbert, *op. cit.*, p45.
23. Atkin, *op. cit.*, p92.
24. Archaeology at Worcester Cathedral, Report of the Seventh Annual Symposium (March 1997).
25. VCHW ii, p255.
26. Burton, *op. cit.*, pp174-5.
27. Rev. Edward Bradley, *The Leisure Hour* (1872), p505.
28. John Hamilton Davies, *The Life of Richard Baxter* (1887), p431.
29. Christopher Hill, *The World Turned Upside Down* (1972), p330.
30. J.W. Willis Bund (ed.), *Diary of Henry Townshend* (1915), pp40-1; Nuttall, *op. cit.*, p76.
31. See Davies, *op. cit.*, pp274-7 and Nuttall, *op. cit.*, pp90-1.

### Chapter Four: The Nonconformists

1. R.A. Lewis, *Kidderminster Stuffs* (1959), p27.
2. Lewis, *op. cit.*, pp1, 31-5.
3. In 1961 the walls began to bulge, and it was found that large amounts of timber from the earlier house had been built into the brickwork to save on bricks. The timber was riddled with woodworm and could no longer bear the weight of the structure. The house was condemned and pulled down. Ian Walker, *op. cit.*, TWAS 'Excavations at Caldwell Hall Kidderminster 1961-69' (1992).
4. Nigel Gilbert, *The Rise and Fall of Franche Hall* (1999).
5. WRO 10470/27.
6. VCHW iii pp169, 172 and 173.
7. George Hunsworth, *Baxter's Nonconformist Descendants* (1874), p14.
8. Bewdley Historical Research Group, *Bewdley in its Golden Age* (1991), pp15-16, 26.
9. J.R. Burton, *A History of Kidderminster* (1890), p176-80.
10. T.R. Nash, *Collections for the History of Worcestershire* (1782), ii p42.
11. Lewis, *op. cit.*, p34.
12. I thank David Everett for drawing my attention to this. The assistance was by means of a 'brief', i.e. a royal mandate for the parish church to organise a collection for a supposedly deserving object. See W.E. Tate, *The Parish Chest* (1983), p120.
13. Burton, *op. cit.*, pp16-18; W. Pitt, *General View of the Agriculture of the County of Worcester* (1813),

p207; BWJ 15.6.1833.
14. WRO 10470/91.
15. SRO D/1317/6/20/5
16. Benjamin Hanbury, *Extracts from the Diary of Joseph Williams* (1826), p29.
17. Don Gilbert, 'Kidderminster's Early Carpet Industry', TWAS (1990), p213.
18. Hanbury, *op. cit.*, pp2, 48, 55 and 101.
19. Rev. Richard Pearsall, *The Power and Pleasure of the Divine Life exemplify'd in the late Mrs Housman of Kidderminster Worcestershire* (1744), entries for 28 March 1724 and 9 October 1731.
20. Lewis, *op. cit.*, p35.
21. Lewis, *op. cit.*, p38.
22. Edmund S. Morgan, *The Puritan Family* (1966), p5.
23. Hanbury, *op. cit.*, pp106, 108-9.
24. Hanbury, *op. cit.*, pp53-4.
25. Hanbury, *op. cit.*, pp2, 5, 79, 87-8.
26. Don Gilbert, *op. cit.*, p214.
27. WRO 10470/151.
28. Len Smith, *Carpet Weavers and Carpet Masters* (1986), p6.
29. KS 29.12.1900.
30. Don Gilbert, *op. cit.*, p216.

**Chapter Five: Industrialisation**
1. Len Smith, *Carpet Weavers and Carpet Masters* (1986), p187, refers to Lord Foley as 'far sighted'. Don Gilbert, 'Kidderminster Early Carpet Industry', TWAS (1990), p223, has noted that it was even claimed that 300 houses were to be built.
2. BWJ 20.3.1753 and 7.3.1754.
3. WRO 8955.
4. Ebenezer Guest VII, KS 6.5.1905.
5. WRO 10470/82. These were probably no. 28 Church Street.
6. Benjamin Hanbury, *Extracts from the Diary of Joseph Williams* (1826), pp 112 and 374.
7. Len Smith, *op. cit.*, p220.
8. Nigel Gilbert, *Ridiculous Refinement* (2001), pp8-11.
9. BWJ 5.7.1770.
10. SRO D1317/6/20/2/1-29.
11. R.A. Lewis, *Kidderminster Stuffs* (1959), pp47-8.
12. BWJ 5.9.76; Rodney Hampson, 'Kidderminster Pottery', *Journal of the Northern Ceramic Society* (1994); Ian Walker, *West Midlands Annual Archaeological News Sheet* (1965).
13. Lewis, *op. cit.*, p59, broadly follows Nash, though the latter, writing in 1780, painted a worse picture. He said that the number of looms then in the town 'hardly amount to seven hundred'.
14. Lewis, *op. cit.*, pp45, 49 and 59.
15. BWJ 15.2.76.
16. *Universal British Directory of Trade* 1793.
17. Sophia Kelly (ed.), *The Life of Mrs Sherwood*, p64.
18. Lewis, *op. cit.*, pp57 and 62.
19. His will, probate 21.12.1775, is held at WRO, and contains a gift of 'that coppice ground in Habberley'. This bequest confirms that almost certainly he was a member of the Crane family of Habberley.
20. Don Gilbert, *op. cit.*, p219.
21. The wills of Pearsall and Lea are held at the PRO, probate Dec. 1794 and Aug. 1780 respectively.
22. KS 22.6.1935.
23. WRO 5278/63 and 5012.
24. R.L. Downes, *The Kidderminster Enclosure Award of 1775*, available in Kidderminster Public Library.
25. Nigel Gilbert, *op. cit.*, pp12-13. Rebecca was the daughter of Sergeant Crane and granddaughter of Henry, the wealthy Church Street woolstapler.

26. Kelly, *op. cit.*, pp60-62.
27. George Hunsworth, *Baxter's Nonconformist Descendants* (1874), p40.
28. E.D. Priestley Evans, *History of New Meeting House* (1900), pp34 and 178.
29. Priestley Evans, *op. cit.*, pp221, 237-8.
30. PRO, probate 20.10.1798.
31. Bill Gwilliam, *Worcestershire's Hidden Past*, p195.
32. BWJ 28.6.1804.
33. KT 30.11.1951; BWJ 17.5.1792.
34. KT 29.1.1954; KS 25.3.2004.

**Chapter Six: A Carpet Town**
1. Taken from an undated cutting from the *Birmingham Post* seen by the author. The letter was to be auctioned, probably in the late 1990s.
2. Nigel Gilbert, *Ridiculous Refinement* (2001), pp 16-18, 76.
3. Nigel Gilbert (ed.), *Kidderminster Foreign* (2002), pp14-16, 111-12.
4. BWJ 1.7.1813; BWJ 27.1.14.
5. KS 2.7.98. The details of the buildings affected by the fire in Barn Street provide further evidence that the Foley plan of 1753 for weavers' cottages never came to pass.
6. Len Smith, *Carpet Weavers and Carpet Masters* (1986), pp12 and 185.
7. *Worcester Herald*, 27.11.1817.
8. Len Smith, *op. cit.*, p88.
9. WRO 10470/130 and 2838.
10. George Hunsworth, *Baxter's Nonconformist Descendants* (1874), p71. For some reason Orchard Street became known as Fish Street for a time.
11. The information in this paragraph is from the authors of a history of Brintons, Len Smith and Don Gilbert, commissioned by the company some years ago and still unpublished. In 1874 John Brinton himself was to provide conclusive proof of the approximate year of foundation, when he referred to their 'fifty years standing', KS 24.10.1874.
12. WRO 10470/75.
13. David J. Martin, *The Kidderminster Paving Commissioners 1813-1856*, p11. Birmingham had four such acts by 1812, Droitwich had one in 1755, Ludlow in 1756, and both Dudley and Stourbridge in 1791.
14. Martin, *op. cit.*, pp37-47.
15. Mr Laird, *Description of the County of Worcester* (1820).
16. *Kidderminster Messenger* 29.7.1836.
17. R.A. Lewis, *Kidderminster Stuffs* (1959), pp62 and 65.
18. Ebenezer Guest V, KS 22.4.1905.
19. A date stone of 1821 in Bromsgrove Street is recalled by former resident, Brian Smith. The 1921 OS map shows back-to-backs on South Street and Cross Street.
20. Melvyn Thompson, *Woven in Kidderminster* (2002), p144.
21. WRO 10765/3.
22. Ebenezer Guest XIX, KS 29.7.1905; WRO 9526/35.
23. WRO 10470/91 for sale to Willis; other information is derived by analysis of poor rate lists, WRO 4766 and 10470.
24. TTM 30.6.1838. Presumably Lea's country retreat was at Blakeshall.
25. Ebenezer Guest V and VII, KS 22.4.1905 and 6.5.1905. By 1833 Barn Street had become Dudley Street, BWJ 10.10.1833. The name change probably occurred in that year, during which Viscount Dudley died and the trustees of his son, Lord Ward,

purchased many of Lord Foley's Kidderminster estates.
26. Kevin Simpson, 'Anglican Church Extension in and around Nineteenth Century Kidderminster', TWAS (2000).
27. Len Smith, op. cit., p223.
28. The Times 2.6.1824.
29. E.P. Thompson, The Making of the English Working Class (1968), p564.
30. Len Smith, op. cit., pp93, 99, 103, 107, 108, 110, 111 and 115.
31. Len Smith, op. cit., pp114, 118.
32. Ebenezer Guest VII, KS 6.5.1905 and WRO 5278/45.
33. Len Smith, op. cit., pp125-6.
34. Len Smith, The Carpet Weaver's Lament (1979), pp66-73.
35. Len Smith, Carpet Weavers and Carpet Masters (1986), pp133-4.
36. Len Smith, op. cit., pp145-6.

**Chapter Seven: Hard Times**
1. Len Smith, Ph.D thesis, The Carpet Weavers of Kidderminster, 1800-1850 (1982), p332.
2. Len Smith, Carpet Weavers and Carpet Masters (1986), pp147-51.
3. Ebenezer Guest VII, KS 6.5.1905.
4. BWJ 4.10.1832.
5. Commission of Enquiry into the Employment of Children in Factories (1833).
6. Reports from Assistant Hand-Loom Weavers Commissioners (1840).
7. H. Gibbins, A History of the Grammar School of Kidderminster (1903), pP70-1.
8. BWJ 22.3.38. The only building still standing from the workhouse is the later lodge, built in 1874 on Sutton Road. The original plan, in the possession of the author, shows a stone yard and stores for 'broken' and 'unbroken' stones.
9. TTM 24.8.1838 and 31.8.1838.
10. Len Smith, op. cit., pp233-4.
11. David J. Martin, The Kidderminster Paving Commissioners 1813-1856, pp29-30; WRO 5278/76.
12. KS 23.1.1986.
13. Kevin Simpson, 'Anglican Church Extension in and around Nineteenth Century Kidderminster', TWAS (2000).
14. E.D. Priestley Evans, History of New Meeting House (1900), pp102-9.
15. Ebenezer Guest, KS 8.4.1905.
16. Reports to the Commissioners on the Employment of Children (1843).
17. Supplement to the Second Report of the Commissioners of Inquiry into the State of Large Towns and Populous Districts (1845).
18. TTM 2.9.1843, 8.1.1847 and 13.8.1847.
19. TTM 10.11.1848.
20. Susan Ann Smith, The Response of Kidderminster Town Council to the 19th Century Public Health Legislation 1848-1872 (1992), p42.
21. I am indebted here to the unpublished work of Chas Townley.
22. A. Patchett Martin, The Life and Letters of the Right Honourable Robert Lowe, Viscount Sherbrooke (1893), pp153-71; Ebenezer Guest XXIV, KS 2.9.1905.
23. Arthur Marsh, The Carpet Weavers of Kidderminster (1995), p61.
24. Susan Smith, op. cit., pp50, 59-61.
25. Brierley Hill Advertiser 2.11.1867.
26. Brierley Hill Advertiser 17.12.1868.

**Chapter Eight: Renewal**
1. J. Neville Bartlett, Carpeting the Millions, p32; KS 12.10.1872.
2. Church Street Baptist Church 1808-1958, available at Kidderminster Public Library; Ebenezer Guest VIII, KS 13.5.1905.
3. KS 21.5.1887.
4. Whiteoak, Kidderminster Infirmary 1880-1914, pp 5,6, 50 and 53.
5. KS 1.5.1875 and 12.1.1878.
6. KS 22.6.1878 and 10.4.1880.
7. Susan Ann Smith, The Response of Kidderminster Town Council to the 19th Century Public Health Legislation 1848-1872 (1992), pp48-9. Lea was reputed to have been satisfied with meeting his constituents annually, KS 29.12.1923.
8. KS 10.10.1874 and 12.12.1874.
9. KS 3.10.1874; Owen Ashton and Stephen Roberts, The Victorian working-class Writer (1999), pp70-4.
10. I am grateful to Scott Pettitt, a descendant of the Paget family, for this information.
11. KS 17.12.1887.
12. KS 16.5.1874.
13. KS 29.5.1875.
14. Ken Tomkinson and George Hall, Kidderminster since 1800 (1975), p12.
15. KS 28.10.1871.
16. KS 21.5.1876.
17. KS 24.3.1888.
18. Ebenezer Guest XXV, KS 9.9.1905; Arthur Marsh, Kidderminster (1995), p159.
19. Tomkinson and Hall, op. cit., pp 227-8.
20. Tomkinson and Hall, op. cit., pp29 and 32.
21. KS 22.3.1884; WRO 9526/35. The information on Larches Land Club comes from a small arbitrary collection of deeds and papers stored by Bewdley museum among the artefacts formerly housed by Kidderminster museum.
22. KS 26.6.1880.
23. Bertram Jacobs, The Story of British Carpets (1968), p68.
24. KS 28.1.1893; 1903 Industrial Number published by KS.
25. KS 1.3.1884 and 19.4.1884.
26. KS 29.12.1983.
27. The Sun, 7.2.1885, carried the full report.
28. KS 3.4.1880, 24.4.1880, 24.9.1887 and 26.3.1893.
29. KS 14.3.1891.
30. Bartlett, op. cit., p79.
31. KS 10.01.1891.
32. KS 9.3.1895.
33. E.P. Thompson, The Making of the English Working Class (1968), pp69-70; Bartlett, op. cit., pp111-12.
34. Bartlett, op. cit., p83.

**Chapter Nine: War and Empire**
1. KS 18.11.1899 and 20.1.1900.
2. KS 14.10.1899.
3. KS 21.10.1899 and 4.11.1899.
4. KS 11.11.1899 and 20.1.1900.
5. Ken Tomkinson and George Hall, Kidderminster since 1800 (1975), p166.
6. KS 20.9.1902.
7. I am indebted here again to Chas Townley who, in October 2000, printed a summary of his research on Richard Eve for a talk he gave to the Civic Society.
8. Report of an Enquiry by the Board of Trade into Working Class Rents, Housing and Retail Prices (1908).
9. J. Neville Bartlett, Carpeting the Millions, p75.
10. E.P. Thompson, The Making of the English Working Class (1968), p163.

11. Bertram Jacobs, *The Story of British Carpets* (1968), pp95-6; KS 17.7.1943.
12. T. Carter, 'The Dissemination of Anthrax from Imported Wool: Kidderminster 1900-1914', *Occupational and Environmental Medicine* 2004; KS 31.12.1965.
13. Jacobs, *op. cit.*, pp81, 97 and 111; KS 21.6.1902.
14. KS 18.10.02; Whiteoak, *Kidderminster Infirmary 1880-1914*, pp18-19.
15. KS 27.1.1912.
16. KS 9.3.1912 and 12.10.1912.
17. KS 28.9.1912.
18. Jacobs, *op. cit.*, p117; Arthur Marsh, *The Carpet Weavers of Kidderminster* (1995), pp163-4; KS 22.8.1914.
19. KS 19.9.1914, 26.9.1914 and 7.11.1914.
20. H.P. Slacke, *The Worcestershire Regiment in the Great War* (1928), pp32-6; Martin Marix Evans, *Over the Top* (2002), p73.
21. KS 21.11.1914 and 28.11.1914.
22. KS 17.7.1943; Marsh, *op. cit.*, p164.
23. KS 30.9.1916 and 14.10.1916; Marsh, *op. cit.*, pp165 and 167.
24. Tomkinson and Hall, *op. cit.*, p169.
25. KS 27.1.1917 and 3.2.1917.

**Chapter Ten: Homes for Heroes**
1. J. Neville Bartlett, *Carpeting the Millions*, p189.
2. E.P. Thompson, *The Making of the English Working Class* (1968), p94; Bertram Jacobs, *The Story of British Carpets* (1968), p97; Arthur Marsh, *The Carpet Weavers of Kidderminster* (1995), pp162 and 179.
3. KS 20.2.1926.
4. Marsh, *op. cit.*, p174.
5. Ken Tomkinson and George Hall, *Kidderminster since 1800* (1975), p102.
6. KS 9.5.1925.
7. A.J.P. Taylor, *English History 1914-1945* (1966), p206.
8. KS 30.4.1921 and 28.5.1921; council minutes 1.2.1922.
9. KS 30.4.1921 and 23.7.1921; council minutes 1.3.1922.
10. Council minutes 15.7.1925.
11. Council minutes 2.1.1924.
12. Tomkinson and Hall, *op. cit.*, p72.
13. KS 26.3.1926.
14. *The Royal Visit to Kidderminster July 1926*, available from Kidderminster Public Library.
15. Thompson, *op. cit.*, p98.
16. Council minutes 8.7.1929.
17. Council minutes 9.1.1929.
18. Council minutes 16.3.1931. This site would be the starting point of any archaeological work to locate the medieval settlement of Sutton.
19. KS 5.12.1931.
20. Council minutes 27.5.1931, 10.1.1934 and 28.4.1937; KS 2.1.1932.
21. KS 19.9.1931 and 24.10.1931.
22. KS 30.1.1932, 7.1.1933 and 30.12.1933; Bartlett, *op. cit.*, p191.
23. Marsh, *op. cit.*, p188; Harry Dutfield, *Carpet Manufacturer and Fisherman*, available in Axminster public library.
24. KS 15.10.1932 and 11.11.1933.
25. KS 15.10.1932.
26. KS 3.6.1933.
27. Council minutes 20.9.1933.
28. KS 7.1.1933.
29. KS 12.8.1933.
30. KS 21.10.1933, 28.10.1933 and 11.11.1933.
31. Letter to council dated 27.8.1934.
32. KS 13.5.1933, 5.8.1933 and 28.10.1933.
33. KS 25.5.1937.
34. Marsh, *op. cit.*, pp191,196 and 198.
35. Marsh, *op. cit.*, p193; KS 18.3.1939.
36. Thompson, *op. cit.*, p98.

**Chapter Eleven: War and Recovery**
1. Ken Tomkinson and George Hall, *Kidderminster since 1800* (1975), p171.
2. My source is an undated *Express and Star* cutting, for which I must thank Dave Nobes and his wife.
3. KS 26.3.1941.
4. KS 9.5.1942; Reports of Maternity and Child Welfare Committee 11.3.1942 and 8.7.1942; KS 2.9.1942.
5. Council minutes 10.12.1941.
6. Quarterly Report of Borough Education Committee, 28.9.1940.
7. KS 22.12.1945.
8. Arthur Marsh, *The Carpet Weavers of Kidderminster* (1995), p202; E.P. Thompson, *The Making of the English Working Class* (1968), p100.
9. KS 9.11.1940 and 10.11.1945; Tomkinson and Hall, *op. cit.*, p173; Nigel Gilbert, *Kidderminster Foreign*, pp7-8.
10. KS 22.9.1945.
11. KS 29.12.1945; Marsh, *op. cit.*, p205.
12. KS 12.1.1946.
13. Council minutes 27.12.1945 and 31.12.1946. My thanks go to Mr Hipkiss' daughter, Mrs Frances Bradley, for information on the Newlands.
14. KT 30.11.1951; KS 20.7.1955; souvenir programme for opening of the Rose Theatre 21.11.1981.
15. Council minutes 16.4.1953; KS 1.5.1953.
16. Tomkinson and Hall, *op. cit.*, p144; council minutes 13.4.1953 and 20.7.1954; KS 24.9.1953.
17. KT 28.1.1955; Nigel Gilbert, *The Rise and Fall of Franche Hall*, pp47-8.
18. KS 1.4.1955.
19. Thompson, *op. cit.*, p112.
20. Marsh, *op. cit.*, pp207 and 233.
21. J. Neville Bartlett, *Carpeting the Millions*, p191.
22. KS 1.1.1954 and 4.1.1957.
23. Bertram Jacobs, *The Story of British Carpets* (1968), pp155 and 161; KS 11.5.1956 and 29.3.1957.
24. KS 8.10.1958.
25. KS 27.9.1957 and 1.1.1960.
26. John Moyle & Tony Pearson, *Kidderminster College 1879-1979*.
27. KS 29.1.1960.
28. KS 10.1.1958 and 17.1.1958.

**Chapter Twelve: Permanent Redevelopment**
1. KS 22.6.1956 and 17.4.1959.
2. KS 10.2.1961.
3. KS 3.1.1969.
4. Nikolaus Pevsner, *The Buildings of England: Worcestershire* (1968), p204.
5. KS 11.10.1963 and 31.12.1965.
6. KS 11.9.1964 and 5.3.1965.
7. KS 6.3.1964, 19.3.1965 and 9.4.1965.
8. KS 6.3.1964; KT 14.1.1966.
9. KS 14.1.1966 and 27.12.1968. The council's confidence about the ring road knew no bounds. In the centenary edition of the *Kidderminster Times* in 1967 the Town Clerk, John Evans, claimed a 'utopia' was being created.
10. At HER is a copy of a list of recommendations for listing of 24 buildings in January 1952. In every case the council's estimation was lower than that of the Ministry, including 15 buildings which the council

wanted deleted from the list.
11. KS 7.8.1953. The fourth inn was the *Anchor Hotel* in Worcester Street, which was pulled down in the 1950s to accommodate Co-op expansion.
12. KS 15.1.1965 and 12.2.1965; council minutes 11.6.1968 and 20.8.1968.
13. KS 2.2.1968; Mabel Payne was the granddaughter of Charles Payne, the Cherry Orchard Chartist.
14. BWJ 29.8.1754; KS 12.2.1965.
15. *Worcestershire Archaeology Newsletter* No. 2, July 1968.
16. The story is created from a scrapbook of press cuttings kindly lent to the author by the present chairman of the Nonentities, Colin Young. The date and source of many of them have not been identified.
17. KS 1.9.1967.
18. KS 14.4.1967 and *Centenary Supplement* 13.2.1970.
19. KS 24.1.1969.
20. KS 8.3.1968.
21. KS 13.2.1970 *Centenary Supplement*.
22. KS 13.2.1970 *Centenary Supplement*.
23. Arthur Marsh, *The Carpet Weavers of Kidderminster* (1995), p215. In fact, the union was still issuing the necessary weaving papers in the 1990s to those who had the required four years 'at the back of the loom' before the age of 21. Marsh, *op. cit.*, p226.
24. KS 13.2.1970 *Centenary Supplement*.
25. Article by Town Clerk, John Evans, in KS 13.2.1970 *Centenary Supplement*.
26. KS 12.1.1946.
27. KS 13.2.1970 *Centenary Supplement*, p30.
28. KS 10.1.1969.
29. Nigel Gilbert (ed.), *Kidderminster Foreign* (2002), pp73-9.
30. KS 13.2.1970 *Centenary Supplement*, p37.
31. Robert Barber, *Kidderminster – The Second Selection* (2002), p82.

**Chapter Thirteen: Wyre Forest**
1. See for example letter in KS 14.12.1973 and article in KS 7.1.1983.
2. Council minutes 25.2.1969; KS 14.12.1973.
3. KS 20.11.1970.
4. KS 6.11.1970.
5. KS 8.10.1971.
6. KT 20.10.1972.
7. KT 17.11.1972.
8. KT 27.10.1972; KS 21.9.1973 and 14.12.1973.
9. KS 24.1.1975, 31.1.1975, 28.3.1975 and 18.4.1975.
10. KS 24.1.1975 and 4.7.1975.
11. KS 31.1.1975. Brinton was charged £1255 for his rent strike by the council. However, he took the matter to the High Court, which ordered the council to repay the money. KS 11.4.1975 and 26.3.1976.
12. KS 7.2.1975 and 4.4.1975. Now, nearly twenty years later, a flood barrier has been built in the Stour valley above the town near Puxton.
13. KS 7.3.1975.
14. KS 24.8.1973 and 30.11.1973.
15. KS 13.12.1974 and 3.10.1975.
16. E.P. Thompson, *The Making of the English Working Class* (1968), p175; KS 17.1.1975 and 21.5.1976.
17. *Carpet Review*, December 1970, Kidderminster supplement, p23.
18. KS 5.1.1979 and 2.3.1979; Thompson, *op. cit.*, p182.
19. Arthur Marsh, *The Carpet Weavers of Kidderminster*,

pp 218-20.
20. KS 4.1. 1980 and 22.2.1985; Thompson, *op. cit.*, p183.
21. KS 4.1.1980, 22.2.1980, 1.1.1982 and 30.12.1983.
22. KS 5.1.1979 and 23.2.1979; KT 17.11.1972, supplement p5.
23. KS 2.11.1973.
24. KS 1.1.1982.
25. Private letter to the author. Alan Brooks is editing a new edition of Pevsner's *Buildings of Worcestershire*.
26. KS 20.4.1984.
27. KS 31.12.1976 and 16.2.1979.
28. *Express and Star* 28.1.85. John Cotterell argued that the council should have purchased the cinema for recreational and cultural facilities. He was ahead of his time.
29. KS 4.12.1981, 17.2.1984, 23.8.1985, 2.1.1986 and 13.3.1986.
30. KS 14.12.1973, 19.3.1976, 30.5.1980 and 2.1.1986.
31. KS 5.4.1985 and 6.12.1985; Thompson, *op. cit.*, pp158-9.
32. KS 16.1.1986.
33. Marsh, *op. cit.*, p222; KS 14.6.1990.
34. Marsh, *op. cit.*, p224.

**Chapter Fourteen: Rebellion**
1. Private letter to the author.
2. The story is put together from letters and documents held by Kidderminster Civic Society.
3. KS 25.2.1993. The same tactic was to be used a few years later in similar arguments over the Piano Building, which the demolition party claimed to be the only possible site for a cinema.
4. *Kidderminster Chronicle* 25.9.1992.
5. A shy council has never released a record of this named vote, despite the efforts of John Cotterell.
6. KS 21.1.1993.
7. KS 30.12.1993.
8. KS 3.4.2003.
9. E.P. Thompson, *The Making of the English Working Class* (1968), p150; KS 23.6.1994.
10. *Birmingham Post* 22.10.1997, 3.11.1997 and 14.2.1998; KS 6.11.1997 and 4.12.1997.
11. *Express and Star* 18.3.1998, 23.3.1998, 28.3.1998, 2.12.1998 and 3.12.1998.
12. *Worcester Evening News* 3.3.2001; KS 23.11.2000; *Kidderminster Chronicle* 16.7.1999; *Public Finance*, May/June 2000; *Birmingham Post* 10.2.2001.
13. KS 5.8.1999; *Worcester Evening News* 3.11.2000; KS 9.11.2000.
14. *Kidderminster Chronicle* 1.12.2000.
15. *Public Finance* June/July 2001.
16. KS 25.10.2001 and 18.7.2002.
17. KS 3.10.2002.
18. KS 4.2.1999.
19. The proposals for Crossley Park, published in March 1996, claimed that in order to be economically viable the Brintons scheme required a food superstore as an anchor tenant.
20. John Parle of Morbaine Ltd in a talk delivered to the Civic Society 11.6.2003.
21. KS 27.3.2003. At the time of writing the 'useless' Horsefair cottages are to be renovated.
22. KS 3.10.2002. Prior to entering the electrical trade, the Russell family had a small foundry in Clensmore.
23. KS 2.9.1999 and 22.5.2003; E.P. Thompson, *The Making of the English Working Class* (1968), p159.
24. KS 9.8.2001; *Daily Telegraph* 6.9.2003.

# Index

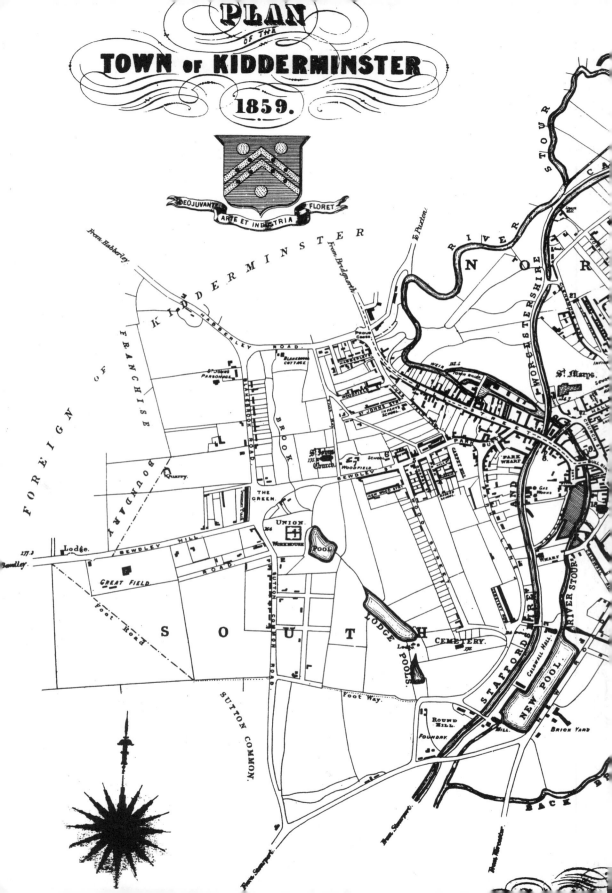

# PLAN
### OF THE
# TOWN OF KIDDERMINSTER
## 1859.

DEO JUVANTE FLORET · ARTE ET INDUSTRIA

From Habberley

From Bridgnorth

To Puxton

RIVER STOUR

KIDDERMINSTER

FRANCHISE

FOREIGN OF

FRANCHISE BOUNDARY

HABBERLEY ROAD

PROUD Cross

WEIR

TOWN HALL

St Marys

WORCESTERSHIRE

N OR R

St Johns Parsonage

BLAKEBROOK COTTAGE

FIREBROOK ROAD

BROOK

St Johns INFANTS SCHOOL

PARK

PARK WHARF

GAS WORKS

St John's Church

WOODFIELD

SCHOOL

School

BEWDLEY

Quarry

THE GREEN

UNION WORK HOUSE

POOL

RAGGED SCHOOL

BEWDLEY HILL

ROAD

Lodge

Bewdley

GREAT FIELD

SUTTON ROAD

LODGE POOLS

CEMETERY

STAFFORD STREET

CALDWELL MILL

RIVER STOUR

NEW POOL

S O U T H

Foot Road

Foot Way

ROUND HILL FOUNDRY

MILL

BRICK YARD

SUTTON COMMON

From Stourport

From Worcester

BACK BR